Exchange Rates, Capital Flows, and Monetary Policy in a Changing World Economy

Exchange Rates, Capital Flows, and Monetary Policy in a Changing World Economy

Proceedings of a Conference
Federal Reserve Bank of Dallas
Dallas, Texas
September 14–15, 1995

Edited by
William C. Gruben
David M. Gould
Carlos E. Zarazaga

Springer Science+Business Media, LLC

Library of Congress Cataloging-in-Publication Data

Federal Reserve Bank of Dallas. Conference (1995: Dallas, Texas)
Exchange rates, capital flows, and monetary policy in a changing world economy: proceedings of a Conference, Federal Bank of Dallas, Dallas, Texas, September 14–15, 1995 / [editors], William C. Gruben, David M. Gould, Carlos E. Zarazaga.
p. cm.
Includes bibliographical references.
ISBN 978-1-4613-7831-0 ISBN 978-1-4615-6175-0 (eBook)
DOI 10.1007/978-1-4615-6175-0
1. Foreign exchange rates—Congresses.
2. Capital movements—Congresses.
3. Monetary policy—Congresses. I. Gruben, William C.
II. Gould, David, 1962- III. Zarazaga, Carlos Enrique. IV. Title.
HG205.F427 1995
332.4'5—dc21 97-7927
CIP

Originally published by Kluwer Academic Publishers, New York in 1997
Softcover reprint of the hardcover 1st edition 1997

Printed on acid-free paper.

CONTENTS

PREFACE: EXCHANGE RATES, CAPITAL FLOWS, AND MONETARY POLICY IN A CHANGING WORLD ECONOMY

The dramatic growth of international capital flows has provided unprecedented opportunities and risks in emerging markets. Investors, policymakers, central bankers, and other practitioners who interact in these markets participated in a lively exchange of ideas about these risks and opportunities during a Federal Reserve Bank of Dallas Conference on September 14–15, 1995. *Exchange Rates, Capital Flows, and Monetary Policy in a Changing World Economy* is the proceedings of that conference.

In Part I, "Exchange Rates and Monetary Policy," Jeffrey A. Frankel concludes that the system is broken "in the sense that it is not working in the perfect, idealized way that our theories say." He cautions against radical reforms but says "some intelligent intervention from time to time cannot hurt and sometimes can help." Leonardo Auernheimer and Steve Hanke offer comments.

Part II consists of Sebastian Edwards', "Optimal Exchange Rate Policy for Stabilizing Inflation in Developing Countries," with discussion from Graciela Kaminsky and John Welch. Edwards focuses on the use of exchange rates as stabilization devices in anti-inflationary programs. He looks for determinants of success and considers dangers and challenges of such policies.

In Part III, Vittorio Corbo discusses his work with Patricio Rojas of Chile's Central Bank, "Exchange Rate Volatility, Investment, and Growth: Some New Evidence." Corbo examines how macroeconomic uncertainty about the inflation rate and the real exchange rate affect economic growth through two mechanisms:

the rate of investment and the overall level of efficiency. Commentary is from David Gould and Liliana Rojas-Suárez.

In Part IV, "Speculative Attacks," Peter M. Garber reviews theories about speculative attacks and considers what happens in the days or hours before a fixed-exchange-rate regime collapses. He relates his comments to two recent cases, the collapse of the European Exchange Rate Mechanism (ERM) in 1992 and 1993 and the collapse of the Mexican peso at the end of 1994. Discussion from Guillermo Mondino and Miguel Savastano follows.

Part V is Alan S. Blinder's assessment: "The Role of the Dollar as an International Currency." Although Blinder finds many claims about the decline of the dollar as a reserve currency, he concludes that they are remarkably undisciplined by facts. "Wherever we have data," Blinder says,

> the message seems to be more or less the same: the dollar is still unquestionably the world's dominant international currency by any conceivable definition. But its preeminent position is eroding slowly, as mainly the Deutsche mark and, secondarily, the yen move up on the pecking order.

In Part VI, "International Capital Flows: Direct vs. Portfolio Investment," Michael P. Dooley challenges conventional wisdom about capital flows, control of capital flows, and what countries might hope to accomplish with capital controls. "Both lenders and the borrowers often see international capital flows as a welfare-reducing phenomenon," Dooley says. But he finds that the motivation for capital flows derives from government policy: the size of the capital inflow will be a function of the credibility of the insurance fund. Thus, policy reforms, particularly fiscal reforms, generate capital inflows, but the size of the capital inflow will be just sufficient to exhaust the insurance fund, he says. "The only way, in my view, to break the insurance chain and discourage these kinds of capital inflows is to introduce uncertainty in the exchange rate and . . . make the private sector investor bear the risk of that investment," Dooley concludes. Agustín Carstens and Edwin M. Truman offer comments.

Part VII, "Central Bank Coordination in the Midst of Exchange Rate Instability," is a panel discussion by Miguel Urrutia, John W. Crow, Ricardo Hausmann, and Allan Meltzer.

This conference would not have been possible without the efforts of many people. We wish to thank Bob McTeer, Harvey Rosenblum, Sherry Kiser, KaSandra Goulding, Agnes Mitchell, Daniel Sanchez, and all the contributors, who made this conference possible. We also thank our editorial staff—Anne Coursey, Rhonda Harris, Monica Reeves, and Kathy Thacker.

William C. Gruben
David M. Gould
Carlos E. Zarazaga

ABOUT THE PARTICIPANTS

Alan S. Blinder, now Professor of Economics at Princeton University, was serving as Vice Chairman of the Federal Reserve Board of Governors in September 1995. Before that, he was a member of President Clinton's Council of Economic Advisers, where he worked on forecasting, budget, international trade, and health-care issues. He is the author or coauthor of 10 books, including *Economics: Principles and Policy*.

Vittorio Corbo is Professor of Economics at the Catholic University of Chile. From 1984 to 1991, he served at the World Bank, most recently as chief of the Macroeconomic Adjustment and Growth Division. He has written more than 80 articles and edited eight books in the field of macroeconomics, economic adjustment, and development.

John W. Crow is an adviser to the American International Group of companies and Lévesque Beaubien Geoffrion, Inc. He served as Governor of the Bank of Canada from 1987 to 1994. Formerly chief of the North American Division of the International Monetary Fund, Crow is a fellow in residence at C.D. Howe Institute.

Michael P. Dooley, Professor of Economics at the University of California, Santa Cruz, was formerly Assistant Director of Research at the International

Monetary Fund. He has authored more than two dozen articles on international capital flows and exchange rate policy, including "Capital Flight, External Debt, and Domestic Policies," "Exchange Rates, Country-Specific Shocks, and Gold," and "Portfolio Capital Flows: Hot or Cold?".

Sebastian Edwards is Professor of Economics at the University of California, Los Angeles. In September 1995, he was Chief Economist for Latin America and the Caribbean at the World Bank. Coeditor of the *Journal of Development Economics*, he has authored several books, including *Exchange Rate Misalignment in Developing Countries* and *Real Exchanges, Devaluations, and Adjustment: Exchange Rate Policy in Developing Countries.*

Jeffrey A. Frankel is Professor of Economics at the University of California, Berkeley, where he is also Director of the Center for International and Development Economics Research. In addition, in 1996 he served on the Council of Economic Advisers at the Executive Office of the President. He also has been a Senior Fellow at the Institute for International Economics and Director for International Finance and Macroeconomics at the National Bureau of Economic Research.

Peter M. Garber, Professor of Economics at Brown University, is a consultant for the International Monetary Fund. Among his published articles are "The Operation and Collapse of Fixed Exchange Rate Regimes," "The Collapse of the Bretton Woods Fixed Exchange Rate System," and "The Linkage Between Speculative Attack and Target Zone Models of Exchange Rates: Some Extended Results."

Ricardo Hausmann is Chief Economist for the Inter-American Development Bank and Professor of Economics at IESA, Venezuela's leading graduate school of business. Previously, he was Minister of Coordination and Planning for Venezuela, the country's Governor in the Inter-American Development Bank and the World Bank, and Chairman of the Joint Development Committee of the International Monetary Fund and the World Bank.

Allan Meltzer is Professor of Political Economy and Public Policy at Carnegie Mellon University. His work on money and capital markets has led to frequent consulting assignments with Congressional committees, the U.S. Treasury Department, the President's Council of Economic Advisers, the Board of Governors of the Federal Reserve System, and foreign governments and central banks.

Miguel Urrutia is Governor of Colombia's Central Bank, having previously served the bank as Director. He was formerly Director of the Inter-American Development Bank's Department of Economic and Social Development and was Vice-Rector of Development Studies at United Nations University in Tokyo.

Part I EXCHANGE RATES AND MONETARY POLICY

The enormous volatility of floating exchange rates has led to a call for limits on exchange rate fluctuations. An increasing number of countries have begun to question the benefits of floating exchange rates. Can central banks limit exchange rate fluctuations, and are there benefits from doing so?

Presenter:
Jeffrey A. Frankel
Professor of Economics
University of California, Berkeley

Moderator:
William C. Gruben
Research Officer
Federal Reserve Bank of Dallas

Discussants:
Leonardo Auernheimer
Professor of Economics
Texas A&M University

Steve Hanke
Professor of Applied Economics
Johns Hopkins University

Frankel:
Something seems to be wrong with the international monetary system, but we are not sure how to fix it. This conclusion that things are not working entirely right, particularly in the foreign exchange market, is fed in part by some recent developments and in part by an accumulation of academic findings. I will review that evidence and those arguments and then discuss proposals for possible reform.

Bubbles and Crises in the Foreign Exchange Market

Is it "broke"? Should we fix it? And if so, how? The 1970s, in a sense, were the peak of enthusiasm for floating exchange rates. Certainly, a majority of economists had come to favor floating rates over fixed rates. This policy was thought to be the way to avoid misalignments, such as the overvaluation to which the dollar had become increasingly subject in the 1960s. The logic was that the market is the best judge of the true value of a currency.

Our host reminded us of Milton Friedman's very prophetic views from the 1950s. If the concern is that evil speculators will be destabilizing, Friedman said this is not very likely. The argument, of course, is that for speculators to be destabilizing, they would have to buy the currency when it was already high to drive the price up and sell it when it was already low to drive the price down. That's what *destabilizing* implies. Yet such speculators, who buy high and sell low, are not likely to last too long before going bankrupt. The argument seemed pretty convincing.

In the 1980s, the pendulum began to swing back for a number of reasons. The episode that convinced the most people that maybe all was not optimal with the system of floating exchange rates was the tremendous appreciation of the dollar. In the early 1980s, this appreciation seemed to fit standard theory: the overshooting model, the monetary fiscal mix, and high real interest rates. But by late 1984 and 1985, the last 20 percent appreciation of the dollar seemed difficult to explain by any macroeconomic fundamentals. Some people, who had been strong proponents of floating rates, began to have doubts. It seemed as if the markets are not always right; maybe they sometimes got it wrong.

What about Friedman's argument that destabilizing speculators would have to lose money and be driven out? A number of articles citing abstruse counterexamples were published. But the most powerful counterexample came up almost accidentally. It was the theory of rational speculative bubbles. Its initial motivation was purely a theoretical curiosity: an extra term kept popping up in the solution to the differential equations. But gradually it dawned on people. This term actually was an important counterexample to Friedman.

A rational speculative bubble is simply one in which investors buy the currency because they expect it to go up in the future. And sure enough: they drive the price up, it goes up in the future, and they are right. Nothing in the logic of speculation in efficient markets rules out a bubble of that sort. The concept of rational speculative bubbles makes a pretty disturbing counterexample to Friedman's argument. But the theory is not very complete. It does not tell us anything about when the bubbles get started or how to stop them. I think one wants to consider speculative bubbles more broadly.

Another reason the pendulum swung back in the 1980s was rising interest in the nominal anchor argument for monetary policy. After the high inflation rates of the 1970s and, in many countries, the high output cost of disinflating in the early 1980s, there was interest in a nominal anchor. The monetarists thought the anchor should be money, but that did not always seem to work.

So there was much interest in using the exchange rate as a nominal anchor. Many countries in Latin America and elsewhere began to try monetary stabilizations based on the exchange rate. Even the International Monetary Fund said maybe this was okay; maybe devaluation was not always the answer. In Europe, one primary motivation for the formation of the European Monetary System (EMS) and later plans for the European Monetary Union (EMU)—at least from the viewpoint of some of the southern European countries—was to establish a nominal anchor commitment, a credible commitment for monetary policy to break inflationary expectations.

It seems to me that in the 1990s there has been renewed disenchantment with fixed rates and that the pendulum is swinging away from attempts to stabilize. I am not sure it is swinging toward pure floating rates; it may be swinging in some third dimension, if pendulums are capable of doing that.

In part, this change is happening because we have had several very disruptive crises in countries that have tried to stabilize their exchange rates. The September 1992 crisis in the European Exchange Rate Mechanism (ERM); the August 1993 ERM crisis, with France in particular; and, of course, Mexico's December 1994 peso crisis have also given people some cause to worry.

These crises all had many predecessors in history. I do not know exactly why the financial markets seem so surprised by these 1990s events, so surprised that politicians who had made promises not to devalue did, in fact, devalue. There had already been a long history of promises that were not kept: the United Kingdom in 1931, 1949, and 1967; the dollar in 1973; and Chile in 1982, which offers many parallels to Mexico in 1994 and Great Britain in 1992. The mainstream view among most economists, I think, is that these crises were not primarily the fault of the markets but the fault of governments. The governments were pursuing policies that were not really consistent with fixed exchange rates.

Nevertheless, unwarranted speculative attacks can happen. Many speculative attacks are based on fundamentals, but some are not. In particular, I would cite the example of the French franc in 1993. It is hard to say what the French were doing wrong. If you look at the fundamentals, France's inflation rate was lower than Germany's. It is hard to say that this was some profligate policy that was inconsistent with the goal of trying to keep up with the mark in the ERM, and yet a speculative attack forced the French to abandon the previous regime. There is now a theory of speculative attacks for fixed rates, which is the analogue of the theory of speculative bubbles for floating rates.[1]

The Academic Literature on the Foreign Exchange Market

Those are the recent developments. I will briefly discuss seven empirical findings we have accumulated.

The first category is volatility. The volatility of floating rates has turned out to be high, judged by any standard. High volatility is what we might have expected, certainly compared with goods prices, with apparent monetary fundamentals, or with just about anything.

The second set of results is the possible adverse effects of this high volatility on trade and investment. Here the academic literature has been pretty muted. It is usually summarized by saying that there is no evidence of large effects of exchange rate volatility on trade, but many studies find evidence of some effects. For example, the idea that exchange rate variability discourages trade is certainly one of the major motivations behind the formation of the Exchange Rate Mechanism and the European Monetary Union on the part of European leaders.

On the econometrics, I recently did an estimate along with Shang-Jin Wei, looking across pairs of countries rather than across time. We found that bilateral exchange rate variability did seem to have a statistically significant effect. Using ordinary least squares regression and hypothetically eliminating all exchange rate variability in the world, our statistical estimate was that, as of 1980, trade would have been stimulated by 22 percent.[2]

There are three important qualifiers to that number. First, we found that the effect that was there in the 1960s and 1970s disappeared in the 1980s. Perhaps this is because of the increased use and availability of hedging instruments so that importers and exporters could protect themselves against exchange rate variability. Second, that estimate of 22 percent does not take into account the likelihood of simultaneity between who you are going to stabilize your exchange rate vis-à-vis and who your important trading partners are. When we take that simultaneity into account, the estimate, although still significant, is much smaller. Third, the defenders of floating rates would say: "Well, even if that's true, even if there is an effect of exchange rate variability on trade, that effect is reflecting some real shocks that are going on in the world economy. And if you try to suppress them, they are just going to show up somewhere else." The idea is that if fluctuations in exchange rates always stem from real disturbances, the impact is going to show up as an appreciation of the dollar in real terms one way or another. For example, if appreciation of the dollar results from an increase in demand for U.S. goods, and if policymakers try to suppress the effect in the foreign exchange market, the impact of appreciation is going to show up as higher U.S. prices. The mechanism is that, to suppress the appreciation, the monetary authorities must print more dollars and add to their foreign exchange reserves, and this increase in the U.S. money supply will be inflationary. So the effect on the real exchange rate, the loss in price competitiveness, is going to occur anyway, and you are better off stabilizing the price level. This argument—that there's a real amount of uncertainty out there that's going to show up one way or another, based on the fundamentals—is addressed by the third and fourth category of findings.

The third finding is the failure to explain most exchange rate movements, especially in the short term, according to fundamentals.[3] Over the longer term, we can explain some movements by fundamentals, but in the short term we can explain very little. Many studies come up with the same answer. So if you cannot explain exchange rate movements by obvious monetary fundamentals—money supplies, interest rates, inflation rates, or gross national product—that leaves two possibilities: either they are the result of fundamentals we cannot observe, or they are not the result of fundamentals. These two possibilities are logically all-inclusive. Many academic economists, perhaps real business cycle types, have argued that there are fundamentals we cannot observe. There are many theories related to something that is not observable, some marginal rate of substitution of currencies over time. The problem with such theories, of course, is that they are not testable. The other possibility is that the movements are not related to fundamentals, which is what I mean by speculative bubbles.

In my view, the most convincing piece of information has to do with the comparison of real exchange rate variability across different regimes. When countries shift from fixed rates to floating rates or back, or if they peg to one currency versus another one, that has effects on nominal *and* real variability. This is a pretty persuasive piece of evidence.

The upper half of Figure I–1 shows the nominal exchange rate variability, and the lower half is real exchange rate variability for the Deutsche mark–dollar rate before and after the switch from fixed to floating. It is not surprising that

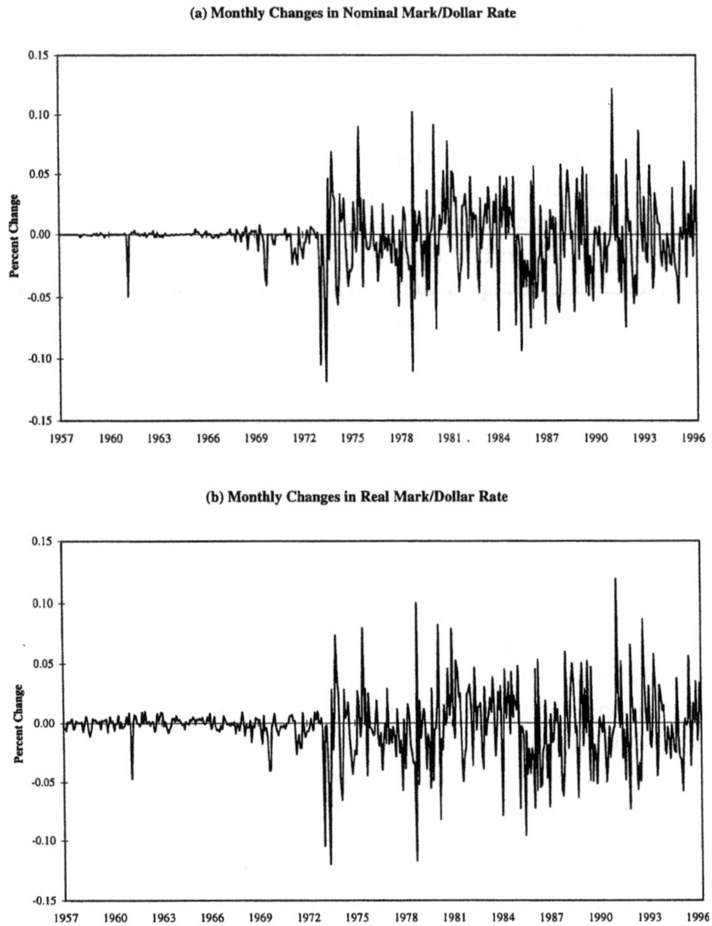

Figure I–1. Volatility of German/U.S. exchange rate since 1957.

Source: IMF *International Financial Statistics* series ae (end of period exchange rate) and series 64 (CPI).

after the switch from fixed to floating rates in 1973, nominal exchange rate variability went up. But some people say it is a coincidence. Those real fundamentals are out there and they are going to determine the real exchange rate no matter what, and the choice of fixed versus floating is immaterial. Is the real variability the same no matter what, whether it shows up in the form of nominal exchange rates or prices?

I think there is pretty persuasive evidence against that because a shift in regime does have a big effect. There are many examples that when you shift nominal variability, real variability goes up, as, for example, when Ireland switches from a dollar peg to a pound peg to a mark peg.[4]

The fact that those two graphs are matched very closely, that the correlation between the movements in the nominal rate and the movements in the real rate is very high (0.98), suggests that what is really happening is that there is some stickiness in goods prices and that nominal variability is creating a lot of the real variability. To me, this evidence argues against the idea that the variability is invariant to the regime. I think the regime does make a difference and that speculative bubbles are prime candidates to explain many of these movements.

Further down the list of empirical findings from the academic literature suggesting all is not quite right with the current system: Number four is apparent bias in expectations, particularly as reflected in the forward exchange rate. There are many tests to determine whether the forward market is an unbiased predictor of the future spot rate, and virtually all of them say no, it is not. In other words, it is biased; you can make money in expected value by betting the opposite direction of the forward rate, a fact that some see as evidence against efficiency of the markets. The more common interpretation, certainly among academic economists, is that this is not evidence of market inefficiency but rather a compensation for risk, the exchange risk premium. The reason is a long story that I will not go into, but I think there is evidence against the exchange risk premium idea and that there is indeed some bias in expectations.

The fifth finding is evidence from survey data on exchange rate expectations,[5] which is related to the sixth finding, the apparent tendency for exchange rate forecasters and traders—the people who are actually in the market—to make forecasts about the future that tend to extrapolate past trends, at short horizons of one week, two weeks, one month.[6] Most trading takes place within these horizons, if not even shorter horizons of a few hours. At these horizons, it appears that traders use technical analysis or various other methods that, on average, tend to extrapolate past trends. Also at these horizons, there is little use of the models based on fundamentals that say: "The dollar is overvalued, whether it's by purchasing power parity or the trade deficit or whatever. We expect it to return to equilibrium."

Traders do tend to use those models at longer horizons of, say, one year. An investor deciding what country's securities to buy or a CEO deciding where to build a factory takes fundamentals into account. But at the very short-term horizon of most trading, it just does not seem to be there.

The seventh category is studies of the effects of exogenous changes in monetary policy. The finding is that there is an effect on the exchange rate, but the effect is not instantaneous as, in theory, it should be. Rather, it is drawn out over time. It takes maybe a year or two before the peak effect occurs, and then it comes back down.[7]

I like to try to explain this finding, and a lot of the others, through speculative bubbles. I call it overshooting of the overshooting equilibrium. This explanation is my attempt to be more specific than just saying *speculative bubbles*, to suggest how a speculative bubble starts. It starts by a movement that is based on fundamentals, but once the trend gets going, the speculative bubble keeps going for a while longer before it catches up with the fundamentals and turns around.

This hypothesis, though unattractive from the viewpoint of rational expectations theory, seems to explain a lot. For example, the finding that the forward rate points the wrong direction is consistent with this theory because the forward rate is also equal to the difference in interest rates by covered interest rate parity. The pattern is this: interest rates increase because of fundamentals, making the country's assets more attractive. Next the currency appreciates—so far so good, just what the textbooks say, as in Dornbusch's overshooting theory. But if the currency has been appreciating for a couple of years, these chartists' or technical analysts' models seem to be giving the right answers because extrapolation for a certain period of time has given the right answer and the currency has not returned to fundamentals. If these conditions continue on for a year or two, momentum builds, and people start throwing away the models based on fundamentals and pay more attention to the models based on technical analysis. You get this extrapolation, which keeps it moving.

Eventually there is a turnaround. It's like the *Roadrunner* cartoon in which the coyote runs off the edge of the cliff. For a few seconds, the market is still going, though not supported by fundamentals—the cliff is the fundamentals. When the market notices that nothing is supporting the fundamentals, it suddenly becomes aware that nothing is holding up the dollar or the yen, and down goes the currency. That is my characterization of the dollar in February 1984 and of the yen in the spring of 1995. In both cases, the bubble burst.

Proposed Cures for the Foreign Exchange Market

I have covered the question "Is it broken?". Now I will turn to "Should it be fixed?". Usually the reply to this question is, "If it's not broken, don't fix it." The implication is, "If it is broken, you should fix it." My answer is not necessarily going to come out that way. The fixes would have to be an improvement for that to be right, and I am not sure that they are.

Let me explain what I mean by going through the major proposals for reforming the monetary system, and, in particular, the foreign exchange system. I will go from the more extreme proposals to the less extreme proposals, although that judgment is partly subjective.

To me, the most extreme proposal is a fixed exchange rate. I am not talking about "fixed but adjustable." I mean irrevocably fixed. Under fixed rates, one might distinguish several variations: irrevocably fixed with your own currency, a currency board, the gold standard, or the most extreme case, a monetary union in which one country actually adopts another's currency. I hope from our discussions we will hear some tales of far-off lands that are experimenting with some of these proposals.

This really is the nominal anchor argument, the idea that if the monetary authorities make a sincere commitment to an exchange rate peg, the policy will work and will allow the country to attain monetary stability with less output cost than might have been suffered in an attempt to disinflate without a nominal anchor or without any way to convince people you were serious. The argument, of course, is that if the nominal anchor is really credible, and if people see there is no going back even if you want to, they will expect lower inflation. And if the public expects lower inflation, inflation will be lower. Workers will settle for lower wage increases, firms will settle for lower prices, and inflation actually will be lower without output costs.

Whatever else can be said, I think, recent experience has cast some doubt on the idea that all that is necessary is for the monetary authority to be sincerely committed to a nominal anchor. A sincere commitment is not all that is needed. The authorities, in the cases of Mexico in 1994 and the ERM, really did want to keep the exchange rate fixed and intended to do so, but the system did not work, and they were not able to keep the rate fixed.

Here I am distinguishing between the monetary authorities and the government or, more broadly, the political process. The monetary authorities might be willing to suffer very high interest rates to stay in the exchange rate mechanism. (Sweden had 500 percent interest rates for awhile.) Yet that might not be good enough if the rest of the government is not prepared to support the monetary authority for fear of losing an election or popular support. If unemployment is very high, there may be revolution in the streets. Or if the banking system is vulnerable, there may be a banking collapse, which may be a price too high to pay. Even if the government is committed, it may get thrown out of office. These possibilities are part of the fundamentals, and in a sense the ultimate fundamentals are politics. In our models, we typically assume monetary policy is just this exogenous M that the government gets to set, but that may not always be the case.

If the speculators sense trouble, there may be a big speculative attack even before the workers are in the streets, or before the poll results are in, as in the case of the French and Danish referenda on membership in EMU. There may be massive speculation that the monetary authority cannot resist.

There is a current fashionable view, for which one of my discussants bears a lot of responsibility (and I say this to his credit—not many of us can have an effect on the regimes that countries are choosing out there). This view is that you need an even stronger commitment than just saying the exchange rate is irrevocably fixed. What you need is a currency board.

Currency boards do have their place. I think they have helped Argentina, and perhaps some of the Baltics. Here are the requirements to be a desirable candidate for a currency board: a very small, very open economy that is well integrated into the world; a *desire* to be integrated, particularly into some specific neighbors (for example, a desire on the part of the Baltics to be integrated into Western Europe, or perhaps for some Central American and Caribbean countries to be integrated into the United States); a desperate need to import monetary stability due to a history of hyperinflation or to an absence of stable institutions (such as a country just coming out of communism that lacks no trustworthy institutions); and the ability to come up with enough reserves to really make the currency board work (it may not be enough to have reserves to back up the monetary base; you may need more than that, possibly enough to buy out the whole M1). Stanley Fischer says that without adequate reserves, a currency board is a recipe for changing what would otherwise be a currency crisis into a banking crisis. If a country lacks all those requirements, as most do, it is not a good candidate for a currency board.

Those are all the proposals that come under fixed rates. There's an alternative set of proposals that come under the realm of capital controls. The Tobin tax is getting more attention now than it did when Tobin first made the proposal 15 years ago.[8] The attention is coming not so much from academic economists but elsewhere. The conventional critique is in two parts: one, a Tobin tax cannot reduce undesirable destabilizing speculation without hurting desirable investment; and two, it cannot be enforced.

On the first, I have an answer. I think there is evidence that short-term speculation, which the Tobin tax would hit proportionately more, does tend to be destabilizing in the sense that it is often based on extrapolative expectations. Long-term investment is stabilizing but minimally so. I am not really willing to say I am in favor of the Tobin tax per se, though a tax of 0.05 or 0.10 percent would certainly be better than the 1 percent tax that has been discussed. My doubts have more to do with the second criticism, enforceability.

Proposals from Dornbusch and others call for various forms of capital control. I will not go into that too much.[9]

Another category that is more moderate is to have more formal institutions for intervention, such as a multilateral intervention fund. Michel Camdessus has proposed something like this.[10] Another subset of these formal institutions is target zones in the manner proposed by John Williamson.[11] He answers the

Table I–1. Four schools of radical reform.

	Do we think that markets always know best?	*Do we think there is some role for government tinkering?*
Want national independence	Pure free float works best (Monetarists)	Anti-control of speculators (Tobin, Dornbusch)
Want an international agreement	Discipline from fixed rates/ currency board/gold standard (Supply-siders)	Activist, international cooperation (Bergsten, Williamson)

critique that target zones do not work: the collapse of the exchange rate mechanism, he says, is not the kind of target zone I have been talking about. The kind of target zone I have been talking about has an automatic adjustment of the central parity when fundamentals change. If one country has a higher inflation rate than another, you regularly change the central parity. You do not wait for a crisis at the bend.

The Williamson version does have the advantage that it makes it more practical and less likely that you could have these crises. But on the other hand, it also vitiates the two main arguments in favor of a target zone. The nominal anchor argument is basically out the window, and if there is always a possibility of a realignment, the argument that speculation will stabilize the rates under a target zone becomes more questionable. Of course, there is also the question of who and how you would determine what the central parity is.

My list of radical reforms that have been proposed would not be complete without mentioning Ron McKinnon.[12] I will do this by putting the radical schools of thought into four categories in a two-by-two graph (Table I–1). The top question is, Do we think that markets always know best, or is there some role for government tinkering? And on the side we ask, Do we want national independence? Is it desirable for each country to be able to follow its own monetary policies, or would we like to have national cooperation and international agreement?

The monetarists are in the upper-left corner. They say pure free-floating works best. Each country gets to choose its own policies; markets can pick the appropriate exchange rate, and everything is fine. It is like the Adam Smith argument for free markets in general.

Tobin and Dornbusch are in the upper-right corner. They say we need some government tinkering, some antispeculator controls.

Those who think the markets know best are in the lower-left box. These people are just as strong on free markets as the monetarists, but they come to the opposite conclusion regarding the exchange rate. I put supply-siders here, but

Table I–2. When does intervention work, and when is it desirable? Four cases.

	The market is sure of itself. ⇒ Intervention will not work.	*The market is unsure of itself. ⇒ Intervention can work.*
Market perceptions of fundamentals are better than the government's.	It is just as well that intervention fails, as with the pound and lira in 1992.	The effect is to keep the exchange rate away from fundamentals, as with the ERM in 1991.
Government may know better than the market.	It is too bad that intervention fails, as with the franc in August 1993 and the yen-dollar rate in March and April 1995.	The effect is to move the exchange rate toward fundamentals, as with the dollar in 1985 and the yen-dollar rate in the summers of 1993 and 1995.

there are a lot of other people who fall into this category, saying we need the discipline from fixed exchange rates such as a currency board or gold standard, which enables each country to go its own way and be responsible for its own errors and yet provides the discipline of fixed rates.

Fred Bergsten and John Williamson are in the lower-right corner. They say we need some government tinkering, and we need it in a cooperative way; we need international cooperation to stabilize currencies.

Ron McKinnon defies classification; he is in a category by himself. I would say he takes ideas from each of the four schools. Like Tobin and Dornbusch, McKinnon thinks a free float does not work very well and speculators give us excessively variable exchange rates. Like the monetarists, however, he thinks purchasing power parity is a good, useful guide to determining the exchange rate. Then he thinks like the supply-siders, believing devaluation is not a useful tool for changing relative prices and for improving the trade balance. And finally, like the fourth camp, he thinks we need a tripartite monetary agreement, a cooperative agreement among the United States, Japan, and Europe to stabilize the world monetary system. I think it is a little hard to combine all those, but he gets points for originality.

Where do I come out? I am not a radical. I have a very moderate view that floating with some occasional intervention is really about the best we can do. This does make me different from, perhaps, most economists, or at least from academic economists, who take the view that intervention can never have an effect unless it changes money supplies, that sterilized intervention can never have an effect (and that even if it did, it would not be desirable to have an effect that was inconsistent with fundamentals).

In Table 1–2, another two-by-two box, I make a distinction across the top about whether or not the market is sure of itself—whether the market really has a firm idea of what the exchange rate should be. If it does, you know these critics are right. The magnitude of the market is $1.2 trillion a day as of April 1995. This is too big for the authorities to fight with intervention, if the markets really know what they want.

But the idea that intervention can never work is just not right. I did a study with Katherine Dominguez in which we looked at the record of daily intervention since 1985. We found that often it does have an effect. It is more likely to have an effect when the market is unsure what it wants, when the intervention catches the market by surprise, when it is coordinated among the authorities, when it is publicly announced, and to be sure, when it is ultimately backed by fundamentals. But the idea that intervention can never work unless it is backed by fundamentals is not right. We found many episodes in which it did work, at least for a month or so, which is long enough to matter. And I would say that interventions in the summer of 1995 have had a real effect on the dollar-yen rate.

The market represented in the second column of Table I–2 is unsure of itself, so intervention can work? The other distinction, along the side, is, Are market perceptions better or worse than government perceptions? I would agree that most of the time, we are in the first box: intervention is probably not going to work if it bucks fundamentals because the market could prevail. Markets are usually, but not always, right; sometimes we are in the other boxes. I will give examples.

Intervention with the pound and the lira in 1992 ultimately failed, which is just as well because it was inconsistent with the fundamentals. Given the shocks of German monetary unification, increased German spending, high interest rates, and upward pressure on the mark, it was inevitable that the ERM was going to give way. And that is what happened.

But sometimes we are in the other categories. Intervention can work. The ERM worked for two years. For two years between the German shock and the collapse, the authorities succeeded in propping up the ERM.

I have examples in which the government, in fact, may know better than the market. That is not impossible. It happens sometimes. I would say the French franc in August 1993 is a case where the speculative attack was not justified by fundamentals. In my view, the movement of the yen against the dollar in 1994–95 was excessive and was a replay of the bubble for the dollar in reverse. During 1984–85, it was the dollar that overshot the overshooting equilibrium, and in 1994–95, it was the yen that overshot the overshooting equilibrium.

In June 1995, I published a couple of articles, one in *Foreign Affairs* and one in *International Economy*, saying the market had just gotten carried away, that the yen-dollar rate of 80 did not make sense.[13] I wrote that the exchange rate was based on perceptions that the Clinton administration wanted a weak dollar (perceptions that were wrong) and that intervention might be useful in turning the situation around. I think these things were exactly what happened in the months that followed.

Sometimes intervention can work if it is done correctly and cleverly, and if the market is unsure of itself. Sometimes that can actually help move things in the right direction.

So is the system broke in the sense that it is not working in the perfect, idealized way that our theories say? Yes. Should we fix it? No. I think the radical reforms would not be an improvement. But some intelligent intervention from time to time cannot hurt and sometimes can help.

Notes

1. See Obstfeld (1994).
2. Frankel and Wei (forthcoming).
3. Meese and Rogoff (1983) and Campbell and Clarida (1987).
4. Flood and Rose (1993). Also, see Frankel and Rose (1995) for a recent survey of the empirical literature on exchange rate determination.
5. Frankel and Froot (1989) and Engle (1995).
6. Frankel and Froot (1987).
7. Eichenbaum and Evans (1995).
8. See Tobin (1978) and Frankel (1996).
9. Dornbusch (1986) and Eichengreen, Tobin, and Wyplosz (1994).
10. See Camdessus (1994). T. Hosomi proposed such an international intervention fund 10 years ago.
11. Williamson (1987).
12. McKinnon (1988) and McKinnon and Ohno (forthcoming).
13. Frankel (1995a and 1995b).

References

Camdessus, Michel (1994), "The IMF at 50: An Evolving But a Constant Mission," speech delivered at the Institute for International Economics, Washington, D.C., June 7 (excerpted in *IMF Survey*, June 13, 1994).

Campbell, John, and Richard Clarida (1987), "The Dollar and Real Interest Rates," *Carnegie-Rochester Conference on Public Policy* 27, August.

Dornbusch, Rudiger (1986), "Flexible Exchange Rates and Excess Capital Mobility," *Brookings Papers on Economic Activity* 1, 209–226.

Eichenbaum, M., and C. Evans (1995), "Some Empirical Evidence on the Effects of Monetary Policy Shocks on Exchange Rate Expectations," NBER Working Paper, no. 4271.

Eichengreen, Barry, James Tobin, and Charles Wyplosz (1994), "Two Cases for Sand in the Wheels of International Finance," CIDER Working Paper, no. C94–45, December.

Engle, Charles (1995), "Why Is There a Forward Discount Bias? A Survey of Recent Evidence," University of Washington and NBER, July.

Flood, Robert, and Andrew K. Rose (1993), "Fixing Exchange Rates," NBER Working Paper, no. 4503.

Frankel, Jeffrey A. (1996), "How Well Do Foreign Exchange Markets Work? Might a Tobin Tax Help?" in Inga Kaul et al. eds. *The Tobin Tax* (Oxford: Oxford University Press).

Frankel, Jeffrey A. (1995a), "Still the Lingua Franca: The Exaggerated Death of the Dollar," *Foreign Affairs* 74 (July/August): 9–16.

Frankel, Jeffrey A. (1995b), "What Dollar Bashing?" *The International Economy* (May/June): 14–15.

Frankel, Jeffrey A., and Kenneth A. Froot (1989), "Forward Discount Bias: Is It an Exchange Risk Premium?" *Quarterly Journal of Economics* 104 (February): 139–161.

Frankel, Jeffrey A., and Kenneth A. Froot (1987), "Using Survey Data to Test Standard Propositions Regarding Exchange Rate Expectations," *American Economic Review* 77 (March): 133–135.

Frankel, Jeffrey A., and A. Rose (1995), "A Survey of Empirical Research on Nominal Exchange Rates," NBER Working Paper, no. 4865, for G. Grossman and K. Rogoff (eds.) *Handbook of International Economics* (Amsterdam: North-Holland).

Frankel, Jeffrey A., and Shang-Jin Wei (forthcoming), "Regionalization of World Trade and Currencies: Economics and Politics," in J. Frankel (ed.) *The Regionalization of the World Economy*, proceedings of the NBER Conference in Woodstock, Vermont, October 19–21, 1995 (Chicago: University of Chicago Press).

McKinnon, Ronald (1988), "Monetary and Exchange Rate Policies for International Financial Stability," *Journal of Economic Perspectives*, Winter, 83–103.

McKinnon, Ronald, and Kenichi Ohno (forthcoming), *Dollar and Yen* (Cambridge: MIT Press).

Meese, Richard, and Kenneth Rogoff (1983), "Empirical Exchange Rate Models of the Seventies," *Journal of International Economics* 14, 2–24.

Obstfeld, Maurice (1994), "The Logic of Currency Crises," *Cahiers Economiques et Monetaires* (Paris: Banque de France), 189–213.

Tobin, James (1978), "A Proposal for International Monetary Reform," *Eastern Economic Journal* 4, 153–159.

Williamson, John (1987), "Exchange Rate Management: The Role of Target Zones," *American Economic Review* 77, 200–204.

Auernheimer:

Professor Frankel has given us coverage that should be commended because it shows that he has a surprising, efficient sense of synthesis. His is a very balanced, complete survey of the state of affairs.

Essentially, I concur with Professor Frankel. The current system is showing too much volatility, and there is the question of what to do. In determining how to proceed, Professor Frankel seems sympathetic to (1) the possibility of the Tobin tax, aside from the question of practicality; and (2) the idea of intelligent intervention. He also supports the establishment of some rule for monetary policy. His rule is certainly not a monetarist (as opposed to *monetary*) rule for monetary policy that would seek to stabilize nominal income.

Here I am reminded of Friedman's theory of nominal income from the late 1960s or early 1970s. There are some things I like a lot in Frankel's work and some things I like less. I like Professor Frankel's suggestion that fluctuations in exchange rates reflect some real risk, and if that if we suppress that reaction, the effect will show up elsewhere. However, he does not bear his idea to final consequences, suggesting instead that it is difficult to prove any real risk in terms of exchange rate fluctuations. But I think that the idea has merit if it guides us in asking more questions.

Something else that I liked a lot is the notion that expectations can differ among market participants. This idea, of course, is very old; it was King's idea, and the one we use in Macroeconomics 101 to explain the shape of the preference schedule. Economists throw away information when we do not look at the volume of transactions because, in the strict models in which everyone shares the same expectations, there is no need for transactions to move the price of something up and down.

The concept that I could take an asset and sell it to you signifies in general that you and I have different expectations about what the price will be in the next period. This idea has not been sufficiently explored, and I mention it with respect to the Tobin tax.

We do have too much volatility, in the sense that there are certain things we do not explain by fundamentals, especially in the short run. But evidence is mixed as far as how that volatility affects trade. There are some empirical works that indicate trade declines by 20 percent, a very big number. Other empirical evidence suggests that the variability of the real exchange rate is sometimes higher under fixed exchange rates systems. The jury is still out.

I think that the concern is not so much with very short-term, day-to-day variability. After all, one might conclude that this is a pseudo-sum gain among short-term participants and does not affect the long-run plans or trade.

Professor Frankel focuses on longer swings that can take several quarters, as in the dollar appreciation during the mid-1980s, for example. He then explores various views of what to do about it. I will not get into a discussion of fixed exchange rates or currency boards. But with regard to his idea about some of the work done by rational expectations people, I think he tends to dismiss some works that are trying to find out not so much what is different between exchange rate regimes but what is common among them. In other words, the question is, Is there a fundamental difference? I refer to situations in which certain outcomes of policy experiments are attributed to the regime when, in fact, the cause is something more fundamental that would be common to both regimes. A recent paper by Aaron Tornell and Andes Velasco, for example, bases the criteria for distinguishing between two regimes essentially on public finance.

In some Latin American experiences, the failure of programs has been laid at the door of the exchange rate rule. Yet it is very easy to show that, given the government's fiscal situation, the same outcome might have occurred under a different policy, such as a monetary rule set at too low a rate of monetary expansion.

Professor Frankel makes a persuasive case for the Tobin tax. He combines McKinnon's complaint about too little intervention and Tobin's complaint about too little speculation in a very smart way. These two issues are the heart of Professor Frankel's discussion of what happens when some fundamental changes in a small way and the market gains its own impetus, raising questions about corrections.

He also distinguishes between daily operators who have lasting expectations and so-called chartists—the long-term investors, the good guys who look at fundamentals and have regressive expectations. This idea is certainly very interesting, but I relate it to the dispersion of expectations among market participants. In pursuing this idea about the chartists who look at the fundamentals, one can get quite a bit of mileage by asking, What is the consequence of the dispersion of expectations among each of these groups? In other words, do all the chartists have or hold the same expectations?

If they do not hold the same expectations, then perhaps the effect of the Tobin tax would be to eliminate the more moderate daily operators and leave the extreme ones. (Although the Tobin tax is a very small tax on transactions, it can have a big effect on daily operators.) The elimination of some transactions does not necessarily mean there will not be a spot exchange rate, but its determinant can vary greatly.

In closing, I think the Tobin tax idea (to which I sometimes react more positively than even to intervention because it implies the rule provides a permanent base) should be distinguished from the general idea of imposing capital controls. In particular, when a fixed exchange rate is not carefully managed and on a permanent basis, it can be destabilizing.

Yes, we are all for intelligent intervention. The question is, Are we able to come up with any rules for intelligent intervention? What are the costs and benefits of guessing correctly or incorrectly? Is there a moral hazard problem in that intervention? In other words, bubbles normally burst, and timely intervention can assure a soft landing. What happens here to credibility or reputation in terms of incentives to future speculators? Should we expect that they will not land softly?

Professor Frankel asserts that the success of certain interventions, such as those in 1985–1987, was that they were kept secret. But in more recent experience, he commends making interventions public and says the effect of an announcement is almost as important as the intervention itself. Also, while not always explicitly, Professor Frankel seems to be talking about sterilizing intervention, which is another discussion that leaves the rule monetary policies to be whatever rule one would like.

Hanke:

As I was listening to Professor Frankel's remarks and his excellent review of the issues, I was reminded of a story that Professor Friedrick Von Hayak once told me. After someone had given a speech, he went back to the back of the room and started to talk to Ludwig Von Mises about the speech. Hayak said, "Well, that's great." Von Mises was unresponsive, so Hayak figured out Von Mises was deaf and told him, "You need to get a hearing aid. I just got one, and they are terrific." Von Mises looked at him and said, "I'm not buying one of those things. I've already heard enough."

I must say, Professor Frankel, about halfway through I was in kind of a Von Misian mode, but I switched into Hayakian mode. You left me extremely stimulated, and I will remark on several topics you have raised.

First, on the motivation for the European Monetary System and European Monetary Union, I think there was absolutely no economic rationale for the monetary union whatsoever; it was completely political. The economists have come in ex post facto to rationalize it, avoid competitive devaluations, eliminate volatility, reduce transactions costs, and all the rest. But primarily, the French want to defang the Bundesbank. As a sometime resident of Paris, I know this.

But I think the proof that it is true is that if the French or other Europeans really wanted to be in a unified currency area in Europe, the easiest way to do that immediately would be to form currency boards, issue their own domestic currency, and use the Deutsche mark as the anchor reserve currency. There is absolutely no way they would even contemplate getting on board with that because they really want to get the mark out of the system. As my old colleague, Bela Balassa, has shown in a French Academy paper, the French have suffered tremendously from being in the shadow of the Deutsche mark. It has really knocked a lot off their potential growth.

Second, Professor Frankel talks about what's wrong with the foreign exchange market, about exchange rates not always being on target with the fundamentals. This is typical of most markets, not just the foreign exchange market. Once one of my economist friends called me after he had just purchased a new house for, say, $200,000. Ten days later, he got his tax notice, and the assessed fair market value of the house was $250,000. So he went storming down to the tax office and said: "I just bought this thing 10 days ago for $200,000, and that was the market exchange. Now you are assessing me at $250,000." The assessor looked up at him and said, "Well, sir, you have to realize we are in the middle of a recession right now." The foreign exchange market really isn't that unusual in regard to these fundamental versus market value determinations, at least over the short run.

Regarding currency boards, we have Professor Frankel's three basic criteria for currency board introduction based on principle: (1) very small, open, well-integrated economies; (2) governments that crave further integration; and (3) countries that need to import monetary stability. There's actually a fourth item, and that is the practical matter of the issue of reserves.

With regard to reserves and currency boards, I think Professor Frankel is somewhat skeptical, thought not downright hostile. At any rate, he's left the door open for me to make a few remarks. At the end, this debate about currency boards and central banks is really just a rules-versus-discretion debate, so that's one point just to keep in mind. But let's review his three principles.

If you apply those three principles, excluding this feasibility (let's assume we can always get enough reserves to cover whatever we have to cover in a currency board system), my view is that most of the 132 developing countries in the world should have currency boards and be part of unified currency areas.

So Frankel and I agree in principle, almost. The qualifier comes in regard to the very small economies; I would drop this constraint. For example, after 1997, the Hong Kong monetary authority will be retained by China. I think it would be great if China went all the way to establish currency boards regionally—in other regions outside of Hong Kong and South China—because the Chinese, particularly as they go through a transition and are monetizing their economy, don't have a clue what the demand for money is. There's no way you can run a central bank, whether it's on a discretionary basis or a rule-driven system, without some idea of the demand for money. My view is that currency boards make a lot of sense in a place like China, which is certainly outside of the very small category. I think currency boards would work because in South China, where all the action is in China, about 60 percent of the money in use is Hong Kong dollars from the currency board in Hong Kong. Whether Chinese currency boards would work or not in terms of blackboard economics is irrelevant; one is working right now in the real world.

Let's consider the reserves and feasibility issue. In my view, this issue is something thrown up by opponents of currency boards to give some fig leaf of respectability to their arguments. They can't just say, "We're against it, period, and that's the end of it and we're not discussing it." The theoretical arguments, I think, get a little bit flimsy with regard to the currency board system. You don't see critics coming out with much by way of substantive theoretical or practical critique. But there are questions about feasibility, and the big question is whether you have the reserves to cover the monetary base or the liabilities of a central bank 100 percent.

Now when this debate started, the only skeptic who gave serious consideration to currency boards, while not being favorably disposed to them, was John Williamson. John has done a lot of work on this subject and, incidentally, given me a lot of help. And he has a new monograph on currency boards that is a good survey of the whole scene.

When we started proposing a currency board for Russia, of course we heard from opponents. There really wasn't much of an economic argument against the suggestion; the questions were about feasibility. John argued that, at the time, the exchange rate was about 420 rubles per dollar, a level that would have meant reserves had to be just over $5 billion to cover the monetary base. John's argument was that, based on purchasing power parity, the exchange rate should have been not 420, but about 25 rubles per dollar. The effect of John's numbers, of course, would be to pump up the required reserves considerably, to about 85 billion versus five billion rubles. So currency boards kind of go off the boards, if I can use that term. That was a very effective piece of grit in the works that really slowed things down, and, of course, Russia does not have a currency board. The exchange rate isn't 420 to the dollar, either.

Moving to phase two, the argument about what exchange rate you should use worked for awhile, but it was fairly transparent. The new argument is that you must eliminate fractional reserve banking and go to 100 percent of broad money covered, an approach that gets into serious reserve requirements.

I think my counterargument is fine. If you want to maintain not only the solvency but liquidity of banks, go to the old Chicago plan: have 100 percent reserve banking with no fractional reserve system, and apply it every place in the developing world, whether the country has a central bank or currency board. I don't think it makes a bit of difference. After all, no central bank guarantees that you can exchange all broad money into foreign exchange. My suggestion would apply this on a level playing field everywhere. Incidentally, over the history of currency boards, there have been very few banking problems—liquidity problems, let alone insolvency problems—in countries that have had currency boards, as compared with countries that have central banks. In looking at this coverage of broad money with 100 percent of reserves, I think we have ignored history and focused a little bit too much on Argentina's contemporaneous experience.

Let me make a remark about Argentina, Lithuania, and Estonia. Each of these countries has a relatively new currency boardlike system. There is not an orthodox currency board in any of the cases. These boards have a limited amount of discretion. This discretion creates tremendous problems, particularly when the boards are not mature and do not have full credibility, because with a currency board there is still an exchange rate and exchange rate risk. The only way to avoid the risk is to do something like El Salvador is planning—dollarize and get rid of the exchange rate. As long as there is a board, there is, in principle, some exchange rate risk that remains quite significant, particularly in Argentina.

In Lithuania in December 1994 and January 1995, the country used its lender-of-last-resort facility. Lithuania substituted some litas-denominated reserves for dollar reserves, which is a no-no, and pledged some of its reserves as collateral for a $10 million loan from the Germans. Clearly, this is not a currency board. Lithuania is breaking its own law in this case. The Lithuanians have cleaned the thing up, but while there were no bank runs or anything, an external flow of money out of the system did result.

Argentina also has a lender-of-last-resort facility. If the country has excess reserves beyond that 100 percent cover, it can use them, as it did in the 1995 crisis. A limited amount of funds—up to 20 percent of the dollar-denominated reserves—can be issued by the government of Argentina. These are low-quality, dollar-denominated reserves, the Bonex bonds. During the crisis, Argentina increased that proportion from about 5 percent to about 15 percent, so the quality of the reserve cover went down. Argentina's monetary policymakers also controlled the reserve requirements of the commercial banks, something currency boards usually do not do. Usually, in fact, there is no reserve requirement. This lowering of reserves rattled the market. All at once, Argentina had the repos going on, the lowering of reserves, and the Bonex increase; all these things inflamed the speculation and stimulated the attack that was under way.

The real killer, though, was something that, to my knowledge, is unique in the history of currency boards. I am referring to what happened with foreign branch banks. Usually, foreign branch banks are a wonderful thing for a currency board system. Currency board countries usually have a lot of foreign branch banks because they have credit lines to their mother house and, when the currency board country has a liquidity squeeze, liquidity immediately comes in through arbitrage opportunities. (Such squeezes do not last long. In Hong Kong, for instance, rates can go up to 50 percent or so for 24 hours, and then the squeeze is over.)

In Argentina, the situation obviously had started to deteriorate after the December 1994 Mexican peso crisis. But Argentina's situation did not become severe until February 27, 1995. On that day, the credit lines of the foreign branches were cut by their mother houses, and the foreign branches had to go into the interbank market. Interbank rates went up from about 20 percent to 60 percent in one day, and what did that do? Already there had been some external drains out of the system and some internal drains in the system. The cutoff of foreign branches' credit line stimulated tremendous internal drains. The bank runs began, and Argentina was left in a tough spot. The country had no protection from the internal drain of bank runs in this scenario. There was no deposit insurance, only limited powers as lender of last resort, and no 100 percent banking. The only resort under a currency board system or gold standard is suspension of convertibility of deposits into cash. But, in effect, Argentina did not have this out either because they had suspended in 1989; to do so again would have been a complete disaster.

To conclude, I love Professor Frankel's taxonomy. It is very effective. I offer only one slight modification. And just to clarify my position, there are three basic regimes:

1. on one extreme is the fixed rate, with either a pure gold standard or an orthodox currency board that is a free market mechanism for international payments
2. on the other extreme is the floating rate without intervention, which is a free market mechanism for international payments
3. in between the fixed and floating rates is the adjustable peg, which is to be accomplished by managing the exchange rate, domestic liquidity, and, usually, the capital account. (This approach is a completely impossible task; that is why we had ERM 1992, France 1993, and Mexico 1994.)

I think where we should go is to take one of those two extremes. For the 32 industrialized countries, let's float. For the 132 developing countries, the only way to keep the clamps on the politicians is to enter unified currency areas with the 32 that float or one of the large currencies that floats.

Frankel:
I would like to thank both discussants for their comments, and most of what they said I agree with. But I will choose one item from each of them that I do not entirely agree with and make a further point.

First, I agree with most of what Professor Auernheimer said. But I want to emphasize this point about whether there is a fundamental amount of real exchange rate variability out there that is invariant to whichever regime you adopt. I think the evidence is clear that this idea is not right.

When you move from a fixed rate regime to a floating rate regime, of course, nominal variability goes up—by almost any definition. Real exchange rate variability does go up, too. I cite the example of pre- and post-1973, but some people say, "That's a coincidence. There are other things going on. We had oil shocks; the world has become a more variable place."

Other examples from other regime shifts support my view. My favorite is one Mike Mussa has discussed about Ireland's bilateral exchange rates. Instead of a two-by-two table, think of a three-by-three table. We have Ireland's bilateral exchange rate variability vis-à-vis first the dollar, then the pound, then the mark. And think of the 1960s, the 1970s and the 1980s. In the 1960s, Ireland was pegged to the dollar like everybody else. In the 1970s, Ireland pegged to the pound, which floated against other currencies. And in the 1980s, Ireland's currency was closely tied to the mark through the ERM. In the nine cells are the bilateral variabilities. In each case where the Irish currency was pegged to the other currency in question, nominal variability was very low, and nominal variability was high vis-à-vis whichever currencies they were not pegged to. The key point is that the pattern of real exchange rate variability mirrors the pattern of nominal exchange rate variability. It always collapses almost to zero vis-à-vis the country that's being pegged to, and it always goes up against the currencies that are not being pegged to. Those shifts happened, I think, for political, exogenous reasons. The evidence is pretty convincing that there is a lot of variability that is related to the choice of regime rather than to underlying monetary fundamentals.

The comment from Steve Hanke I want to discuss is the part about the reserves in the currency board being sort of a red herring, an excuse. I think it is more serious than that. First, if you are worried about banking crises, then you need enough reserves. That issue is separate from the issue of the currency board, but you see that the two are interrelated when you remember what the guarantee is under a currency board. When a country declares that it has a currency board, what the country is declaring is that if there is a crisis, a speculative attack, it will allow the domestic money supply to contract. Money will flow out of the country, and the domestic money supply will contract however much it takes; the country will allow interest rates to rise however far it takes. That is what Argentine policymakers said they would do last year, and the policy seemed to work with some help from the IMF.

But it is no coincidence that this view raises the issue of banking crises. If you let interest rates rise however much it takes, the banking sector will have problems, and that is why having enough reserves to back the monetary base is not enough. Having some extra reserves to bail out the banking sector is a substantial issue, not just an excuse. (As Professor Hanke notes, I have made a proposal for how some Eastern European countries might be able to come up with the reserves.)

Look at the countries that have had currency boards that have worked so far. Where did Estonia get reserves? Estonia had gold, or as I understand the story, the U.K. was generous. They had gold on deposit from Estonia that they had returned to the Soviets. When Estonians asked for it 40 years later, the U.K. said, "Well, okay" and gave the money again to the Estonians.

In Argentina after such great hyperinflation, the real money supply was very low. It was easy to get reserves.

I think reserves are a real issue. I have made a proposal for how other small Central or Eastern European countries that meet the criteria I laid out, such as the Czech Republic, could get reserves. My proposal is that they go to Brussels and say, "We are going to be the first country to adopt the Euro as our legal currency. This will give you a real shot in the arm. You folks in Brussels have been depressed since these EMU crises, and you want to move forward. This will help the movement to EMU; you actually are going to have the Euro circulating somewhere. There is just one catch. You have to give us enough Euros to do this." This proposal illustrates how a currency board could be made to work for countries that otherwise might have trouble coming up with reserves.

To sum up, Steve Hanke and I agree that the United States should float, we agree that Estonia should fix, and it is just the countries in between that we have to talk about.

Question:
(from Liliana Rojas-Suárez)
With respect to currency boards, one of the prerequisites that, in my view, has not been stressed enough is the pressure on the banking system. In the recent case of Argentina, there were pressures on the trade rate and problems with the banking system.

The reason the Argentine banking system was able to manage pressures on the exchange rate without an even greater crisis in the banking sector was because banks had a lot of liquid reserves, and they used those liquid reserves to satisfy the demand for deposits. When those reserves were gone, the central bank was able to manage the crisis because rather than letting the interest rate go as far as the currency board would have required, the central bank had a short-term facility with the banks called a swap operation. The swap operation, within the norms of the comparability law, allowed the central bank to extend a certain amount of cash to the banks.

What I am saying is that, unlike industrial countries where assets are in all kinds of maturities and liquidity, in the countries we are discussing, especially Latin American countries, most of the assets are very liquid, with short-run maturities. Under a currency board, defending the exchange rate implies high increases in interest rates. So if the banking system is not strong enough, it will lead to a collapse of the financial sector. This trade-off needs to be taken into account when discussing currency boards in Latin America.

Hanke:
I completely agree.

Question:
I was surprised that there was no discussion about how, if the currency board is to work, there must be an adjustment of the real exchange rate and how

inflationary pressure builds. Perhaps we need a lot of flexibility in the labor market.

Frankel:
I think that might be worth discussing. I assume part of the argument for a small open economy is that flexibility is greater. At least this is true in Hong Kong.

Part II OPTIMAL EXCHANGE RATE POLICY FOR STABILIZING INFLATION IN DEVELOPING COUNTRIES

Many developing countries, especially in Latin America, have used the exchange rate as a nominal anchor to help stabilize inflation. But highly managed exchange rate regimes in developing countries have had a tendency to fail, with dramatic consequences. Should developing countries manage the exchange rate or let it float?

Presenter:
Sebastian Edwards
Professor of Economics
University of California, Los Angeles

Moderator:
Evan Koenig
Research Officer
Federal Reserve Bank of Dallas

Discussants:
Graciela Kaminsky
Economist
Board of Governors
Federal Reserve System

John Welch
Chief Economist, Latin America
Lehman Brothers

Edwards:
There is little doubt that exchange rates are today at the very center of the economic policy debate. They appear on the front page of newspapers, in the news, and even in dinner conversations when people try to decide whether to speculate or go on vacation.

There are, I think, four fundamental issues in exchange rate economics that occupy most of the time, at least of economists. One, shall we use the exchange rate as an anti-inflationary tool and, in particular, should we use a fixed rate to bring down inflation? Two, what should be the exchange rate regime over the longer run once inflation has been obtained? Three, do exchange rate regimes affect policymakers' behavior and, in particular, is it the case that a fixed exchange rate imposes discipline on fiscal and monetary behavior? And four, how do we know if the real exchange rate is out of line and overvalued?

What I would like to focus my discussion on is the first of these issues: the use of exchange rates as stabilization devices in an anti-inflationary program. And I would like to ask whether this is a good idea, whether it makes sense. Are countries that adopt this strategy likely to succeed? If so, what are the determinants of this out of the possible outcomes of this type of policy, and what are the dangers and the challenges?

Without any doubt, after the Mexican crisis, this particular question has become once again very important. It has become important not only because we would like to understand what actually happened in Mexico but also because other countries are considering embarking on similar paths in efforts to bring down inflation. It is particularly important for those of us who follow Latin America because one of the most important countries in the region, Argentina, has adopted that kind of system to bring down inflation. And there are a number of skeptics about the fate of Argentina.

I think that in discussing the merits of using the exchange rate as a policy tool in an anti-inflationary program, it is useful to distinguish among a number of aspects of the problem: what are the initial conditions from which most economies that have adopted this kind of policy have started; what are the other policies that are usually undertaken jointly with a fixed exchange rate; what are the short-run effects of these policies; and how has the situation historically unfolded? In discussing this issue, I will refer again and again to the case of Mexico. I will tell you my reading of the Mexican story and relate what happened to Mexico to the experience of Chile in the early 1980s. In Chile, a very similar program was adopted that, as in the case of Mexico, ended in crisis, frustration and sorrow.

Inflation: Where Exchange-Rate-Based Stabilization Programs Begin

What is usually the starting point in an exchange-rate-based stabilization program? Usually, it is a situation of high inflation, triple-digit inflation. Mexico's inflation was about 157 percent to 160 percent at the start. We have a situation in which inflation has been going on at this type of rate for a sufficiently long period of time for people to begin to internalize. And the way it is internalized is that indexation starts to take hold of the economy. Indexation takes hold of contracts, and contracts are adjusted according to some index periodically. Depending on the initial rate of inflation, the periodicity may be every six months or every three months. And if the inflation rate becomes too high, the adjustment becomes a monthly one.

Indexation also takes over wages, and wages are guided by a combination of forward-looking expectations and backward-looking indexation that takes into account accumulated inflation in between wage adjustments. In most cases, the exchange-rate-based stabilization program starts from a situation in which the exchange rate up to that point also has become indexed through the adoption of some kind of purchasing power parity (PPP) approach toward adjusting the nominal exchange rate every period according to accumulated inflation differentials between the country in question and some partner or group of partners.

In this type of scenario in which inflation is high, higher than 100 percent, and where contracts are readjusted according to some index, a very high degree of inertia and persistence occurs. From a technical point of view, it is very easy to show that in this type of regime, the rate of inflation can be represented as a first-order outer regressive mechanism in which inflation today depends on a number of variables but fundamentally on what inflation was yesterday.

The degree of persistence from period to period depends on how generalized indexation is, how backward-looking wage contract adjustments are, and exactly what exchange rate policy the government follows. What we have seen in the initial phases of a stabilization program of this type is that the rate of inflation can be characterized by having a unit root. That means inflation in the previous period is totally passed into the current period and the degree of persistence is complete. And what this means is that the system has completely lost its nominal anchor. Depending on what happens to other policies, including external shocks, inflation could go anywhere. Indeed, this is what we have seen in a number of Latin American countries.

Possibly the best example is Brazil. For a number of years, Brazil followed this type of policy, and the rate of inflation was 40 percent per year stable. The first oil shock came, and inflation just jumped—no anchor, no force to bring it back down to a different level. The rate of inflation jumped to around 200 percent. A new shock came, and it jumped to 400 percent and stayed stable for a time. A new shock came, and it went up to 2,000 percent. There were no forces in this setting that would make inflation revert toward some kind of lower equilibrium level, such as international inflation.

It is in this context that at some point, the authorities decide to bring down inflation. In the well-behaved cases—such as Mexico's and, in the 1970s and 1980s, Chile's—the first thing the authorities do, and rightly so, is tackle the fiscal problem. And when the fiscal problem is tackled and inflation continues to be high and to be extremely stubborn, the decision is usually made to use the exchange rate as a stabilization device.

The exchange rate is fixed, and by fixing the exchange rate, it is argued that the prices of tradable goods will have some kind of limit in terms of how fast they can grow and, in that way, it is thought that inflation will come down.

In general, there are two variants of this policy. The first one aims at eliminating inflation very quickly. We have seen very few of those examples in the world when the starting point is one of very rapid but not hyperinflation. Possibly the best-known example is France's stabilization in the 1920s.

The other variant, and it's the one that Mexico followed, is where fixing the exchange rate does not have the purpose of eliminating inflation immediately but has as its main purpose reducing the degree of inertia, the degree of persistence —the extent to which inflation yesterday affects inflation today.

If the degree of inertia is indeed reduced this way, there is a very serious danger of the exchange rate's becoming highly appreciated because, of course, as inertia is reduced but inflation is not eliminated, the real exchange rate begins to appreciate.

The Mexican authorities were clearly aware of this danger. But they thought Mexico would be exempt of the effects of this appreciation for three reasons: one, because Mexico had ample international reserves; two, because Mexico started the experiment in a situation of undervaluation and, thus, had a cushion in which the real exchange rate could appreciate without leading to an overvaluation; and three, because Mexican policymakers thought there would be very rapid productivity gains that would compensate or more than compensate for the appreciation of the real exchange rate that would come with the adoption of the exchange-rate-based stabilization program.

Finance Minister Pedro Aspe in 1988, when the program was adopted as a longer term feature of the stabilization efforts in Mexico, went to the Mexican congress and said: "For the exchange rate to serve as an anchor, it is required that the balance of payments starts from a favorable surplus position. The use of the exchange rate according to a downward trend is fully justified if we consider that there is an ample margin of antivaluation of our currency."

Indeed, the Mexican authorities were aware of the appreciation syndrome but were confident because of these three reasons: an ample surplus in the balance of payments, enough international reserves, and an initial situation of antivaluation that provided a cushion.

The exchange-rate-based stabilization program was applied in Mexico, the fiscal side had been fully corrected, the primary balance was in surplus on the order of 7 or 8 percent of GDP, and the system then was put into place.

Let's see what happened. Inflation did initially come down very quickly; it then hit about 20 percent and got stuck at that level. It persisted at 20 percent, while the rate of devaluation of the peso was significantly lower and declining. As a consequence, the real exchange rate started to appreciate the Latin American way, where appreciation moves downward in a very significant way. At some point, some people became concerned that the cushion had been used.

Let me now compare this with what happened to Chile during the 1970s and 1980s. In 1978, Chile adopted an exchange-rate-based stabilization program, and in 1979, the exchange rate was fully fixed to the dollar at 39 pesos per dollar. What we see is a pattern that is very similar to the Mexican pattern: a rapid reduction in the rate of inflation, which gets stuck at some point at around 20 percent and then slows. For the same reasons as in Mexico, the real exchange rate, however, appreciates very significantly. And the accumulated rate of appreciation in Chile between 1978 and 1981 was around 28, 30 percent, depending on how one measures it. The rate of appreciation in Mexico is on the order of 33, 35 percent.

In the case of Mexico, as the authorities had argued, the degree of inertia was reduced. But the degree of inertia was not reduced significantly. As these figures suggest, the residual degree of persistence was still considerable, and that helps explain why the real exchange rate continued to appreciate.

By 1989, a number of people were seriously concerned about the viability of the Mexican system. Many observers began to argue that the cushion from an undervalued currency had already been fully used and that the exchange rate was becoming not only appreciated but overvalued.

In early 1990, however, the international financial community rediscovered Latin America. And it rediscovered Latin America years, if not decades, earlier than most of us thought it would. In particular, the international financial community rediscovered Mexico.

After the Brady deal was signed, the Mexicans began to privatize the banks, and all of a sudden Mexico, with its reforms, its privatization, its stellar group of policymakers, looked like an extremely attractive alternative. In two years,

Mexico jumped in the Euromoney country risk ranking from 77 to 34, way ahead of Chile in 1990, way ahead of many other countries that one would consider a very good and sure bet.

The great reduction in risk that took place at this point, the enthusiasm for Mexico, the privatization of banks, and the notion that NAFTA may actually happen, resulted in massive inflows of capital into Mexico. These massive inflows did basically two things. First, they allowed Mexico to finance the emerging trade deficit and do away with concern about the decline of international reserves. Second, they allowed people to finance a truly tremendous consumption boom that was reflected in a decline in private savings rates in Mexico that was staggering—from around 14 percent to around 8 percent of GDP.

As this capital came into the country, people were able to increase their expenditures. As part of these expenditures went into real estate and domestic goods, the real appreciation that we had seen because inertia had not been fully eliminated became even more serious. Of course, the other side of the coin of this capital inflows phenomenon was a very large current and trade account deficit.

Let's see what the data show, both on capital inflows and on the deficit. We can see how capital inflows into Mexico jump from being negative in 1988 and very small in 1989 to a level of roughly 9 percent of GDP by 1993.

Let's see the parallel in the case of Chile in the 1970s and 1980s. You can see how imports just explode and the trade deficit becomes tremendously large in the case of Mexico. What is very important to note is that export growth is rather modest. That, to a large extent, is because the exchange rate continued to appreciate throughout the period, and despite what the authorities expected, productivity in Mexico did not grow throughout this period.

The case of Chile, of course, is similar. In fact, in Chile, the exports not only did not grow very fast, at the end of the overvaluation appreciation period they actually declined. The fact that capital flew into the country at a very fast rate —allowing the financing of the trade deficit, allowing an increase in the current account deficit, and, in a way, justifying the real exchange rate appreciation —became an issue of concern to many analysts. The concern in 1989 about the real exchange rate appreciation was now compounded by the fact that not only had the real exchange rate appreciated significantly, the current account deficit financed by these capital flows was extremely large, on the order of 8 percent of GDP in Mexico and 12 percent of GDP in Chile.

When people expressed their worries and their preoccupation about this case, the reply by Mexican and by Chilean officials more than a decade earlier was that we shouldn't worry: these were private capital inflows, and the fiscal conditions were under control.

The governor of the Bank of Mexico told economists in January of 1994 that the current account deficit was not a problem because it was associated with inflows of private foreign funds rather than an expansionary fiscal or monetary policy, and that's a quote from the economists.

The Bank of Mexico annual report expressed in 1993, and I'm quoting:

> The current account deficit has been determined exclusively by the private sector's decisions to save and invest. Because of the above and the solid position of public finances, the current account deficit (which had been around 8 percent) should clearly not be a cause for concern.

What had Chilean authorities said back in 1981? The minister of finance said:

> There is no doubt that privately financed current account deficits are highly beneficial for the country and that we should make an effort to maintain them at the highest possible level and for the longest possible period of time.

So not only was there no reason to be concerned, in fact, they should be promoted.

Of course, from a factual point of view, it was true in both cases that the fiscal situation was under control, although it was lucent in Mexico in 1994. In that regard, we did not see the kind of situation that we usually see in typical balance-of-payment crises and currency collapses. What is missing in the argument that we shouldn't worry because these are private capital flows is that these private capital flows during the early stages of the reform process are due to a stock adjustment. They are due to the fact that there have been reforms and that the country risk associated with the country has declined significantly.

Because the country risk has been reduced significantly, all of a sudden there is a tremendous demand for the country's securities. And for this demand for the country's securities to take place, a very large capital inflow has to occur in a short time. But capital inflows at that level are temporary and will only stay at those tremendously high levels while the stock adjustment takes place and is resold.

When the stock adjustment has been resold and international investors are holding the amount of Mexican or Chilean or Argentine securities that they want to hold, capital inflows will have to come down to a new, sustainable level. They don't have to become negative. They don't have to reverse themselves. We don't have to see a transfer going in the other direction necessarily, but in the long run, it is highly unlikely that a country can run a current account deficit of 8 or 12 percent of GDP.

In fact, any portfolio model would suggest that in a country like Mexico, where the rate of economic growth at the time and the rate of growth expected for the near future was not spectacular—rather modest, indeed—the sustainable current account deficit was on the order of 2 to 4 percent, not 8 percent of GDP, as we observed in 1992 and 1993. So the question by late 1993 was not whether the capital that was flowing into Mexico or the rest of Latin America, for that matter, was sustainable. That was not the question, because it clearly was not sustainable at that level.

The questions were different, although related. And the relevant questions were when and to what extent will we see a slowdown of this capital inflow? And when we see a slowdown of this capital inflow, what kind of mechanism will our countries use to adjust to the lower availability of foreign financing, and what kind of mechanism will they use to make sure the economy has a smooth landing?

Finding the Formula for a Smooth Landing

The problem is that a fixed exchange rate makes a smooth landing difficult. It makes a smooth landing difficult because when capital comes into the country and helps finance the increasing trade and current account deficit, there are no impediments to appreciation of the real exchange rate.

But when these flows stop flowing in, slow down, or even worse, when, for any reason—be it a kidnapping, a political assassination, or a crisis in another country—the demand for that country's securities is reduced, the required real devaluation is much harder to engineer, especially because inertia continues, prices and wages are rather inflexible, and the situation is very different.

Mexico had built into its system some flexibility through the existence of the band, but once the band was used up, we were in a different regime. Once the exchange rate was at the ceiling of the band, for all practical purposes, we were under a fixed-exchange-rate regime. And it was necessary at that time to play by the rules of the fixed-exchange-rate regime if we were to see a successful, although costly, adjustment.

The problem is that, at that time, of course, the game was not played according to the rules. There was sterilization of the laws of international reserves, interest rates were not allowed to go up, *tesobonos* were substituted for *cetes* and, in the end, instead of having a smooth landing, we had a tremendous crash.

Chile went through the whole adjustment Mexico has seen. Once the adjustment took place, Chile was forced to generate in order to reverse the transfer. Capital inflows not only slowed down, they were completely reversed, as has been the case of Mexico, arguably, today. Imports had to be compressed a tremendous amount. The magnitude and the speed of the imports adjustment in Chile we have not seen in too many countries in the modern history of economics. And this decline in imports to 50 percent of what they had reached clearly captures the severity of the Chilean crisis, where unemployment went up to 30 percent and where GDP declined in just the first year by 14 percent.

What I would like to argue is that, to a large extent, this kind of outcome, which does not occur in all exchange-rate-based stabilization programs, is so costly that even if one attaches to them a limited probability, it is an extremely risky way to go.

So, what shall we do? I think the historical evidence, including the two stories that I have just told you, increasingly points toward the notion that there may be some merit to using a fixed exchange rate to bring down inflation during the early phases of a stabilization program, but the key is to know when to exit that program. Once inflation expectations are broken, it is time to get out of the system and move to a different type of regime, as Israel did successfully.

And I would argue that the regime that should be adopted once the policy has been exited successfully is a regime based on either a crawling peg or a managed float that would provide this system landing gear. I think that a comparison of the Chilean, Colombian, and Mexican cases in that regard is very illustrative. Mexico during the 1980s and 1990s followed its pegged program. After the 1980s experience, Chile, in contrast, decided very clearly not to peg the exchange rate. Chile followed a policy that was basically geared at not letting the exchange rate become overvalued. While Chile averaged 6 to 7 percent growth during this period, Mexico grew an average of 2.8 percent. Colombia, which at the same time did not fix the exchange rate, grew at 5.1 percent. While inflation in Mexico eventually came down to a single-digit rate, Chile lived with double-digit inflation until 1994.

In the trade-off between inflation and growth, clearly both Colombia and Chile have decided to very strongly favor growth. If one takes the index of real wages in 1980 equal to 100, today Chilean wages are 126. Colombian wages are 123. Mexican wages in 1994, before the crisis, were 99.4 percent. And if one goes on through a number of indicators, one can see that both Colombia and Chile were able to maintain a rapid rate of growth with livable, and, in the case of Chile, declining inflation, and at the same time not put the system into the straitjacket that the fixed exchange rate means. I think the lesson of all of this is that at the end of the road, the straitjacket, the rigidities, the inflexibilities associated with a fixed exchange rate are too great to gamble on. And countries such as the Latin American countries in general should opt for flexible exchange rate regimes. In the debate between fixity and flexibility, I think that increasingly, flexibility is getting the upper hand, notwithstanding the currency board supporters.

Let me end with the one case in Latin America that I think is an exception. I think that Argentina is a case where clearly it is justifiable, understandable, and that one should support strongly the type of exchange rate regime and monetary system that the country has followed. In a country that has been used to very high rates of inflation, to fiscal and monetary indiscipline with almost no parallel, a country where the authorities debase the currency every time they have a chance, there was very little alternative but to choose the route that the Argentines chose: the convertibility law, the opening of the capital account early on, the one-to-one exchange rate policy, the quasi-currency-board system.

But I think what is more important than that is that the Argentines understood that having that kind of system not only allows inflation to come down very quickly and brings stability not seen in Argentina for decades, it also means there are very serious responsibilities that monetary and fiscal authorities must follow. That means when the tables turn against you, you must be willing to play by the rules of the game of a truly fixed—fixed but not adjustable—exchange rate. Argentina has played by those rules, and the system is responding in an admirable way because, I think, the country is moving in the right direction. The probability of a crisis has been greatly reduced, but at the same time we are seeing that the cost is a very deep recession. What Argentina has done has been very courageous. It is paying off at a cost, but no one said that was not going to be the case.

Conclusion

Let me end by saying that if one really gets a lesson from Mexico, it is the importance of economic history. Had we all paid more attention to the previous experiences in Latin America, we would not have had to look very far to find out that the Mexican crisis had close predecessors, in fact, a very close one in the case of Chile. If economic history had been looked at with greater care and less arrogance, maybe some of these problems would have been avoided.

Kaminsky:

In his presentation, Sebastian asked three different questions. The one that he emphasized was whether fixed exchange rates help anchor inflation. He discussed why some countries have adopted the fixed exchange rate while others haven't, and whether a fixed exchange rate imposes discipline on central banks.

I will be mostly concerned with the analysis of the first point, whether fixed exchange rates help anchor inflation. I will try to condense the other two questions by asking what conditions are necessary for a fixed exchange rate to be viable.

Although Sebastian didn't present it, I will discuss some evidence from Latin America and EMS countries that illustrates how successful fixed-exchange-rate regimes are in anchoring inflation. Data from the stabilization programs in the 1970s and 1980s in Argentina, Chile, Israel, and Mexico show that inflation ranged from 3 percent to 23 percent per month in all these countries. Under stabilization programs like the Austral plan, the Israeli plan in 1985, and the

Mexico plan at the end of 1987, inflation fell drastically during the first year, moving into the one-digit range.

So from this point of view, it seems that fixed-exchange-rate regimes have helped anchor inflation in these countries. It is important to consider how the fixed exchange rate works. The fixed exchange rate imposes a binding constraint on central banks. They cannot accommodate different shocks in the economy. Therefore, because monetary policy is not a commodity, inflation must lose persistence.

In fact, inflation's persistence seems to have been reduced drastically in three of these cases. For example, in the case of Argentina's inflation, if you have something like a unishock in one period before the plan, in the next period, about 80 percent of the shock persisted. After 10 months, one-year inflation still was on the order of 40 percent to 50 percent. After the plan, inflation's persistence was drastically reduced. The case is similar for Israel and Mexico. As Sebastian has pointed out, in Chile this persistence was not eliminated. One reason was the indexation of wages.

In principle, this evidence seems to suggest that fixed exchange rates work. But let me give you some further evidence from EMS countries. In the first part of the table, you can see data from EMS countries and non-EMS countries before and after EMS's inception. Inflation was higher in non-EMS countries before EMS, and inflation decreased substantially in the EMS countries relative to non-EMS countries after the fixed-exchange-rate regime or the target zones regime was adopted. This evidence seems to support the idea that anchors work. I want to point out that during the first three years of the EMS, inflation was not reduced. Four years after the inception of EMS, however, inflation patterns of EMS countries and non-EMS countries start to show different patterns.

I also examined and tried to reproduce some results from a paper by Sue Collins in which she asks whether the EMS helped reduce inflation. She compares EMS and non-EMS countries. We cannot look just at when the exchange rate was fixed. We must be able to compare which type of shocks affected inflation in these countries before and after EMS, and we have to control for them. I examine an equation for inflation in which we test whether the EMS was, in fact, a leading force in the reduction of inflation in the EMS, or whether the early 1980s inflation was reduced throughout Europe and the United States. From this analysis, I observe that in the 1979 and 1985 episodes, whether we consider EMS countries or non-EMS countries, inflation was reduced. In fact, if you look at whether the EMS had additional explanatory power in the reduction of inflation in EMS countries, we observe that this is not the case.

The evidence on how successful these fixed exchange rates have been is mixed. Research should continue in this direction because fixed exchange rates, by enhancing the credibility of central banks, should reduce the persistence of inflation, and we should be able to examine how attitudes about inflation change under fixed-exchange-rate programs and under more flexible exchange rate regimes. We should be looking at how flexible wages become after the imposition of the fixed-exchange-rate regime and whether this increasing credibility encourages workers to moderate wage demands and enhances wage flexibility.

I want to support Sebastian's view that, even if the adoption of the fixed-exchange-rate regime helps anchor inflation, the movements of prices and wages have been slow. As a result of the adoption of the fixed exchange rate regime, we observe large appreciations of the domestic currency, some loss of competitiveness, and large current account deficits. We cannot say that all this real exchange rate appreciation is the result of fixing the exchange rate and the stickiness of wages and prices. We must consider that, aside from the adoption of fixed exchange rates in all these countries, there have been some sweeping reforms.

In Argentina, reforms in the fiscal sector have helped open the economy. So changes in productivity alone could explain this real appreciation as an equilibrium phenomenon. If we want to cast doubt on how flexible prices and wages are, we cannot just look at the real exchange rate and conclude that this is a disequilibrium phenomenon. Still, as a result of the adoption of a fixed-exchange-rate regime, we observe that, with the qualifications and caveats, these countries have lost some competitiveness. During the period of fixing, we observe the increase in the current account deficits.

In closing, I will comment on the viability of these fixed-exchange-rate regimes. When the ERM and the Mexican crises started, some people said all these currencies were overappreciated, prices and wages did not come rapidly enough, and, therefore, competitiveness requires more flexibility on the exchange rates. Whether we agree or not, it is true that at the time of each crisis, these countries had suffered some other shocks. In the case of the ERM, we can talk about the monetary and economic unification of Germany that, by itself, requires some appreciation of the German currency in terms of other currencies. And in the case of Latin America, we've seen the change in monetary policy in the United States and a decrease in the demand for assets of Latin America countries.

Those shocks require some real depreciation of the domestic currencies. The question is how to achieve this real depreciation. Mexico has chosen one way. Argentina, perhaps due to the history of chronic hyperinflation, has chosen the other way. There are trade-offs between credibility and real adjustment. The cost of maintaining central bank credibility has led Argentina into a large recession. But we have to consider that the situations in Mexico, the EMS countries, and Argentina are different. So choosing this fixed exchange rate might be appropriate for countries that have experience running hyperinflation, but at the same time, the choice bears some costs.

Welch:
Dr. Edwards has taken a stand on which type of exchange rate policy he likes, especially in the debate between more rigid and more flexible exchange rates. He clearly provides evidence that he likes more flexibility in exchange rates, although not necessarily a floating rate over a more rigid one. Rigid regimes tend to collapse, allowing speculators like George Soros to make a lot of money at the expense of other investors, and, probably more important, the central bank.

Flexible rates tend to preclude this type of situation. I wish he had pursued this thought further because he doesn't discuss the role that financial markets and financial institutions had in the Chilean, Mexican, or ERM crisis. Yes, fortunes were made and lost in the ERM crisis, but in the most recent Mexican crisis, fortunes mostly were lost. Why is that?

In the ERM crisis, speculators were allowed to short-sell currency. In other words, they could sell currency they didn't own. Shorting in the first instance may increase instability and make a currency more vulnerable to attack, as in ERM's case. In 1992, when the shorts were clearly much bigger than those going the other way for the British pound, everyone headed for the exits. But to make a profit on a short, you have to cover it. In other words, you must buy the assets you've sold that you do not own.

What happened almost immediately in the next week was a huge short-covering rally that gave a supporting bid to the British pound. On top of that, because those investors had to buy pound-denominated assets, a very large bond market rally began, despite the loss in credibility the Bank of England suffered from leaving the ERM.

In Mexico, there was no such dynamic. Shorting or hedging the peso is very difficult and very expensive. The first devaluation occurred on December 20, 1994, and signaled to investors who had not been getting the reserve data for some time that reserves were much worse than most had feared. Everybody headed for the exits, and for a couple of reasons: one was fear that dollar reserves would not cover short-term dollar obligations, most notably *tesobonos*, and two, fear that the first devaluation may have seriously injured the banks that were already in very serious condition. There was no supporting bid that emerged until the United States and the International Monetary Fund stepped in.

So the question here, at least in terms of the exchange-rate-regime choice and floating rate, is, Are certain levels of financial development and infrastructure necessary to accommodate a floating rate? We come to the same conclusion in the end about how to make a transition—especially using Chile as an example —to that particular type of regime if you do not have this infrastructure.

If regulation restricts the ability to short a currency or to hedge oneself, investment will be lower and the central bank will face political pressure, both internal and external, to provide that hedge through a fixed rate or similar policy. Although investors could not short the peso, it did not keep a collapse from occurring, particularly after the devaluation of December 20. These comments, however, do not detract from Dr. Edwards' main conclusion on flexible rates or the semiflexible rates I believe he prefers. But the role of financial institutions has many important dimensions not only to the question of collapse, but also to the question of persistence of inflation.

The framework Dr. Edwards chose to look at how this overvaluation occurred, in my mind, puts undue emphasis on backward indexation. No matter what exchange rate regime is in place, real appreciation follows huge capital inflows. It's not really a question of exchange rate regime at this point. However, Edwards concludes that the increasing rigidity of the exchange rate regime lowered inflation in both Chile and Mexico and led to overvaluations. Although his framework encompasses wage indexation, I find his choice puzzling because Dr. Edwards also concludes that the Mexicans had no longer had a true link between wages and inflation.

Work by Guillermo Calvo and Carlos Vegh has shown that the persistence of inflation may have more to do with credibility of monetary policy than with backward indexation. Similarly, if a central bank must compromise its monetary policy by providing liquidity to financial institutions after a run, that event may involve an issue of credibility because most agents know the central bank will intervene in a crisis.

I had questions about the econometrics in the way I understand Taylor's model. If you look at a model with backward-looking indexation, especially when you have inflation as a unit root, the autoregressive part of it isn't the most important component; the moving-average part is. In other words, most countries have random-walk-type inflation, and all sorts of policy regimes can generate that random walk, not just those with backward-looking indexation. If a government maximizes inflation tax revenue, you will get a unit root. So a better technique would be to fit an arm to the first difference of inflation and look at whether the moving-average part of the equation is significant.

Anna Novize of the World Bank applies this technique to Brazil, until recently the most notoriously indexed economy. She finds that inflation persistence, although significantly different from zero, is much smaller than most people believed due to backward-looking wage indexation.

Some of the clues to what happened in Mexico and in Chile lie in the financial system, as Dr. Edwards and his wife have shown in a number of works. If a central bank cannot credibly commit to refrain from expanding the money supply in a banking crisis, its monetary policy will not have full credibility in bringing down inflation, and there will be forward-looking persistence in the inflation rate.

In general, however, I agree with Dr. Edwards' conclusions in regard to Latin America (with the possible exception of Argentina) and other countries. Instead of statically looking at how these countries' exchange rate regimes are chosen, it is more interesting to look at how they have evolved over time. We clearly see a compendium of all the different options. Typically, Latin American countries have tried to introduce rigidity into their exchange rates. And, typically, the devaluation doesn't happen for the reason you see in Europe and elsewhere—to achieve growth.

Countries run out of reserves. But as the reserve accumulation process goes on, some rigidity returns, perhaps because of capital flows and so forth. However, it's hard to argue that the region of the Americas is an optimal currency area. That means a flexible exchange rate system is clearly in order. The question is how you get from a more rigid rate to a more flexible rate.

Colombia, Chile, and Ecuador now seem to have gradually adopted what Dr. Edwards favors—a floating-type band system—that seems to work quite well. Maybe we'll see it elsewhere in Latin America.

Edwards:
I would like to address some of the important points that the discussants made. First, I want to clarify that I have nothing against George Soros. I think that he and other speculators perform a great service to the international financial system. I am referring to the debate that we had when Jeff Frankel was talking about the need to have the optimal, as it were, degree of speculation for the exchange rate system to work appropriately.

The only way for the type of regime I have suggested to work is for the financial sector to be developed, not only in the sense of allowing people to shorten the currency, but also by having strong financial regulation that makes sure banks that intermediate these flows are healthy and are not going to behave in a reckless way.

The second point has to do with indexation and the question of whether I have exaggerated the role of backward-looking indexation in the case of Mexico, especially since what Mexico did was use the back toss to get away from backward-looking indexation in trying to introduce some kind of forward-looking elements.

Wages are a very important and key price in the economy but not the only one; a very important component in determining the overall aggregate degree of inertia in the system is the de facto optimal degree of indexation that comes off the willing and free negotiation between different parties.

What the data show in the case of Mexico is that although Mexico, unlike Chile, didn't have a legal backward-looking wage indexation system, the degree of backwardness of the indexation of other contracts, materials, rent, and so on was still significant in the sense that it maintained a residual degree of inertia that was very, very high.

This brings me to my third point: that inertia and unit root type of inflation behavior can be the result of many different types of models. What is really important is to compare whether the degree of inertia changes and whether there are breaks in the features and the characteristics of the time series of inflation when different policies take place. It is exactly in this type of analysis where we find that in Chile, there was not such a change. I was gratified to see that Graciela's results confirmed my previous results. But in Mexico at the time the *pactos* were adopted, there was a break in the degree of inertia, in inflation, but not one sufficient to eliminate inflation. That created the real exchange rate appreciation that I mentioned.

I'm not trying to make the point that only the inertial element was responsible for the real appreciation. What I'm trying to say is that there are two periods. One can distinguish that up to 1990, inertia and persistence were mostly what created the appreciation; after 1990 came the capital inflows, which made the overvaluation even worse.

Let me discuss three points that Graciela Kaminsky made that I think are very important. She rightly calls our attention to the distinction between equilibrium changes in the real exchange rate changes that are justified by changes in fundamentals and actual changes in the real exchange rate. She tells us, and very rightly, that not every appreciation of the real exchange rate is a situation of disagreement that should call for policy action. Every time the real exchange rate strengthens, we shouldn't get concerned and start devaluing. She mentions that Latin America went through numerous changes and reforms that surely affected the real exchange rate. I am absolutely in agreement with that. The problem, of course, is that most changes that Latin America went through (especially the opening of international trade, which is the great difference between Latin America today and 20 years ago) call for an equilibrium real depreciation, not appreciation.

It is exactly in that context where, on one hand, the trade reform was calling for a more depreciated exchange rate that would encourage exports and allow the trade reform to be successful but, on the other hand, was producing this great appreciation and was opening a gap between actual and equilibrium in the sense of creating an overvaluation.

Graciela also asks about the viability of fixed exchange rates in the long run. I think, in that sense, we must specify what we mean by the "long run." Paradoxically, Latin America offers the best historical episodes to look at this type of situation. Honduras had a fixed exchange rate between 1918 and 1990. That, as far as I know, is the longest fixed-exchange-rate experience in modern history. Guatemala had a fixed rate from 1926 to 1986. Central America's viability started to crumble in the 1980s as a result of three things: increased straight shocks whose magnitude was many times greater than those seen in the past, increased capital mobility, and a very serious social conflict that exacerbated the temptation to abuse the printing presses around the political process. Lars Stenson pointed out not too long ago, after reflecting on the ERM, that fixed exchange rates are not a shortcut to low inflation. I think that is a very important lesson.

Graciela states correctly that fixed rates worked because inflation went down in the first year. Of course, inflation will go down in the first year. If you fix the variable that governs one-half of the tradable prices, inflation will go down. The problem is, fixed rates tend to generate a situation of overvaluation that, most of the time, generates a very acute process of self-denial among policymakers, who just say it's not happening, it's justified, or it can be explained. In the end, they cannot explain it to you, and it's too late. The economy has already crashed. So the thing to take into account is that the true anchor must be fiscal policy.

Let me end by saying that for those of you who have not noticed it, I am not in favor of currency boards.

Question:
Liliana Rojas and John Welch brought up a key point. In looking at any of these exchange rate regimes, you have to look at the financial institutions outside the central bank. I would like some clarification from John. He said you couldn't short the Mexican peso because there weren't organized futures markets, but that just wasn't so. The Mexicans were shorting the peso like crazy beforehand. The constraint was that you had to have real assets that you could use as collateral to the banks to get loans. And as long as there weren't exchange controls between the United States and Mexico, you could cover your shorts. It was no problem.

Welch:
I totally agree with you. You can always short a currency by borrowing it. What I meant was an infrastructure that gave a dynamic that creates a bid for the currency on the other side. I totally agree with you. In that type of situation, sterilizing capital outflows is going to foresee your doom on the exchange rate regime.

Questions and Comments from the Floor

Question:
I found John Welch's idea of the Mexican crisis' being related to the fragility and the vulnerability of the banking system to be very interesting. I quite agree this is the key aspect of the crisis, especially with the fear that the central bank eventually could bail out banks with problems and expand the monetary supply.

These arguments may have more to do with self-fulfilling prophecies and the problems of fragility of the banking system than with the existence of an overvalued or extremely overvalued real exchange rate.

In the 1994 case, after the initial devaluation, there was a further real exchange rate devaluation for the following three months. It was not until the news came that there was money to support the adjustment problem in the banking system that we started seeing an overvaluation. So the problem might be a combination of an initially appreciated real exchange rate and a self-fulfilling crisis because of the bank fragility and vulnerability. This has to do more with the policies toward dealing with banking vulnerability and not so much with real exchange rate management.

Edwards:
That's a feasible story line. I think, however, one has to have some kind of event that ignites the whole process. In the case of Mexico, we had political shocks —the assassination of Luis Donaldo Colosio and Chiapas and so on—but also an economy—if one wants to follow your line of argument—that was vulnerable not only because the banks were in worse shape than many people had anticipated, but also because the real exchange rate reached a level at which many people in Mexico—in the financial sector, academia, the multilaterals—questioned its viability. Even if one is to take your argument, the real exchange rate overvaluation and the difference between stocks and flows in the capital flows adjustment process are very, very important.

Another question is why almost everyone was so wrong in figuring by how much the exchange rate had to be devalued before things would calm down. Most analysts had been concentrating the real exchange rate's role in generating a flow equilibrium in the current account. Analysts were ignoring the fundamental importance of helping generate a stock equilibrium and asset equilibrium. Once one takes that into account, the mystery disappears, and things become much easier to understand.

Appendix to Part II

Exchange Rate Policy and Macroeconomic Stability

Sebastian Edwards

During the crisis of the Exchange Rate Mechanism of the European Monetary System in September of 1992, fortunes were made and lost. It is reported that George Soros made close to $1 billion speculating against the pound. From a public policy perspective, this episode has added a new dimension to the debate, to what extent are "rigid" exchange rate regimes beneficial in the longer run?

This appendix briefly discusses some of these issues from a policy and comparative point of view. My approach is to develop a simple analytical framework, a model, and then contrast its implications with real-world experiences using statistical methods, namely regression analyses.

I assume that, initially, most contracts, including wages, are indexed to past inflation, and that the authorities follow a passive crawling peg exchange rate system, in which the exchange rate rule consists of adjusting the nominal exchange rate by a proportion ϕ ($\phi \leq 1$) of lagged inflation: $d_t = -\phi(\pi_{t-1} - \pi^*_{t-1})$. Monetary policy is assumed to be passive and to accommodate inertial inflationary forces. In this case, inflation will tend to perpetuate itself.

In a high-inflation setting, inertia is high and the coefficient a_1 is close to unity. The main purpose of using a fixed nominal exchange rate as an anchor is to lower the value of this coefficient and accelerate the convergence of domestic inflation toward world inflation. The effectiveness of this strategy will depend on two factors: (1) accompanying macroeconomic policies (behavior of z); and (2) behavior of inertial components in the rest of the economy, especially in wages.

Two important historical experiences with nominal exchange rate anchors during a stabilization occurred in Chile (1978–1982) and Mexico (1987–1994). In the late 1970s and after having eliminated a stubborn fiscal deficit, Chile adopted an exchange-rate-based stabilization program. Initially, from February 1978 to June 1979, the program consisted of a preannounced *declining* rate of devaluation of the domestic currency. In June 1979, with inflation standing at an annual rate of 34 percent, the government put an end to the system of a preannounced declining rate of devaluation and fixed the nominal exchange rate at 39 pesos per dollar. It was expected that this move to a fixed rate would accelerate the convergence of domestic to world inflation.

In 1988, the Mexican government embarked on an ambitious stabilization program. As in the case of Chile, the manipulation of the nominal exchange rate became an important component of the stabilization plan. In both cases, the rate of inflation declined, reaching a one-digit level. In both cases, however, the program eventually collapsed and major crises ensued.

An important question, however, is to what extent the adoption of the anchor policy accelerated the rate of convergence of domestic inflation toward world inflation. In terms of our equation, did the coefficient a_1 decline significantly after the adoption of the anchor? Technically, this can be analyzed by statistically estimating a_1 before and after the adoption of the anchor policy. If the anchors program is effective (and credible), the estimated coefficient of b_2 should be significantly *negative*, indicating that this policy successfully reduced the degrees of inertia in the system. $(b_1 + b_2)$ is the inertia coefficient after the anchor program is in effect.

As can be seen, in Chile, the program did not reduce the extent of inertia; in Mexico, it did. In the end in both cases, however, there was a substantial degree of real exchange rate overvaluation. This reduced the degree of competitiveness of exports and made imports cheaper.

Also in both cases, there was a major increase in capital inflows, putting pressure on the real exchange rate. These two factors, real exchange rate overvaluation plus major increases in capital inflows, allowed both Chile and Mexico to run very large trade and current account deficits. From every possible point of view, these deficits were unsustainable in the long run. In both cases, the capital inflows came to a (sudden) halt, forcing the economy to implement a major adjustment. The rigidity of wages and the inflexibility of the exchange rate made the adjustment particularly difficult.

Now I turn my attention to the selection of exchange rate regimes in the long run. In 1973, the international monetary system created in Bretton Woods came to an end, as the major industrialized countries abandoned fixed-exchange-rate regimes. In the 1990s, however, a large number of countries—88 in 1992, according to the IMF—continue to have some kind of fixed-exchange-rate regime. Most, but not all, of these countries are developing nations.

The most important economic factors are the degree of "external vulnerability" of the economy, its degree of openness, and its history of external difficulties. More open and vulnerable countries will tend to prefer flexible rates, as will countries with a history of external sector difficulties. The most important structural variables include the degree of development and the structure of production.

The key question is whether countries with a fixed-exchange-rate regime are indeed able to maintain a greater degree of monetary and fiscal discipline than are those with a more flexible regime. I use a data set drawn from 70 countries to analyze this issue empirically.

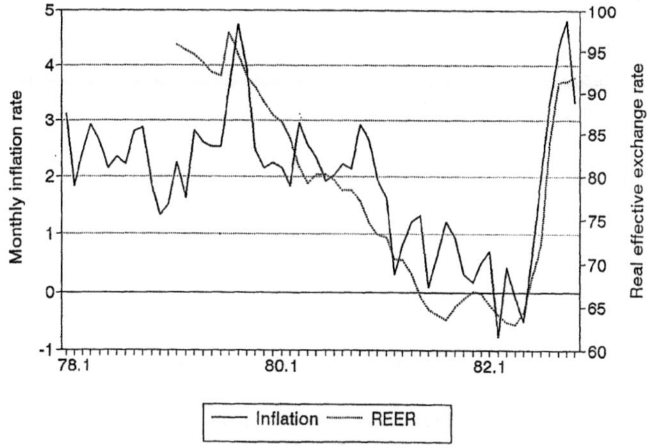

Figure IIA–1. Chile: Inflation and real exchange rate.

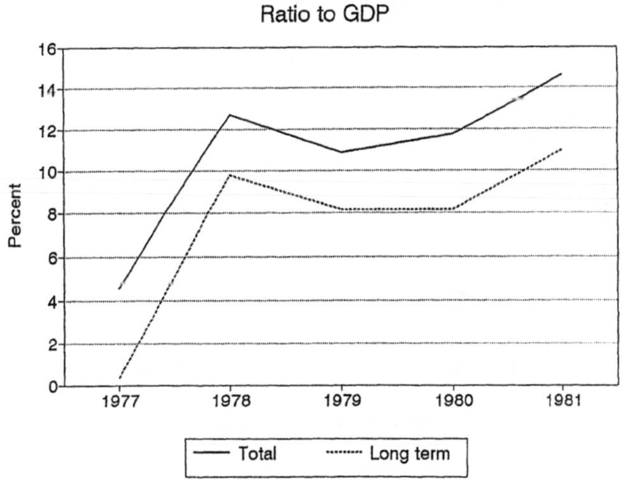

Figure IIA–2. Chile: Net capital inflows.

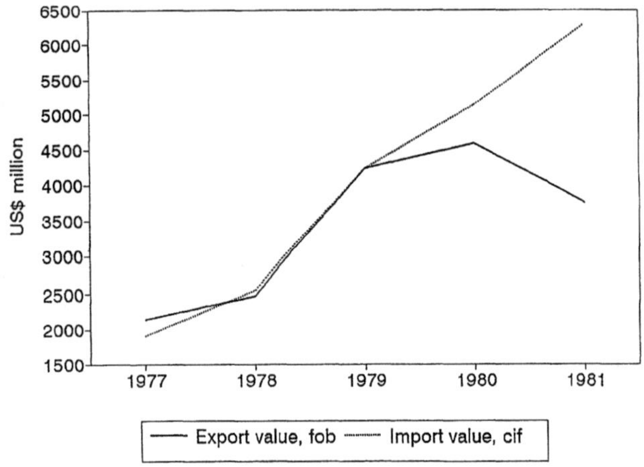

Figure IIA–3. Chile: Exports and imports.

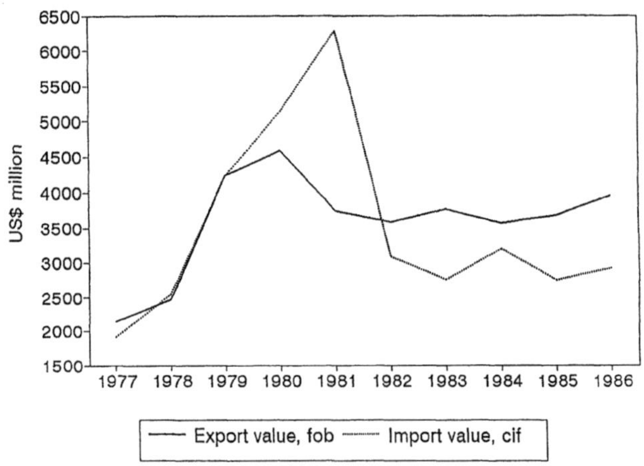

Figure IIA–4. Chile: Exports and imports.

Table IIA–1. Exchange rate arrangements (*as of September 30, 1994*).

Currency pegged to				
U.S. dollar	*French franc*	*Other currency*	*SDR*	*Other composite*
Antigua & Barbuda	Benin	Bhutan (Indian rupee)	Libya	Algeria
Argentina	Burkina Faso	Estonia (Deutsche mark)	Myanmar	Austria
Bahamas, The	Cameroon	Kiribati (Australian dollar)	Rwanda	Bangladesh
Barbados	C. African Rep.	Lesotho (South African rand)	Seychelles	Botswana
Belize	Chad	Namibia (South African rand)		Burundi
Djibouti	Comoros	San Marino (Italian lira)		Cape Verde
Dominica	Congo	Swaziland (South African rand)		Cyprus
Grenada	Côte d'Ivoire	Tajikistan, Rep. of (Russian ruble)		Czech Republic
Iraq	Equatorial Guinea			Fiji
Liberia	Gabon			Hungary
Lithuania	Mali			Iceland
Marshall Islands	Niger			Jordan
Micronesia, Fed. States of	Senegal			Kuwait
Nigeria	Togo			Malta
Oman				Mauritania
Panama				Mauritius
St. Kitts & Nevis				Morocco
St. Lucia				Nepal
St. Vincent and the Grenadines				Papua New Guinea
Syrian Arab Rep.				Slovak Republic
Turkmenistan				Solomon Islands
Venezuela				Thailand
Yemen, Republic of				Tonga
				Vanuatu
				Western Samoa

Table IIA–2. Exchange rate regimes.

Country Code (IMF)	*Country Name*	*d7985*	*d7992*	*Country Code (IMF)*	*Country Name*	*d7985*	*d7992*
111	United States	0	0	343	Jamaica	0	0
112	United Kingdom	0	0	369	Trinidad & Tobago	1	1
122	Austria	1	1	429	Iran	1	1
124	Belgium	0	0	524	Sri Lanka	0	0
128	Denmark	0	0	534	India	0	0
132	France	0	0	536	Indonesia	0	0
134	Germany	0	0	564	Pakistan	0	0
136	Italy	0	0	566	Philippines	0	0
138	Netherlands	0	0	578	Thailand	0	0
142	Norway	1	1	616	Botswana	1	1
144	Sweden	1	1	618	Burundi	1	1
156	Canada	0	0	622	Cameroon	1	1
158	Japan	0	0	626	Central African Rep.	1	1
172	Finland	1	0	628	Chad	1	1
174	Greece	0	0	634	Congo	1	1
178	Ireland	0	0	636	Zaire	0	0

182	Portugal	0	0	644	Ethiopia	1	1
184	Spain	0	0	646	Gabon	1	1
186	Turkey	0	0	652	Ghana	0	0
193	Australia	0	0	662	Cote D'Ivoire	1	1
196	New Zealand	0	0	664	Kenya	1	1
199	South Africa	0	0	666	Lesotho	1	1
218	Bolivia	0	0	684	Mauritius	1	1
223	Brazil	0	0	686	Morocco	0	0
228	Chile	0	0	694	Nigeria	0	0
233	Colombia	0	0	698	Zimbabwe	0	0
243	Dominican Republic	0	0	714	Rwanda	1	1
248	Ecuador	0	0	724	Sierra Leone	1	0
253	El Salvador	0	0	726	Somalia	0	0
268	Honduras	1	0	732	Sudan	1	0
273	Mexico	0	0	738	Tanzania	1	1
278	Nicaragua	1	0	742	Togo	1	1
288	Paraguay	1	0	744	Tunisia	1	0
293	Peru	0	0	746	Uganda	0	0
299	Venezuela	1	0	754	Zambia	0	0

Source: Constructed with data obtained from International Financial Statistics, IMF.

Table IIA–3. Probit regressions for exchange rate regime selection. Dependent variable D79–92 (*t*-statistics in parentheses).

Sample	*All*
Constant	–7.473
	(–1.932)
Log Pol Inst	–1.173
	(–2.690)
Log Inflation (–1)	–1.181
	(–1.491)
RER variability (RERV)	–0.355
	(–2.953)
RERV * Openness	0.005
	(3.065)
Log GNP per capita	1.556
	(2.768)
Urban	–0.084
	(–2.815)
Agriculture	0.106
	(2.528)
Current Account deficit	–2.051
	(–2.394)
N	61
Log Likelihood	–15.50
Chi-square	44.67

Table IIA–4. Regressions for inflation and exchange rate regime choice. (*t*-statistics in parentheses.)

Sample *Dependent variable*	*All* *Inflation*	*LDCs* *Inflation*
Constant	−0.840	1.243
	(−0.990)	(2.191)
Log GNP per capita	0.978	−1.480
	(0.832)	(1.573)
Urban	1.90E-04	−9.10E-04
	(0.040)	(−0.151)
Agriculture	0.017	—
	(2.686)	
Latin America	0.615	0.471
	(3.209)	(2.165)
Asia	−0.241	−0.505
	(−1.090)	(−1.959)
Industrial Countries	−0.409	—
	(−1.306)	
Political Instability	0.974	1.730
	(2.157)	(2.524)
d7980	−0.372	−0.488
	(−2.589)	(−2.604)
N	69	52
R-square	0.433	0.419

Part III EXCHANGE RATE VOLATILITY, INVESTMENT, AND GROWTH: SOME NEW EVIDENCE

It is often argued that exchange rate volatility deters foreign trade and investment. But is exchange rate volatility associated with higher or lower rates of growth? What is the best policy to achieve maximum growth?

Presenter:
Vittorio Corbo
Professor of Economics
Catholic University of Chile

Moderator:
W. Michael Cox
Vice President and Economic Advisor
Federal Reserve Bank of Dallas

Discussants:
David Gould
Senior Economist
Federal Reserve Bank of Dallas

Liliana Rojas-Suárez
Principal Adviser
Inter-American Development Bank

(Vittorio Corbo's presentation was based on this paper he cowrote with Patricio Rojas, Research Division, Central Bank of Chile.)

In recent years, there has emerged a broad professional consensus on the type of economic policies that are more conducive to an improvement of growth and a reduction of poverty. This consensus has resulted from the interpretation of the favorable growth record of the East Asian countries (World Bank 1993) and from the examination of the factors that account for the differences in performance between successful and unsuccessful adjustment programs (Corbo and Fischer 1995). This consensus was initially articulated in Williamson (1990).

Empirical work on the determinants of differences in growth rates across countries has also shown regularities that have reinforced the lessons obtained from the literature on the role of economic policies on growth. This work has incorporated on top of factor accumulation a separate role for the quality of economic policies. The work initiated by Romer (1986), Lucas (1988), and Barro (1990) has provided the analytical underpinning for a mechanism through which economic policies and investment, in human and physical capital, could affect not only the level of output but also its rate of growth. The belief that economic policy and the investment rate are major determinants of economic growth has long been expressed in the writings of economists, but it has only recently found its way into the standard growth literature. A sample of recent work along these lines is Levine and Renalt (1992), Fischer (1993 and 1991), Easterly and Rebelo (1993), King and Levine (1993), World Bank (1991), and Inter-American Development Bank (1995).

More recent work has emphasized the role of macroeconomic uncertainty on investment and growth.[1] Thus, Fischer (1993) investigates the effect of macroeconomic uncertainty on both growth rates and on factor accumulation.

In this paper, we examine the role of macroeconomic uncertainty on economic growth. Two sources of macroeconomic uncertainty are considered: uncertainty about the inflation rate and uncertainty about the real exchange rate. We distinguish two mechanisms through which macroeconomic uncertainty could affect long-term growth: its effect on the rate of investment and the overall level of efficiency or total factor productivity.

Our work is based on the by now standard "new growth theory" type of growth model, in which a country's growth performance is associated with the initial productivity gap with an industrial country, the rate of investment, initial human capital levels, economic policies, and macroeconomic uncertainty. Our empirical work indicates that the uncertainty in the real exchange rate is the single most important measure of macroeconomic uncertainty in explaining growth differences across countries and for the same country through time.

The Nexus Between Macroeconomic Uncertainty, Investment, and Growth

Some Historical Developments on the Determinants of Growth

The recent literature on growth highlights a number of channels through which economic policies could affect growth. Promoting human capital accumulation—for example, by providing adequate nutritional levels, basic educational skills, and investment in research and development—can foster growth (Romer 1989 and Rebelo 1992). Along these lines, Becker, Murphy, and Tamura (1990) show that economies may become stuck in a poverty trap: a situation in which low income and low human capital levels create incentives for high population growth and low investment in human capital that perpetuate the state of poverty. Policies that stimulate investment in human capital can break the economy out of this stagnant situation.

Furthermore, in a series of influential papers, Romer (1993a and 1993b) has singled out the role of the overall policy environment for the development and adaptation of ideas as one of the most important channels for policies to affect long-term growth. The new model also stresses the importance of trade policy, fiscal policy, and financial policy as determinants of long-term growth.[2] Macroeconomic uncertainty could affect growth indirectly through its effect on the investment rate and directly through its effect on total factor productivity. In recent years, Fischer has given a more prominent role to macroeconomic instability in the growth process through both its effect on factor accumulation and in the rate of change of total factor productivity (Fischer 1993 and 1991).

The Effects of Macroeconomic Uncertainty on Growth

We review now the channels through which macroeconomic uncertainty could affect long-term growth. Two types of macroeconomic volatility are considered in this paper: the volatility of inflation and the volatility of the real exchange rate. As most of this volatility in these variables is unpredictable, volatility generates uncertainty on the future value of both variables: the inflation rate and the real exchange rate. The higher uncertainty about the inflation rate will affect the information content of relative prices, resulting in a suboptimal choice of the input and output mix, a lower level of overall efficiency, and ultimately—through endogenous growth channels—in a lower level of growth. A higher level of real exchange rate uncertainty reduces the information content of the relative prices between tradable and nontradable goods and also the relative price of differentiated tradables, with effects on efficiency and growth similar to those associated with increased uncertainty about inflation.

In theory, the relationship between real exchange rate uncertainty and investment is ambiguous. If investment is irreversible, the increase in the uncertainty about future return associated with the increase in real exchange rate uncertainty increases the option value of investment and, in the short run, results in lower investment (Dixit and Pindyck 1993). However, the long-term relationship between real exchange rate uncertainty and investment is ambiguous. For example, Bertola (1989) shows that irreversibility of investment and uncertainty *can* lead to a higher capital output ration in long-run equilibrium, even though the higher uncertainty decreases the investment rate in the short run. In their review of the literature on uncertainty and investment, Pindyck and Solimano (1993, 274) conclude:

> There is little that can be said about the effects of uncertainty on the long-run equilibrium values of investment, the investment-to-output ratio, or the capital–output ratio. Thus, it is left for empirical work to investigate the link between uncertainty and investment.

In their empirical work, Pindyck and Solimano find that their measure of volatility (the volatility of the log of the marginal profitability of capital) is negatively associated with the investment rate, but it is statistically significant only for the developing countries in their sample. Furthermore, they find that the most important source of volatility in the marginal profitability of capital is due to the volatility of the inflation rate.

Real exchange rate uncertainty could also affect growth directly through its effect on the growth rate of total factor productivity. The mechanism here is from higher uncertainty in the real exchange rate to less predictable relative factor and commodity prices, a nonoptimal choice of the factor and output mix, a lower level of aggregate output, and—through endogenous growth channels—a lower rate of growth.[3]

A Framework for Studying the Relationship Between Macroeconomic Uncertainty and Growth

The Growth Equation

The neoclassical framework has provided the starting point for a number of studies to investigate the different sources of growth. The typical methodology of these studies (Levine and Renelt 1992; De Gregorio 1992; Fischer 1991; Barro 1991) is to start with a neoclassical production function of the type

$$Y_t = eF(L_t, K_t), \qquad (1)$$

where K is capital, L is labor input, and μ is a constant rate of productivity growth. Putting this function in growth terms yields

$$y_t = \beta_L l_t + \beta_K k_t + \mu, \qquad (2)$$

where small letters denote rates of growth. With constant returns to scale and perfect competition, the βs represent factor shares in output. Then, the first two terms on the right side of equation 2 represent the contribution of labor and capital to growth, while the last term represents the contribution of technical progress. The standard approach to growth accounting is to obtain input shares directly from the data. Solow (1956) uses the observed factor shares and growth rates of capital and labor to decompose the contributions of both factors to output growth. The part of growth that cannot be explained by input growth represents the growth in total factor productivity, which is assumed to come from exogenous technical change.

Since capital stock data are generally not available, adding the assumption of a constant capital output ratio enables one to write the rate of growth of the capital stock in terms of the investment rate. Then, the equation usually estimated by many empirical studies, both for time series data for a single country and for cross-sectional country studies, is

$$y_t = a_0 + a_1 1_t + a_2 i_t, \qquad (3)$$

where i is the investment rate and, given the assumption that capital–output ratios and technology are the same in all countries, a_1 and a_2 should represent the marginal product of labor and capital share, respectively.

Essentially, most cross-sectional studies begin with this basic model and then include other regressors. Levine and Renelt (1992) present a list of 41 cross-sectional growth studies published since 1980. Each study regresses the output growth rate over a given period against a set of variables that, in addition to variables related to the productivity gap, labor, and physical and human capital, includes variables related to trade policy, fiscal policy, exchange rate policy, political and social stability, and macroeconomic policy and outcomes.

For a sample of 101 countries, Levine and Renelt analyze the effects of including variables in addition to the standard ones—gross domestic product (GDP) per capita, investment rate, rate of population growth, and rate of secondary school enrollment. Levine and Renelt's main findings are that several measures of economic policy are related to long-run growth and that, except for

Table III–1. Macroeconomic variability indicators.

	1960–1964	*1965–1969*	*1970–1974*	*1975–1979*	*1980–1984*	*1985–1988*
Whole Sample						
Inflation	6.61	7.43	12.73	19.57	28.35	63.20
S. Deviation of Inflation	3.71	4.58	8.84	7.99	16.51	76.77
S. Deviation of Real Exch. Rate	9.23	7.52	9.65	9.96	16.92	19.96
Whole, Excluding African Sample						
Inflation	7.78	8.46	13.93	15.74	31.00	30.06
S. Deviation of Inflation	3.97	3.22	10.11	6.95	18.99	22.04
S. Deviation of Real Exch. Rate	7.15	6.36	8.99	7.24	14.47	15.32
Latin American Sample						
Inflation	9.83	10.70	23.83	35.63	58.52	216.10
S. Deviation of Inflation	5.05	4.80	18.64	17.11	44.09	293.13
S. Deviation of Real Exch. Rate	6.86	8.08	9.16	9.83	21.10	15.12
African Sample						
Inflation	3.13	4.82	7.66	17.32	13.07	17.76
S. Deviation of Inflation	3.08	4.14	5.70	6.99	5.05	8.78
S. Deviation of Real Exch. Rate	14.57	10.38	9.06	14.88	14.97	30.79

the investment ratio, the relationship between growth and every particular macroeconomic indicator is fragile.

On the other hand, Fischer (1991), using cross-sectional regression for average growth in a sample of 73 countries and a pooled cross-sectional time series regression for annual growth in the same sample of countries, finds a significant relationship between macroeconomic policy-related variables and growth, supporting the view that the quality of macroeconomic management matters for growth. In this paper, we use the same type of models.

In our empirical work, we use a model of the type provided by equation 3. Our empirical work is done using two databases. The first is a sample of 58 countries that corresponds to the whole sample of Summers and Heston (1991), excluding the African countries. The second sample includes only Latin American countries. The Appendix to Part III presents an overview of the data and defines the data sources.

We investigate now the variability in the two macroeconomic variables of interest: the inflation rate and the real exchange rate. As shown in Table III–1, the level of inflation and the variability of both the inflation rate and the real exchange rate increase slightly between the first and second period and then take a big jump in the period 1970–1974. The last period corresponds to the breakdown of the Bretton Woods agreement.

In industrial countries, it has also been found that the breakdown of the Bretton Woods system of pegged but adjustable exchange rates has coincided with an increase in the variability of nominal and real exchange rates of individual countries (Mussa 1990 and 1986). Furthermore, empirical evidence, based on both cross-section and time series data, has shown that the short-run variability of real exchange rates is higher under floating-rate regimes than under fixed-rate regimes.

Furthermore, recent work on the determinants of nominal exchange rate movements shows that most of the exchange rate variability has not been anticipated. Thus, higher exchange rate variability results also in higher exchange rate uncertainty (Taylor 1995; Obstfeld 1995; and Goldstein 1995).

The increase in variability continues throughout the periods. For the particular case of Latin American countries, there is a large increase in the variability of the inflation rate between the period 1980–1984 and the period 1985–1988. This is not surprising, as the macroeconomic adjustment programs enacted as a response to the severe terms of trade, interest rate, and sudden cutoff of external financing shocks of the 1980–1984 period called for a larger real devaluation and reduced aggregate spending. The sudden collapse of external financing at a time when fiscal deficits were increasing (as a result of the cumulative effect of real depreciation on the budget, the slowdown of economic activity, and the support to the financial system) led to monetization and inflation. Interestingly enough, the variability of the real exchange rate was reduced between the period 1980–1984 and the period 1985–1988. This result is not surprising, as by now most Latin American governments were pursuing real exchange rate targeting to support the development of the export sector.

In the case of the African countries, there is a big jump in the variability of the real exchange rate between the periods 1980–1984 and 1985–1988. This result is due in major part to the increasing misalignment of the CFA countries as a result of the lack of financial discipline in the early 1980s (Devarajan and De Melo, 1991).

We now investigate the direct effect of macroeconomic uncertainty on growth and on the investment rate. In particular, we use two measures of macroeconomic uncertainty: the standard deviation of inflation and the standard deviation of the real exchange rate. Both the growth and the investment model extend the models used in Corbo and Rojas (1993 and 1992), adding to the by now standard Barro type of growth equation the two measures of macroeconomic uncertainty. The investment equation is of the type used by Solimano (1992) and Fischer (1991).

Econometric Results

In this section, we present different specification estimates of growth and investment equations. As we use time invariant variables in our panel data, we cannot allow for fixed effects in our estimates. Therefore, our estimates are obtained using random effects.

The single cross-sectional equation has been the alternative most used in the empirical growth literature. However, averaging over the entire sample period eliminates the information contained in the sample about the effect of changing conditions of growth in individual countries and allows only cross-country variation to inform the estimates. Furthermore, macroeconomic uncertainty is a more short-run, within-period effect that, to be properly captured, requires analysts to work with much shorter periods than the ones used until now in the empirical literature. Thus, in what constitutes a major departure from the empirical work in this area, we work with a mix of a time series and a cross-section of countries. The empirical work is performed as a panel estimation using subperiod averages for the period between 1960 and 1988. However, since we are interested in secular growth patterns, some amount of averaging was required to net out irregular fluctuations in the annual data. For this purpose, the data were pooled using five-year averages and one four-year average. The periods used are 1960–1964, 1965–1969, 1970–1974, 1975–1979, 1980–1984, and 1985–1988.

We discuss now the definition and measurement of a macroeconomic framework conducive to higher investment and higher growth. A stable macroeconomic framework can be described as one in which inflation is low and predictable, real interest rates are positive but not too high, fiscal policy is stable and sustainable, the real exchange rate is competitive and predictable, and the balance-of-payments situation is perceived as viable (Corbo and Fischer 1992). From this list of variables, we use the level and standard deviation of the inflation rate, the standard deviation of the real effective exchange rate, and the size of the trade deficit to GDP. The latter variable is used as an indicator of the sum of the private and public deficit to GDP ratio, a higher value indicating less total macroeconomic discipline.

Whole Sample, Excluding African Countries

Previous work done with the complete database showed that the African countries do not have the same growth and investment equations as the rest of the countries (Corbo and Rojas 1992), and we therefore work here with the whole sample, excluding the African countries. To avoid the possibility of endogeneity in the growth equations, all the regressions were estimated using the instrumental variable technique. Additionally, all the standard errors were computed using White's (1980) heteroskedasticity-robust procedure.

Tables III–2 and III–3 present the results for the whole sample, excluding the African countries. The first column in Table III–2 presents the results for a standard growth equation. The right-hand-side variables are investment rates of the period and of the previous period, the productivity gap vis-à-vis the United States, the government spending to GDP ratio, and a measure of human capital, the primary school enrollment rate. All the equations are estimated using instrumental variables to avoid the standard simultaneous equation bias that can arise in this type of equation. All variables are statistically significant.

Regressions 2 to 5 assess the effect of macroeconomic instability on long-term growth. In regression 2, we add two new variables: the inflation rate and the standard deviation of the real exchange rate. Both variables are highly significant and have the expected signs.

The negative effect of exchange rate uncertainty on growth has also been found in Cottani et al. (1990) and Dollar (1992). However, the two studies do not control for new growth theory-type of variables, and their findings most likely are subject to specification bias, as their equation leaves out important variables. IDB (1995) also reports an important effect of exchange rate uncertainty on growth in a steady-state cross-sectional study of a large database that includes the African countries and uses as its unit of observation the average for the period 1960–1985.

The inflation rate and its standard deviation are highly collinear; therefore, the significance of the inflation rate could be due to the increased uncertainty

Table III–2. Pooled regressions for growth rate in GDP per-capita; five-years averaged data for whole sample, excluding African countries; instrumental variable estimation: 1960–88.

	(1)	*(2)*	*(3)*	*(4)*	*(5)*
Constant	−0.004	0.004	0.004	0.009	0.009
	(−0.343)	(0.279)	(0.266)	(0.593)	(0.584)
Investment ratio in t	0.609	0.532	0.536	0.51	0.512
	(2.436)	(2.051)	(2.069)	(1.968)	(1.950)
Investment ratio in t–1	−0.48	−0.42	−0.422	−0.41	−0.413
	(−2.239)	(−1.882)	(−1.893)	(−1.843)	(−1.828)
Productivity gap	−0.013	−0.013	−0.013	−0.014	−0.014
vis-à-vis USA	(−1.809)	(−1.794)	(−1.771)	(−1.949)	(−2.015)
Government spending (x10E-2)	−0.069	−0.074	−0.074	−0.082	−0.079
	(−2.784)	(−2.924)	(−2.927)	(−3.132)	(−2.844)
Primary school rate	0.014	0.018	0.018	0.018	0.018
	(1.421)	(1.723)	(1.693)	(1.709)	(1.735)
Inflation rate		−1.53E-03			
		(−4.381)			
S. Deviation of inflation rate			−8.69E-02	−8.89E-04	−8.93E-04
			(−4.894)	(−4.951)	(−4.961)
Trade deficit					−0.011
					(−0.222)
Standard Deviation of RER		−3.46E-02	−3.62E-02	−3.16E-02	−3.22E-02
		(−2.928)	(−3.057)	(−2.607)	(−2.556)
Assassinations				−0.004	−0.005
				(−2.133)	(−2.132)
Sample Size	267	263	263	263	263
Corrected R-squared	0.26	0.272	0.271	0.275	0.272

Note: t-statistics in parentheses. The regressions also include time-period dummies for periods 1965–69, 1970–74, 1975–79, and 1980–84.

associated with the higher standard deviation of inflation that goes hand in hand with a higher level of inflation. The results presented in the third column of this table support this hypothesis. Thus, when we introduce the standard deviation of the inflation rate instead of the inflation rate, the results do not change much. The roles of political instability variables on growth were also investigated. Regressions 4 and 5 add as a growth determinant the index of assassinations taken from Barro and Wolf (1989). The estimates indicate that the coefficient of this variable is negative and highly significant.[4] This result is consistent with the hypothesis that political uncertainty has a negative effect on growth. Finally, in column 5, when we add an additional measure of macroeconomic imbalance, the trade deficit to GDP ratio, the results show that after introducing the macroeconomic volatility variables the trade deficit is not statistically significant.

Table III–3 presents results about the determinants of the investment rate, the single most important variable that accounts for differences in growth rates in this sample (Corbo and Rojas 1992). As discussed above, in a world of irreversible investment, theory provides no unambiguous answer with respect to the effect of a higher level of macroeconomic uncertainty on the steady-state investment rate. However, it does predict that increasing macroeconomic uncertainty would result in a postponement of investment. In our database of observations that are five-year averages, the short-run effect of uncertainty on investment should result in a negative coefficient for the macroeconomic uncertainty variable(s). Our panel data results are consistent with this implication, as the coefficients of both the variability of inflation and the variability of the real exchange rate have negative signs and are highly significant. As shown in the last column, the variable number of assassinations also has a detrimental effect on investment rates.

Latin American Country Estimates

The rest of the results are based on a richer database that includes only the Latin American countries. In this sample, we control also for supply shocks in the form of terms-of-trade shocks, and we include a measure of distortions in the exchange rate market. Table III–4 shows the results for the regressions of GDP per capita growth, and Table III–5 shows the results for the regressions of the investment rate.

In general, the most robust determinants of growth are the investment rate, the initial relative productivity gap vis-à-vis the United States, the government expenditures to GDP ratio, the primary school rate, and the measures of macroeconomic stability (the inflation rate, the standard deviation of the inflation rate, the trade deficit, and the standard deviation of the real exchange rate). In most of the regression, the coefficients of these variables appeared to be statistically

Table III–3. Pooled regressions for investment ratios; five-years averaged data for whole sample, excluding African countries: 1960–88.

	(1)	(2)	(3)	(4)	(5)	(6)
Constant	3.533	2.347	1.842	1.837	2.936	2.745
	(2.369)	(1.631)	(1.253)	(1.253)	(1.927)	(1.794)
Growth rate in GDP per-capita in t–1	64.218	61.206	59.63	59.278	58.178	57.989
	(7.402)	(7.268)	(7.271)	(7.250)	(6.981)	(6.987)
Productivity gap vis-à-vis USA	1.509	1.298	1.519	1.494	0.514	
	(0.564)	(0.486)	(0.567)	(0.557)	(0.195)	
Government spending	−0.284	−0.307	−0.318	−0.317	−0.336	−0.346
	(−3.801)	(−3.929)	(−4.057)	(−4.056)	(−4.177)	(−4.279)
Primary school rate	10.735	15.335	15.634	15.644	13.931	14.167
	(2.492)	(3.861)	(3.853)	(3.857)	(3.487)	(3.599)
Inflation rate				−1.42E-01		
				(−2.083)		
S. Deviation of inflation rate		−6.40E-02	−7.43E-02		−7.32E-02	−7.26E-02
		(−1.827)	(−2.232)		(−2.422)	(−2.433)
Standard Deviation of RER			−0.048	−0.047	−0.041	−0.041
			(−2.594)	(−2.585)	(−2.297)	(−2.316)
Assassinations					−3.679	−3.741
					(−4.143)	(−4.043)
Sample Size	290	284	284	284	284	284
Corrected R-squared	0.317	0.335	0.343	0.344	0.361	0.364

Note: t-statistics in parentheses. The regressions also include time-period dummies for periods 1965–69, 1970–74, 1975–79, and 1980–84.

Table III–4. Pooled regressions for growth rate in GDP per-capita; five-years averaged data for Latin American countries: 1960–88. Inst. variable estimation.

	(1)	(2)	(3)	(4)	(5)	(6)	(7)	(8)	(9)
Constant	−0.019	−0.016	−0.012	−0.[illegible]18	−0.01	−0.011	−0.019	−0.019	−0.101
	(−0.643)	(−0.436)	(0.374)	(−0.[illegible]97)	(−0.447)	(−0.274)	(−0.554)	(−0.555)	(−0.907)
Investment ratio in t	0.291	0.34	0.319	0.[illegible]46	0.281	0.333	0.256	0.251	0.256
	(1.517)	(1.967)	(1.798)	(1.[illegible]76)	(1.360)	(1.959)	(1.431)	(1.422)	(1.976)
Investment ratio in t–1	−0.258	−0.307	−0.294	−0.[illegible]11	−0.276	−0.309	−0.24	−0.24	−0.232
	(−1.611)	(−2.073)	(−1.926)	(−2.[illegible]76)	(−1.579)	(−2.106)	(−1.579)	(−1.571)	(−2.134)
Productivity gap vis-à-vis USA	−0.056	−0.079	−0.083	−0.[illegible]78	−0.083	−0.08	−0.077	−0.078	−0.073
	(−2.997)	(−3.805)	(−3.821)	(−3.[illegible]86)	(−3.284)	(−3.757)	(−3.537)	(−3.545)	(5.384)
Government spending (x10E-2)	−0.119	−0.073	−0.078	−0.[illegible]74	−0.101	0.073	−0.09	−0.09	−0.079
	(−4.457)	(−2.350)	(−2.406)	(−2.[illegible]45)	(−1.930)	(−2.374)	(−2.724)	(−2.744)	(−3.726)
Primary school rate	0.044	0.041	0.046	0.[illegible]41	0.047	0.04	0.052	0.052	0.043
	(2.901)	(3.178)	(3.306)	(3.[illegible]72)	(2.822)	(2.903)	(3.792)	(3.821)	(4.709)
Growth rate in terms of trade	0.208	0.188	0.185	0.[illegible]9	0.201	0.179	0.177	0.177	
	(4.565)	(4.172)	(4.274)	(4.[illegible]04)	(4.709)	(3.797)	(4.235)	(4.230)	
Inflation rate		−9.96E-04	−4.45E-03		−7.03E-04	−1.02E-03		−6.36E-04	
		(−2.575)	(−1.487)		(−1.773)	(−2.723)		(−2.234)	
S. Deviation of inflation rate							−4.21E-04		−3.54E-04
							(−2.493)		(−1.737)
Trade deficit		−0.185	−0.209	−0.[illegible]72	−0.180	−0.192	−0.192	−0.193	−0.259
		(−2.022)	(−2.202)	(−1.[illegible]63)	(−1.705)	(−2.091)	(−2.058)	(−2.062)	(−4.016)
Black premium rate			4.10E-04	−9.[illegible]7E-05					
			(1.233)	(−2.[illegible]25)					
Trade ratio					0.008				
					(0.549)				
Standard Deviation of RER							−3.41E-02	−3.34E-02	−4.24E-02
							(−3.554)	(−3.464)	(−4.542)
Assassinations						−0.002			−0.002
						(−1.278)			(−2.029)
Sample Size	100	100	100	100	100	100	100	100	100
Corrected R-squared	0.518	0.539	0.537	0.536	0.53	0.538	0.555	0.554	0.602

Note: t-statistics in parentheses. The regressions also include time-period dummies for periods 1965–69, 1970–74, 1975–79, and 1980–84.

significant regardless of the inclusion of other variables. The black premium rate also appeared to be negatively correlated with growth, but this result was more sensitive to the specification.

Furthermore, in all the regressions reported in Table III–4, the coefficient of the productivity gap variable is negative and highly significant, providing strong evidence in favor of the hypothesis of conditional convergence of per capita GDP growth. That is, holding everything else constant, the countries with the lower per capita income grew at a higher rate than countries with a higher level of per capita income.

The human capital variable (proxied by the primary school rate) shows a positive and significant effect on growth in all the regressions. On the other hand, government spending on GDP has a negative and significant effect on growth in all the regressions of Table III–4.

An important difference between the results for the whole sample, excluding the African countries, and results for Latin American countries only is the large drop in the sum of the coefficients for the investment variables. This sum, which corresponds to the steady-state coefficient for investment, is reduced from 0.099 (column 5 in Table III–2) to only 0.024 (column 9 in Table III–4). Thus, the investment rate has a much smaller contribution to steady-state growth in Latin America than in the whole sample, excluding Africa.

Regressions 4 and 6 assess the effect of trade openness on long-term growth. Two measures of openness were considered: the GDP share of total trade and the black market, or parallel market, premium. The first one tries to use a proximate effect of openness as a proxy for openness itself, while the black market premium is directly related to changes in trade restrictions or in openness, basically because the premium reflects the excess demand for tradable and for foreign assets that is not satisfied by the official foreign exchange market. Thus, the greater the controls on the use of official foreign exchange, the larger the premium on the black, or parallel, market exchange rate. The estimates of regression 5 show that the coefficient of the share of total trade in GDP is positive but not significant. However, in the case of the black market premium rate, its coefficient in regression 4 is significant and negative, indicating that those Latin American countries with more foreign exchange restrictions have recorded slower output growth.

However, the significant effect of the black market premium rate on growth depends on the presence of the inflation rate in the regression. When both variables are included in the specification (regression 3), both variables are not significant and the sign of the black market premium is positive, indicating that this variable could also represent some degree of macroeconomic instability more than the degree of openness of the economy. This caveat to the use of the black market premium as a proxy for openness arises from the fact that the demand for foreign exchange assets is also a function of the degree of political and macroeconomic instability. Thus, when the premium changes because the portfolio excess demand for foreign assets is affected by political or economic "news" or internal civil disturbances, it undermines the usefulness of the premium as a measure of openness. Then, the premium may change due to speculation, even when there is no change in the degree of restrictiveness of the regime.[5]

Equations 7, 8, and 9 in Table III–4 include as regressors the variability of the inflation rate and the variability of the real exchange rate. After including the standard type of Barro-augmented equation and the trade deficit to GDP ratio, the two macroeconomic variability variables are highly significant, and both have a negative sign. Furthermore, the adjusted corrected *r*-square for these regressions is 0.602. From the two macroeconomic variability variables, the standard deviation of the real exchange rate is the most significant in all the regressions. Thus, our empirical work indicates that a higher variability of the real exchange rate and of the inflation rate is associated with lower growth in total factor productivity.

As we mentioned earlier, the second channel through which economic policies and macroeconomic uncertainty could affect growth is investment rates. Table III–5 presents estimates of numerous pooled investment regressions. In all these regressions, the dependent variable is the share of investment in GDP for each of the periods also used for the growth equations. Regression 1 presents the results of the simplest model. In this model, the investment rate is explained in terms of an accelerator model augmented by a human capital variable, the share of government spending in GDP, the productivity gap vis-à-vis the United States, and a terms-of-trade variable that accounts for supply shocks. In this equation, the coefficient of the relative productivity gap vis-à-vis the United States and all other coefficients but one of the terms-of-trade variables are significant and with the expected signs. The latter has the expected sign but is only marginally significant. In particular, the significant coefficient on the lagged growth rate in GDP per capita is consistent with the usual finding that accelerator-type investment functions perform well.

Similar to the results obtained for the larger sample in the investment equation and in the Latin American equation for the growth rate, both human capital and the ratio of government spending to GDP have significant effects on the investment rate in all the regressions in Table III–5. Both effects on investment not only have the expected signs but also are significant at the 1-percent level.

In regression 2, we add the standard deviation of the inflation rate. This variable has a negative and highly statistically significant coefficient; a larger standard deviation of inflation decreases the information content of relative prices and makes more attractive the option of waiting before undertaking an irreversible investment. In regression 3, we also include the standard deviation of the real exchange rate. The coefficient of this variable has the right sign, and it is also highly significant.

Table III–5. Pooled regressions for investment ratios; five-years averaged data for Latin American countries: 1960–88.

	(1)	*(2)*	*(3)*	*(4)*	*(5)*
Constant	6.031	5.749	5.792	7.118	6.568
	(2.963)	(2.771)	(2.829)	(3.620)	(3.470)
Growth rate in GDP	48.604	47.393	45.364	43.977	47.154
per-capita in t–1	(4.271)	(4.136)	(4.060)	(3.916)	(4.590)
Productivity gap	−13.041	−12.923	−12.664	−12.867	−11.237
vis-à-vis USA	(−1.968)	(−1.926)	(−1.949)	(−2.118)	(−1.942)
Government spending	−0.324	−0.307	−0.333	−0.352	−0.342
	(−3.134)	(−2.911)	(−3.190)	(−3.280)	(−3.222)
Secondary school rate	32.222	31.361	34.65	33.951	32.726
	(2.186)	(2.084)	(2.272)	(2.397)	(2.253)
S. Deviation of inflation rate		−7.10E-02	−7.55E-02	−7.25E-02	−7.15E-02
		(−2.028)	(−2.260)	(−2.291)	(−2.229)
Standard Deviation of RER			−0.047	−0.035	−0.035
			(−2.286)	(−1.708)	(−1.716)
Terms of Trade Index	−5.38E-03	−5.47E-03	−5.39E-03	−4.42E-03	
	(−1.537)	(−1.562)	(−1.515)	(−1.281)	
Assassinations				−3.426	−3.502
				(−5.346)	(−5.155)
Sample Size	100	100	100	100	100
Corrected R-squared	0.307	0.308	0.317	0.372	0.373

Note: t-statistics in parentheses. The regressions also include time-period dummies for periods 1965–69, 1970–74, 1975–79, and 1980–84.

Finally, regressions 4 and 5 include a political instability variable. The coefficient of this variable is negative and highly significant, helping improve the explanatory power of the regression by about 6 percentage points. As Barro (1991) maintains, this negative relationship between investment and political instability could involve the adverse effects of political instability on property rights and the linkage between property rights and private investment. However, the correlation could also reflect a political response to bad economic outcomes. From Tables 4 and 5, we observe that the political instability variable is a significant explanatory variable in both the growth and the investment relation. Thus, political instability affects the rate of growth directly and indirectly through the investment rate.

In general, our findings are consistent and extend the results of some recent theoretical and empirical work on the role of uncertainty and the credibility of policies on investment and growth (Pindyck and Solimano 1993 and Fischer 1993).

To illustrate the importance of the relationship between volatility and growth, we decompose the growth differential between the five highest average growth countries and the five lowest average growth countries during 1960–88. We attribute the difference in growth rates to economic and political characteristics. For this decomposition of growth differential, we use the coefficients of equation 9 in Table III–4. The results are presented in Table III–6. As the tables indicate, the average growth in per capita income in the highest growth countries was 2.3 percent per year higher than that registered in the lowest growth countries. However, the group of highest growth countries started in 1960 with a lower per capita income than the group of lowest growth countries. It was expected that the first group would have tended to grow more rapidly than the second group, and then the "catch up" effect should explain 0.9 percent per year of the growth difference. Taking this factor into account, the difference to be explained by other factors between the highest and lowest growth Latin American countries becomes 1.4 percentage points. Basically, the table shows that investment in human capital accounts for a very large proportion, around 42 percent, of the difference, while the share of government spending in GDP accounts for about 21 percent of the difference. On the other hand, volatility of real exchange and inflation rates accounts for 21 and 5 percent of the difference, respectively. However, the difference between the investment rates of both groups of countries accounts for a very small fraction of the difference. The latter result is due to both a small coefficient for the investment rate and a small difference between the average investment rates of both groups of countries.

Further discussion is warranted regarding the robust finding that a lower variability of the real exchange rate has a positive effect on the rate of growth, both through a higher investment rate and through a higher rate of growth—holding

Table III–6. Growth differential between the highest and the lowest growth rate Latin American countries.

	Actual difference	*Percentage of the growth difference*
Difference in average growth	2.30%	
Predicted "catch up"	0.9	
Difference in growth to be explained	1.4	100.0%
Amount due to		
Domestic investment	−0.03	−2.1
Government spending to GDP	0.3	21.1
Primary school rate	0.6	42.3
Trade deficit	−0.2	−14.1
Volatility of RER	0.3	21.1
Volatility of inflation	0.07	5.0
Political uncertainty	0.08	5.6
Unexplained	0.3	21.1

Source: Calculations using estimates presented in Table III–4, equation 9.

constant the rate of investment. A higher level of variability in both variables is usually a manifestation that the macroeconomic situation is getting out of control. Indeed, aware of the detrimental effects of inflation and its variability on overall economic activity, there has been an important movement to introduce institutional arrangements that provide for an independent central bank removed from political pressures. The main objective of the central bank has been to achieve a continuous and gradual reduction in the inflation rate. This movement is most advanced in Latin America, the region with the worst inflation record during the postwar period. Thus, independent central banks have been established in Chile, Colombia, Mexico, Peru, and Argentina, and this process is under way in Bolivia.

There is also increasing awareness of the importance of avoiding the sharp real appreciation and real exchange misalignments that are linked to exchange-rate-based stabilization programs that rely on a fixed exchange rate for too long. But also there is increasing awareness that, depending on the exchange rate system, the authorities could control the nominal exchange rate (in a fixed or adjustable peg system), the money supply, or the interest rate (in a flexible exchange rate system), but independent of the exchange rate system, the real exchange rate—with its variability—is an endogenous variable. Therefore, the way to reduce the variability of the real exchange rate is through a macroeconomic policy that results in a low fiscal deficit—in a world of increasingly integrated capital markets and flexible nominal exchange rate regimes—and a monetary policy in which nominal domestic interest rates are in line with international interest rates, augmented by the expected rate of depreciation. In this type of setting, a domestic interest rate that is not in line with international interest rates will result in large changes in the nominal exchange rate. Given that, as a result of the stickiness of commodity prices and of the inflation rate, in the short and medium run, the variability of the nominal exchange rate is closely associated with the variability of the real exchange rate (Mussa 1990, 1986).

The interest in real exchange rate stability has risen recently in the context of capital inflows toward emerging markets. It could be claimed that a sudden jump in capital inflows could result in a real exchange rate appreciation as well as in a higher real exchange rate variability as nominal interest rates are adjusted to deal with some of the aggregate demand effects of the inflows. In a forthcoming comparison of policies to deal with capital inflows of Asian and Latin American countries, V. Corbo and L. Hernández show that the countries that have received the largest capital inflows (as a percentage of GDP) on average during 1989–1982 *are not* those that have experienced the largest real exchange rate appreciation, implying that the application of different economic policies may have helped contain the appreciation of the real exchange rate, despite receiving significant levels of capital inflows. In particular, those countries that show a decreasing pattern of government consumption (as a percentage of GDP) are also the ones that show a lower real exchange rate appreciation, while those countries that show an increasing share of government consumption in GDP are the same ones that show the highest real exchange rate appreciation. They also found that sterilized intervention is most effective when it is accompanied by fiscal restraint. However, it does not seem to be a sustainable policy in the long run, as sterilized intervention tends to exacerbate capital inflows rather than ameliorate them. This occurs because it tends to increase the differential between domestic and foreign interest rates. Furthermore, sterilized intervention worsens the quasi-fiscal deficit of the central bank.

They finally concluded that an increase in public-sector savings seems to be the only sustainable policy to protect the real exchange rate *in the long run* and seems to be perceived more favorably by the international investors' community. However, a mixed fiscal–monetary policy seems to be more appropriate in the short run than a pure fiscal policy. This occurs because fiscal policy usually lacks the required flexibility to deal with volatile capital flows in the short run.

Conclusions

The new empirical work reported in this paper confirms some of our earlier results. Corbo and Rojas (1993) also provide some new clues on the role of policy on growth. We briefly summarize our main findings.

First, policies can affect growth directly through the law of motion for growth and indirectly through investment rates.

Second, human capital has a positive effect on growth, both through the growth equation and through a higher rate of investment. This result shows that public policy has an important role in promoting growth by enhancing the human capital base. The latter could be done through the direct provision of human capital for the low-income groups of the population or through the creation of an enabling environment that reduces distortions to the accumulation of human capital.

Third, controlling for other factors, the share of government spending on GDP has a negative effect on growth and investment rates. In general, government spending can enhance or hinder growth. Government spending may promote growth by providing essential public goods. However, it could create negative growth effects by wasting resources on programs with low rates of return. Our results show that, on average, government spending has a strong negative effect on growth.

Fourth, and what is a new and very robust result, is the negative effect of macroeconomic uncertainty on growth. Thus, the standard deviations of the inflation rate and of the real exchange rate have a negative effect on growth, both directly through the rate of increase of total factor productivity and indirectly through its negative effect on the investment rate.

Fifth, political instability has also a negative effect on growth, both through the growth equation and through lower investment rates.

From the above analysis emerges a growth strategy. Public policy should be geared to deliver a stable macroeconomic framework, to improve the human capital base of the population, and to keep a low share of government consumption to GDP. Surprisingly, differences in investment rates were not important when accounting for differences in the rate of growth between the high-performing and low-performing Latin American countries. Thus, it is not just the level of investment that matters but also its efficiency.

Notes

1. Inter-American Development Bank (1995) presents a nice summary and provides numerous sources on the recent work along these lines.

2. Most development practitioners have, for a long time, emphasized the role of economic policies and the formation of human and physical capital on the overall growth process. Thus, Díaz-Alejandro (1976) concentrates on poor economic policies to explain the poor long-term growth record of Argentina. Krueger (1978), Little (1982), Feder (1983), and Balassa (1985) have used similar arguments. For these authors, there is not much that is new in the "new growth" theories.

3. Real exchange rate uncertainty also affects growth by denying countries the full benefit of specialization through international trade. Thus, Caballero and Corbo (1989) have shown that exchange rate uncertainty has a negative effect on exports.

4. We report only the result for the variable number of assassinations per million population per year (1960–1985). Other variables were also considered and were found not to have a significant effect on growth. These variables were the index of civil liberties, the index of political rights, and the number of *coups d'etats*.

5. It is surprising that the trade openness variable, measured by the trade ratio, is never significant. There are many reasons the increase in the degrees of openness should be associated with higher growth (Dornbusch 1992). In particular, the new growth theories suggest a link between openness and the long-run output growth rate rather than a rise in the level of output. Grossman and Helpman (1992) suggest that this can occur through the favorable impact of openness on technological changes, and Romer (1993a) introduces the channel of a favorable medium for the adaption of new ideas. For example, openness to trade increases growth rates because trade provides access to a variety of imported inputs that embody new technology. On the other hand, Paul Krugman has maintained that greater openness expands the size of markets facing domestic exporters, thereby raising returns to innovation and thus enhancing the country's specialization in research-intensive production. However, the new growth theories also show that growth can be lowered by increased foreign competition, or it can be increased by import protection if protection promotes investment in the research-intensive sectors of the relevant country. Thus, the direction of the openness–growth relationship is a question open for empirical research rather than a theoretical given.

References

Balassa, B. (1985), "Export, Policy Choices, and Economic Growth in Developing Countries after the 1973 Oil Shock," *Journal of Development Economics*, June.

Barro (1991), "Economic Growth in a Cross Section of Countries," *Quarterly Journal of Economics*, May.

Barro, R.J. (1990), "Government Spending in a Simple Model of Endogenous Growth," *Journal of Political Economics* 18.

Barro, R.J., and H.C. Wolf (1989), "Data Appendix for Economic Growth in a Cross-Section of Countries," mimeo., Harvard University.

Becker, G.S., K.M. Murphy, and R. Tamura (1990), "Human Capital, Fertility, and Economic Growth," *Journal of Political Economy* 98.

Bertola, G. (1989), "Irreversible Investment," unpublished working paper, Princeton University.

Caballero, R., and V. Corbo (1989), "The Effect of Real Exchange Rate Uncertainty on Exports: Empirical Evidence," *World Bank Economic Review* 3(2): 263–78.

Corbo, V., and S. Fischer (1995), "Structural Adjustment, Stabilization, and Policy Reform," in Behrman and Srinivasan (eds.) *Handbook of Development Economics*, vol. 3 (Amsterdam: North Holland).

Corbo, V., and S. Fischer (1992), "Adjustment Programs and Bank Support: Rationale and Main Results," in V. Corbo, S. Fischer, and S.B. Webb (eds.) *Adjustment Lending Revisited: Policies to Restore Growth* (Oxford: World Bank).

Corbo, V., and P. Rojas (1993), "Investment, Macroeconomic Stability, and Growth: The Latin American Experience," *Revista de Análisis Económico* 82 (June): 19–35.

Corbo, V., and P. Rojas (1992), "Crecimiento Económico de América Latina," *Cuadernos de Económica* 87 (August).

Cottani, J.A., D.F. Cavallo, and M.S. Khan (1990), "Real Exchange Rate Behavior and Economic Performance in LDCs," *Economic Development and Cultural Change* 39 (October): 61–76.

Devarajan, S., and J. De Melo (1991), "Membership in the CFA Zone: Odyssean Journey or Trojan Horse?" in A. Chibber and S. Fischer (eds.) *Economic Reforms in Sub-Saharan Africa* (Oxford: World Bank).

Díaz-Alejandro, C.F. (1976), *Foreign Trade Regimes and Economic Development: Colombia* (New York: National Bureau of Economic Research).

Dixit, A., and R.S. Pindyck (1993), *Investment Under Uncertainty* (Princeton, N.J.: Princeton University Press).

Dollar, D. (1992), "Outward-Oriented Developing Economies Really Do Grow More Rapidly: Evidence from 95 LDCs, 1976–85," *Economic Development and Cultural Change* 41: 523–544.

Dornbusch, R. (1992), "The Case for Trade Liberalization in Developing Countries," *Journal of Economic Perspectives*, Winter.

Easterly, W.R., and S. Rebelo (1993), "Fiscal Policy and Economic Growth: An Empirical Investigation," *Journal of Monetary Economics* 32 (December): 417–458.

Feder, G. (1983), "On Exports and Economic Growth," *Journal of Development Economics* 12: 59–74.

Fischer, S. (1993), "The Role of Macroeconomic Factors in Growth: Macroeconomic Stability and Growth," *Journal of Monetary Economics* 32 (December): 485–512.

Fischer, S. (1991), "Growth, Macroeconomics, and Development," *NBER Macroeconomics Annual 1991* (Cambridge, Mass.: MIT Press).

Goldstein, M. (1995), *The Exchange Rate System and the IMF* (Washington, D.C.: Institute for International Economics).

Grossman, G., and E. Helpman (1992), *Innovation and Growth in the Global Economy* (Cambridge, Mass.: MIT Press).

Hausmann, Ricardo, and Michael Gavin (1996), *Securing Stability and Growth in a Shock-Prone Region: The Policy Challenge for Latin America* (Washington, D.C.: Inter-American Development Bank).

Inter-American Development Bank (1995), "Macroeconomic Volatility in Latin America: Causes, Consequences, and Policies to Assure Stability," mimeo., July 17.

King, R.G., and R. Levine (1993), "Finance, Entrepreneurship, and Growth," *Journal of Monetary Economics* 32 (December): 513–542.

Krueger, A.O. (1978), *Liberalization Attempts and Consequences* (New York: Ballinger for the National Bureau of Economic Research).

Levine, R., and D. Renalt (1992), "A Sensitive Analysis of Cross-Country Growth Regressions," *American Economic Review*, September.

Little, I.A. (1982), *Economic Development: Theory, Policy, and International Relations* (New York: Basic Books).

Lucas, R.E., Jr. (1988), "On the Mechanics of Economic Development," *Journal of Monetary Economics* 22.

Mussa, Michael (1990), "Exchange Rates in Theory and Reality," *Essays in International Finance*, no. 179 (Princeton, N.J.: Princeton University Press).

Mussa, Michael (1986), "Nominal Exchange Rates Regimes and the Behavior of Real Exchange Rates: Evidence and Implications," *Carnegie-Rochester Conferences Series on Public Policy* 25: 117–213.

Obstfeld, M. (1995), "International Currency Experience: New Lessons and Lessons Relearned," *Brookings Papers on Economic Activity* 1995: 1.

Pindyck, R.S., and A. Solimano (1993), "Economic Instability and Aggregate Investment," *NBER Macroeconomics Annual 1993* (Cambridge, Mass.: MIT Press).

Rebelo, S. (1992), "Growth in Open Economies," *Carnegie-Rochester Conference Series on Public Policy.*

Romer, P. (1993a), "Two Strategies for Economic Development: Using Ideas vs. Producing Ideas," *Supplement to the World Bank Economic Review*, proceedings of the World Bank Annual Conference on Development Economies 1992, March, 63–91.

Romer, P. (1993b), "Idea Gaps and Other Objects Gaps in Economic Development," *Journal of Monetary Economics* 32 (December): 543–573.

Romer, P. (1989), "Human Capital and Growth: Theory and Evidence," NBER Working Paper Series, no. 3173 (Cambridge, Mass.: National Bureau of Economic Research).

Romer, P. (1986), "Increasing Returns and Long-Run Growth," *Quarterly Journal of Economics*, May.

Solimano, A. (1992), "How Private Investment Reacts to Changing Macroeconomic Conditions: The Case of Chile in the 1980s," in Chhibber et al. (eds.) *Reviving Private Investment in Developing Countries* (Amsterdam: North Holland).

Solow, R.M. (1956), "A Contribution to the Theory of Economic Growth," *Quarterly Journal of Economics* 70.

Summers, R., and A. Heston (1991), "The Penn World Trade (Mark 5): An Expanded Set of International Comparisons," 1950–1988, *Quarterly Journal of Economics*, May.

Taylor, M. (1995), "The Economics of Exchange Rates," *Journal of Economic Literature* 33 (March): 13–47.

White, H. (1980), "A Heteroskedasticity-Consistent Covariance Matrix Estimator and a Direct Test for Heteroskedasticity," *Econometrica* 48: 817–38.

Williamson, J. (1990), "What Washington Means by Policy Reform," in J. Williamson (ed.), *Latin American Adjustment* (Washington, D.C.: Institute for International Economics).

World Bank (1993), *The East Asian Miracle* (Oxford: Oxford University Press).

World Bank (1991), *World Development Report* (Oxford: Oxford University Press).

Gould:

Over the past few months, exchange rate movements have certainly taken center stage. With the dramatic devaluation of the peso in December 1994 and extremely wide swings of the dollar against the yen and the mark, 1995 will probably be noted as one of the most volatile years for exchange rates.

But even though we have seen a lot of volatility recently, it is not new. It is just a continuation of a trend marked by other noticeable events such as the collapse of the European exchange rate mechanism in 1992. In fact, as Jeff

Frankel mentioned earlier, exchange rate volatility has been much higher since the end of the Bretton Woods fixed-exchange-rate regime in 1973.

The Dallas Fed's own Trade-Weighted Value of the Dollar series has been one and one-half times more volatile in the first half of the 1990s than it was in the last half of the 1970s. Despite all this volatility, little research has gone into the study of how exchange rates directly affect long-run growth. But the effect of exchange rates on economic growth is an important issue for many countries because it gets at the heart of which exchange rate regime they should be following over the long run. I think Vittorio Corbo, by looking at economic growth, takes the right approach in his paper.

Often, countries are quick to adopt some new type of managed exchange rate policy hoping it either will provide a painless transition to low inflation or will increase the stability of financial markets. However, what policymakers may not appreciate fully at the time of adopting a managed exchange rate policy are the costs of the abandoning that policy—something that, for one reason or another, usually happens.

Professor Corbo examines the long-run relationship between real exchange rate volatility—the nominal exchange rate adjusted for foreign and domestic inflation differentials—and real economic growth. Whereas he also studies the relationship between inflation volatility and long-run growth, I will comment primarily on his results regarding the real exchange rate volatility and economic growth. I liked Professor Corbo's paper very much, and I think it moves us in the right direction in understanding the relationship between exchange rates and economic growth. It is the first paper that I have seen that directly examines the relationship between real exchange rate volatility and economic growth in such a wide sample of countries and controlling for so many different variables.

Corbo's underlying idea is that exchange rate volatility reflects macroeconomic uncertainty, which, in turn, may have important effects on long-run investment and growth. If exchange rate volatility has important effects on economic growth, then perhaps by implementing policies to alter that real exchange rate volatility, countries may enhance their long-run rate of economic growth.

The context in which Corbo examines this relationship has been called the *new growth theory*, but as he mentions, it is not that new. The idea is that increases in real economic growth are determined by technological progress, which does not happen by accident. Instead, progress occurs as a result of the incentive to make a profit.

The implication is that productivity growth might be related to the structures and policies followed by the economy, rather than the exogenous forces of nature and luck. Anything that enhances technological progress can increase real economic growth. Consequently, a country's macroeconomic environment can have profound effects on its long-run rate of growth.

Exchange rate volatility may create insecurity about the future and decrease the incentives to invest in future development. For example, highly volatile exchange rates may foster uncertainty about the future profits from a new export product and limit investment in its development.

Great exchange rate volatility may also cause firms to diversify production across countries to hedge exchange rate risk rather than choose production locations based on the lowest cost (that is, based on what economists refer to as *comparative advantage*). This last effect, however, may actually increase investment and growth in some countries that gain the foreign facilities. So theoretically, as Corbo mentions, the effects of exchange rate volatility on growth are uncertain.

In looking at the growth experience across more than a hundred countries over 28 years and controlling for such factors as the country's rate of investment, its productivity gap compared with the United States, government spending, and various other factors, Professor Corbo finds that the real exchange rate volatility and inflation negatively affect real per capita GDP growth. This holds true for the whole set of countries as well as just the Latin American countries themselves. Moreover, the results are consistent with several recent empirical studies that have shown that short-term exchange rate volatility is very difficult to assign to economic fundamentals.

There are, however, some areas that may be expanded and some notes of caution in interpreting the results of the paper. As Professor Corbo mentions, real exchange rate volatility or inflation volatility does not necessarily reflect policy uncertainty. Even in the most informed world, where government policies are well known and not subject to change, real exchange rates naturally will move. After all, the exchange rate is a relative price, just like the relative price of apples to oranges, and is subject to change depending on market conditions. It doesn't necessarily have to reflect uncertainty. Given this ambiguity, analysts must correctly discern what this negative relationship between real exchange rate volatility and growth means.

For instance, suppose a country experiences a bad economic shock, such as a drop in the price of oil for an oil-exporting country. Volatility in the real exchange rate will likely result, and later real GDP growth may decline. In other words, it may not be real exchange rate volatility that causes growth to fall. Rather, growth falls because of other real factors, and real exchange rate volatility may just be coincidental. Therefore, making policy conclusions based solely on Corbo's analysis is a bit risky.

To some degree, as Professor Corbo demonstrates, you can control for economic shocks that would affect the real exchange rate and economic growth by controlling for political stability. But one should also control for things such as oil prices, a particularly relevant factor for many Latin American countries. However, it is difficult to control for all relevant factors, which is why this type of analysis should not be taken as sufficient evidence that exchange rate management can increase economic growth.

From a policy point of view, however, it would be nice to evaluate exactly which types of exchange rate policies are associated with greater economic growth. My suggestion is to include both nominal and real exchange rate volatility in the growth equations to get an idea of how nominal exchange rate volatility, which is subject to direct policy control, can influence growth. Because these two variables are highly correlated, the results will probably not show any direct effects. Nonetheless, it would be interesting to see what these effects are, if they are observable.

Another suggestion is to separate countries into different groups and time periods according to their exchange rate regime and then compare their growth rates. It may also be useful to identify the exact mechanism by which volatility decreases economic growth. Does growth decline because of lower general investment or lower trade sector investment? Several studies have shown that exchange rate volatility is negatively associated with growth in trade, although the effects, as Jeffrey Frankel mentioned earlier, seem to be rather small. So it is unclear how exchange rate volatility affects investment and growth.

Finally, as a technical note, the measure of volatility that Professor Corbo uses in this draft is the standard deviation. Using the standard deviation in this cross-country analysis may present a problem because standard deviations are not comparable when the average of the series differs between countries. For example, if the yearly inflation rate of a certain country has a standard deviation of 1 percent, this information alone does not necessarily tell us whether this volatility is great or small. A standard deviation of 1 percent would reflect great volatility in Japan but very little volatility for Argentina. What might be useful is a relative measure of volatility, such as the coefficient at variation that scales the standard deviation by the mean of the variable.

In concluding, I would reiterate that I enjoyed Professor Corbo's paper. It is an important work that helps us move closer toward understanding the long-run effects of exchange rate volatility on economic growth.

Rojas–Suárez:
As Vittorio Corbo's paper clearly put it, volatility matters for growth. Certainly that is the case, but the most important question is, perhaps, what kind of volatility? Many articles in the literature these days stress a number of different forms of volatility affecting growth such as real exchange rate volatility and inflation volatility. As Corbo said, the difference between this kind of literature and his paper is that he analyzes the issue in the context of a more integrated model that starts with a Barro-type equation.

I want to start my comments with a bit of skepticism about the method used in Corbo's paper of adding variables to the famous Barro empirical growth equation. The problem I have with that methodology is that, without a model or some basic fundamental theory about which variables explain growth, it is not clear whether it is the level or volatility of a variable that matters for growth.

The literature on economic growth is replete with a large number of equations to which it keeps adding variables. Sometimes the level matters, sometimes the volatility, sometimes both. I am a bit skeptical about continuing to go that route to explain long-term growth.

Using this methodology, there is a danger that one might misspecify the model that one wants to examine. Vittorio Corbo basically stresses the importance of demand-side variables from the point of view of macroeconomic policy management. However, other studies, such as Hausmann and Gavin (1996), who follow a similar methodology, obtain a different result from Corbo's.[1] They find that although many demand-side variables matter for growth, the most important variable is volatility in changes in the terms of trade. In other words, it is a supply-side variable and not a policy-related demand-side variable that is important. I'm not saying that one is right and the other is wrong. What I'm saying is that the danger of adding variables without a theory is that it can lead to a misunderstanding of what is important for growth.

Moving further into the issue of what variables to consider, I would like to discuss the importance of a variable Corbo does not discuss in his paper—volatility in the premium on the market determined exchange rate.[2] I believe that that variable is very important for explaining the patterns of short- and medium-term growth in the Latin American region.

Let me present my argument by answering two questions: First, why do changes in the nominal exchange rate matter for economic activity? And second, why do we also need to consider the volatility in the nominal exchange rate changes to understand the behavior of economic growth in Latin America? With respect to the first issue, I need to start by stressing that, from my point of view, the exchange rate is the most important signal given to economic participants in Latin America about the state of the economy. Let me explain: In countries such as those in Latin America, everything is short term. By definition, the exchange rate is the foreign price of domestic money, and money is the most liquid and short-term asset of all. Changes in the exchange rate get transmitted into changes in the short-term interest rate extremely quickly. But the short-term interest rate is all there is in Latin America.

There are very few countries where long-term financial markets exist, and where they do, they are not very liquid. So from a market point of view, predictions of what will happen with the exchange rate also send signals of what will happen with the short-term interest rates. And since that's all there is in the economy, economic agents also form expectations about the effect of such movements on real activity.

Imagine a conservative policymaker who is trying very hard to bring inflation down and that faces a shock, say a sudden outflow of capital, that leads to sharp pressures on both the nominal exchange rate and the short-term real interest rate. If the policymaker is constrained by a fixed exchange rate regime and is committed to the target of low inflation, the real money supply and the availability of real credit in the economy will decrease. This in turn will slow down economic activity. In short, nominal variables like the exchange rate get transmitted quickly into the real economy because of two features in Latin American economies: maturities are very short and there's not enough creditworthiness or depth in the domestic financial markets.

Let us now turn to the second issue: why volatility in the nominal exchange rate also is important for growth. In a study that I have just initiated on Argentina, Mexico and Chile, statistical analyses show that there is a strong inverse relationship between economic growth and volatility in expected changes in the nominal exchange rate. It is important to stress that we found that *expected* and not *actual* volatility in the nominal exchange rate is the relevant variable.

Now, what does that say about choosing an exchange rate system? Can we isolate the economy from uncertainty by a system of fixing exchange rates? Here Argentina comes as a case in point. Does Argentina's fixed exchange rate regime mean that uncertainty about changes in the exchange rate have vanished? In my view, the answer to that question is no. Data on the spreads on peso-dollar deposits in Argentina, since the beginning of the convertibility law, show that the spreads are not constant and are not zero. If there were full credibility in the exchange rate, you wouldn't observe this pattern of changes in the spread. So, even with a fixed exchange rate regime, exchange rate expectations can be important.

How do I explain the fact that volatility, and not only the level of expected changes in the exchange rate, also matter in the explanation of real variables? To answer this question, let me refer you to the famous currency substitution model where expected changes in the exchange rate were commonly used to explain the dollarization process in Latin America. The model was very successful when inflation rates were high in Latin America. However, when the inflation rate started to come down in these countries, the currency substitution model began to cease its effectiveness in explaining the persistence of dollarization.

Why, if expectations about the exchange rate changes calmed down, did the countries not come back toward the use of domestic currency as opposed to foreign currency? Well, using an extension of the capital asset pricing model, Paul McNellis and I (1996) found out that over the last two decades, the U.S. dollar has established itself as a safe asset in Latin America, an asset with low returns, but safe.[3]

In contrast, the domestic currency is viewed as a risky asset, where its riskiness is approached by the volatility of expected changes in the exchange rate.

Thus, even though the expectation of large exchange rate changes has declined significantly, volatility is still there. In my work with McNellis, the persistence of dollarization in Latin America can be explained by this expected exchange rate volatility. So volatility on the expected changes in the exchange rate matters, and matters a lot, for the determination of real variables in the American economies. It is then not surprising to find out that uncertainty about behavior of expected changes in the exchange rate also impacts strongly on economic activity.

Notes

1. Hausmann and Gavin (1996), "Security Stability and Growth in a Shock Prone Region: The Policy Challenge for Latin America," OCE, Working Paper No. 315, Inter-American Development Bank.
2. In many Latin American countries under fixed exchange rates, the best approximation to a market-determined exchange rate is the black market rate.
3. See McNellis, Paul and L. Rojas-Suárez (1996), "Exchange-Rate Depreciation, Dollarization and Uncertainty: A Comparison of Bolivia and Peru," OCE, Working Paper No. 325, Inter-American Development Bank.

Appendix to Part III

Description of the Data in Exchange Rate Volatility, Investment, and Growth: Some New Evidence

The data required to generate the trade openness, inflation rate, and direct foreign investment variables are taken from the World Bank database. Black market premium data are from the *World Currency Yearbook*. Terms-of-trade data are from ECLAC statistics, and the real exchange rate is from IMF and World Bank statistics. All other time series data are from Summers and Heston (1991), who have compiled internationally comparable annual figures on output and its composition, prices, and exchange rates for 134 market economies from 1950 to 1988. The data for the time invariant variables are from the database of Barro and Wolf (1989).

The entire sample, excluding Africa, has 58 countries with six periods of data. However, the use of the lagged value of the investment rate and some unavailable data produces a sample of 263 observations for the larger regression growth model, while it has 284 observations for the larger investment model. The Latin American sample consists of 20 countries with six periods of data. After losing 20 observations for the lagged value of the investment rate, we obtained a total of 100 observations for analysis.

Part IV SPECULATIVE ATTACKS

Countries that attempt to manage their exchange rate have been subject to large speculative attacks by a foreign exchange market that now exceeds $1 trillion of transactions a day. Are these foreign exchange markets a stabilizing or destabilizing force?

Presenter:
Peter M. Garber
Economics Professor
Brown University

Moderator:
Carlos Zarazaga
Senior Economist and Executive Director
Center for Latin American Economics
Federal Reserve Bank of Dallas

Discussants:
Guillermo Mondino
Executive Director
Fundación Mediterránea

Miguel Savastano
Economist
International Monetary Fund

Garber:
Normally, it is with some trepidation that I present a paper in the very last session of any day. But today, because of the nature of the topic and the previous discussion, I think it is a very nice position to be in. It allows me to try to wrap up many of the issues that have been discussed during the day.

First, I will talk about the theory we have about speculative attacks, since that is one of the key issues that was discussed this morning. Then I will consider the issue discussed in the background paper (Appendix to Part IV), which is a very micromarket issue involving what happens at the time of an attack, in the days or the hours before the collapse of a fixed-exchange-rate regime in a situation in which capital markets are perfectly open and we have the sort of derivative products and exchange markets that are found in the industrial countries. And then finally, I will try to apply a bit of these results to the Mexico case. The two cases that seem to have crystalized, or recrystalized, interest in speculative attacks were the collapse of the European Exchange Rate Mechanism (ERM) in 1992 and 1993 and the collapse of the Mexican peso at the end of 1994. I will try to weave in those examples as I go along.

Speculative Attack Theory

The theory of speculative attacks actually was developed at the Federal Reserve, starting as a research project having to do with the collapse of the Bretton Woods system in 1971 and 1973. The first paper in this literature was one by Salant and Henderson that was published in 1978 but was circulated before then. They developed the principles we still use today to analyze speculative attacks. Paul Krugman was, I believe, a summer intern at the Fed in about 1977 or 1978 and made use of the basic concepts in the Salant and Henderson paper but applied his results not to an attack on a buffer stock of gold, as did Salant and Henderson, but to an attack on a fixed-nominal-exchange-rate regime. That has been the primary application of these concepts in the literature since then.

Bob Flood and I specialized the Krugman model when Bob was an economist at the Board of Governors, and I did a paper with Herminio Blanco that did some empirical testing of this model for the previous Mexico collapse, back when I was a visiting scholar at the Board of Governors in 1982. So I would characterize this theory of speculative attacks as the Federal Reserve System's theory of speculative attacks.

The models are not necessarily to be taken very literally. They allow us to organize our thinking about speculative attacks and convince ourselves that speculative attacks are quite rational and reasonable responses to imbalances and inconsistencies in government policies. Typically, they are set up in a very simple money market equilibrium framework. They are generally based on a monetary theory of the exchange rate in which a central bank has a secondary policy of fixing an exchange rate but a primary policy of printing money by supplying the government with domestic credit. The primary policy will never be abandoned. It is the secondary policy, the fixed exchange rate, that will eventually be eliminated. It has long been known that a policy of domestic credit creation through a central bank is ultimately inconsistent with a fixed-exchange-rate regime. Sooner or later, the fixed-exchange-rate regime will collapse. That has been shown time and time again.

The contribution of the literature is to show when and under what circumstances the regime must collapse. The usual assumption is that the fixed-exchange-rate system will collapse into a floating rate regime. The problem is figuring out exactly when that will occur. The principles that are used to determine the timing are, first, that there are to be no unusual speculative profits had by speculators. Speculators will compete with each other in determining the time of the attack in order to eliminate expected speculative profits. In so doing, they will cause a discrete collapse in the central bank's reserves. Typically, the assumption is that reserves will fall to zero. In other words, the central bank will not fund itself by going short in foreign exchange; it will let go of the exchange rate beforehand.

That is the basic model. The outcome is driven by a fundamentally inconsistent central bank policy. In addition, there have been some developments of this model in which the central bank policy of domestic credit creation is a contingent policy, not a policy that is necessarily in effect at a given time during the existence of the fixed-exchange-rate regime. By that I mean that the central bank uses the fixed exchange-rate regime to control itself. This would be the view of the fixed exchange rate as a nominal anchor. That is, without a fixed exchange rate, the central bank is effectively a money printing addict. It can't control itself except by pegging solidly to some other country's currency. Speculators in the system will, depending on their expectations, either attack or not attack the fixed-exchange-rate regime. If their expectations revolve around the notion that the central bank is going to go on a money-printing binge, they will attack the regime and the central bank will go on a money-printing binge, even though, before the attack, it had run a perfectly stable policy consistent with the fixed-exchange-rate regime. The attack will, therefore, have been ratified and proper, and so it would be a reasonable equilibrium.

Alternatively, if speculators believe that the central bank will not go on a money-printing binge, they will not attack, the fixed-exchange-rate system will continue to exist, and the central bank will maintain control of itself and not print money. Again, that would be a perfectly consistent equilibrium.

So there is some instability created by speculative expectations. Depending on what they are, they can drive the system either to a floating system and a collapse of the fixed-rate system or to a continuation of the fixed-rate system. This possibility has become interesting in the context of the ERM collapse because of the belief that the attack on the French, in particular, was not justified and perhaps was the result of a self-fulfilling type of attack.

The Case of the ERM

Obviously, it is easy to think of policies that are inconsistent with the maintenance of a fixed-exchange-rate regime. This morning, Jeff Frankel presented two cases: the case of Italy and the case of the UK. Their policies were fundamentally inconsistent with the maintenance of a fixed-exchange-rate regime or with staying within the band, and, therefore, the attacks on their currencies were generally considered to have been based on fundamentals. The attack on the French, whose fundamental policies seemed to be even better than those of the Bundesbank, was generally thought to have been unjustified.

When I was at the International Monetary Fund (IMF), looking at the European capital markets in the aftermath of the collapse of the ERM, the question that came up again and again was, Why were the French attacked? My view was that the whole situation really was not an attack on the French but an attack on the Germans. How far were the Germans willing to go to lend to their partners in the ERM? It was clear to the markets, once they attacked Italy, that the Germans had a limit on how much they would lend to the Italians. It was clear the speculative wolf pack attacked the sled, and the Germans threw the Italians off the sled. Once the wolf pack got the taste of blood, they thought the Germans might feed them some more, so they attacked the British. The Germans threw the British off the sled and made it clear that there was a limit beyond which they would not go. The Germans were unwilling to relax their own monetary policy beyond a certain point to lend to their partners through the Very Short Term Financing facility. As a result, the wolf pack thought that maybe the Germans had a limit in regard to the French. Before, that limit might have been thought to have been quite large, but now it was clear that the Germans were pulling back, that they had reached the limit of their ability to sterilize the impact of their loans in support of the exchange rate mechanism. So the wolf pack thought, let's try the French. Regardless of what French internal policies were, this was a German policy. So France was attacked and tested, and the attack turned out to be mistaken. The French passed the test because the Germans made it clear they were unwilling to let the French franc be devalued as well. The Germans visibly lent an unlimited amount, and even bought francs themselves, and this undid the force behind the attack. So there are good reasons to think that the attack against the French in the autumn of 1992 was a fundamentals-based attack. The summer of 1993 is a different issue. That situation is not as clear.

The reason I am going into this is that the argument that came out of France after the 1992 attack and defense of the franc was that the attack was unjustified and perhaps the result of a self-fulfilling attack, and so perhaps there were reasons to stifle these markets. The huge power of these markets had nearly driven the French off the ERM band, so perhaps it was time to impose some sort of control on them. This was noised about a little bit in official circles, but that quickly ended. Now there is really not much talk, of the sort that existed then, about controlling capital flows.

Again, this was a political decision. The French had devoted a lot of effort to developing their financial markets. Paris, London, and Frankfurt were competing to become the financial center of Europe, and there had been large liberalizations in the system. The French, in particular, had undertaken heavy investment to liberalize and update and upgrade their markets. If they suddenly imposed capital controls, that would eliminate France as the financial center of Europe and would eliminate a very nice, high-wage business.

Run-Up to an Attack

Let me shift a bit now to the issue of what happens in the run-up to an attack. The speculative attack models work on the principle of perfectly free capital movements. So speculators, when they want it, can get whatever credit they need, through whatever instruments they have. They can go to the central bank of the weak currency to acquire the domestic currency they need to buy foreign exchange from that same central bank.

So the first thing to consider is what actually happens when there are perfectly open and free capital markets and free movement of capital under modern conditions. This is where my background paper comes in (Appendix to Part IV). When capital markets are open, obviously, capital moves. And in the few years before the attack on the European exchange rate mechanism, there was a large-scale movement of capital across borders, not only within the ERM countries, but capital came in from the United States as well. This capital was moved in to try to take advantage of the liberalization of the markets and the perceived inappropriate interest rate differentials between what were thought of as weaker currencies and stronger currencies within the ERM. But the risk was hedged, or at least partially hedged. A lot of the capital coming in was from mutual funds or pension funds in the United States. These funds' managers did not want to take all of the currency risks involved, so they engaged in hedging operations. One sort of hedging operation, of course, is to buy a put on the currency that you are interested in. Another is to create a synthetic put on that currency. In addition to people who had moved capital in and were just trying to cover it, there were those we would call classic speculators, people who would take a short position. It was possible for them to speculate in almost unlimited amounts.

The mechanism of speculation for a hedge fund is simply to short-sell the currency in some sort of forward contract, and it is easy to leverage up capital tenfold in the banking system to do this. To get the banking system to take the other side—that is, buy in the weak currency—the banking system itself has to have an outlet for that currency; it has to be able to cover that position.

The world's banks generally do not take a very large position in foreign exchange, or prefer not to. They make their money by trading. So if there is a large sale into the banks of the weak currency, there will be a large sale out of the banks. The way the banks typically cover themselves in forward operations is to sell the currency on the spot market and then do a currency swap to cover the maturity differential. These are wholesale operations that are done with the rest of the world's banking system. So a bank in New York might buy pounds from Quantum Fund on a forward contract but immediately sell the pounds on the spot market and do a swap as well. It has to do the swap with some other bank and the spot exchange rate transaction with some other bank. Let's assume it is a British bank. Ultimately, it is going to have to go to a British bank, which, again, is taking the opposite position—it is buying pounds and engaging in the opposite part of the swap. Now that British bank is also engaged in an imbalance, and it is going to have to cover its position. If it is a one-way market in an attack, it will sell the pounds to the Bank of England, but it also has to get pounds to deliver to the Bank of England. Where does it go to get the pounds? Ultimately, a British bank will go to the Bank of England to get the pounds. It will borrow the pounds through the discount window to get them and then deliver the pounds. So ultimately it gets credit, which it funnels through to the world's banking system in order to finance the attack on the central bank itself. The central bank finances the collapse of its own policy.

That is the basic nature of an attack. A central bank that is posting a Lombard rate or a discount rate, usually at slightly above the market, at which it discounts freely, and fixes the exchange rate is schizophrenic. It is expressing two goals: one goal is to implement the macro policy, fixing the exchange rate, maybe for current account purposes or whatever. The other goal is one of maintaining stability in the financial markets by posting a Lombard rate. That is what Lombard Street is all about, right? You post a Lombard rate to be the lender of last resort in a crisis. If you keep the Lombard rate low, then you are expressing a priority of maintaining financial stability over maintaining the fixed-exchange-rate regime. That is the difference, I think, between a central bank and a currency board. A central bank has a body that is expressed in the form of the fixed exchange rate, but its soul, its true being, is expressed in the posting of a Lombard-type rate. It is willing to give up the fixed exchange rate in a pinch to avoid a financial crisis. A currency board does not have a body. Its soul is keeping the exchange rate, and it does not care about what happens to the financial system. I think that is the difference. One expresses a priority policy of maintaining the fixed exchange rate, while the other expresses a duality of policy and usually a secondary policy of fixing the exchange rate. That secondary policy of fixing the exchange rate ultimately is going to be consistent with a speculative attack, and such central banks will always, at some point or other, be attacked.

That is what the speculators do. But what about the hedgers? The hedgers are, in fact, the same as speculators in an attack on a central bank. You really cannot tell the difference in their behavior. And the hedgers that I have in mind, particularly in the background paper, are those that use dynamic hedging strategies to replicate put options. To hedge a position, a fund that has foreign investments might acquire directly an actual put option, or it might create a synthetic put option by dynamic hedging. If it actually buys a put option, it will usually be an over-the-counter put option on the currency. It will buy that from a bank, and then the bank must cover the currency implications of that position by dynamic hedging. So one way or another, an attempt to hedge the risk of currency movements by investors will lead to a dynamic hedging operation. These operations occur in large amounts, and they are typical in this business now. A dynamic hedge mimics a put in the following sense. In the theory of put pricing, a put on a currency represents a short position in the particular currency and a long position in the currency that was used to buy the weak currency—the currency that is named in the put option. For instance, a put that allows one to sell pounds for dollars at some future date is a position that is short pounds and effectively long dollars, and, in particular, the short position is a fraction of the face value of the put, the notional value of the put. The value of the put, the "premium," changes as volatility changes and as interest rate differentials between the pound and the dollar change.

To cover a put, a bank or a fund can create actual positions in the currency —that is, a short position. If it is a put on pounds, the fund can create a short position in pounds by borrowing and selling pounds, use the proceeds to buy dollar assets, and then add a few additional dollar assets in order to equal the premium value. These positions have to be adjusted, from time to time, as changes occur in the exchange rate, volatility, and interest rate differentials.

So, for example, when British interest rates are very low for a given maturity, only a certain fraction of the notional value of the put is hedged, say, 50 percent of the notional value. This would represent a short position of 500,000 pounds on a 1 million pound notional value. But as the British interest rate rises up to crisis values, the hedging ratio tends to rise. You might go from 50 percent of those million pounds to a short position of 80 percent, so you would short 300,000 pounds more. This would be a standard strategy.

I would like to tie this into the macro effects of these strategies on the financial system. When there is a speculative attack on a currency, it will show up as changes in volatility and the exchange rate. Speculators will show up at the exchange window of the central bank and demand foreign currency. Ultimately, there is a defense against this. If a central bank is really serious about maintaining its exchange rate, it can put up its discount rate or its Lombard rate. By putting up its Lombard rate, it will squeeze the markets. People who are caught short in the currency will have to scramble to get the currency, and the only way they can typically do that is to sell back the foreign exchange to get the central bank to create some new base money. This is the classic interest rate defense of the exchange rate system.

The problem with that defense—in the presence of this large-scale dynamic hedging business, this effectively automated stop-loss selling—is that putting up the interest rate will cause, through dynamic hedging, an avalanche of sales of the weak currency, not a huge amount of buying. That avalanche of sales might push the central bank past its intervention limits, might drive it down to a net negative position in foreign exchange, which it doesn't want to hold, and therefore collapse the exchange rate. So the presence of these sorts of strategies in the system undermines the ability of a central bank to defend the fixed exchange rate.

Moreover, all of these hedging strategies are based on faulty macro models. Embedded in any finance model from which we get a pricing formula for an option is a macro model about relationships between exchange rates and interest rates. In the very simple Black–Scholes or Garman–Kohlhagen model, the relationship is exogenous. The interest rates can drift. Interest rates can fluctuate or move, but that does not change the assumed random walk nature of the exchange rate.

The Case of Mexico

Let us consider, now, the case of Mexico. This example is one in which there are perfectly open capital markets in any number of instruments. There are currently some efforts to try and stifle these markets for causing excessive volatility and speculation, perhaps through a Tobin-type transactions tax. The problem with such taxes is that these markets are extremely plastic. They can move readily from one form to another, and it is easy for them to move in such a way as to avoid the tax. Unless you impose the tax on every kind of financial transaction, it is very difficult to get at these kinds of transactions or to impose capital controls.

In the case of Mexico, these avenues of speculation were much narrower in that it was not easy to take a short position against the peso. The futures market did not exist. You could go over the counter in New York, but it was difficult to cover that position in Mexico. So although there were large forward sales in New York, they were usually on a matched basis and did not spill over into Mexico.

Banco de México and the Mexican government, however, did provide some of the credit necessary to engage in the attack. The attack, in its virulent form, is usually thought to have occurred between the end of November and the end of December 1994, but it actually occurred throughout 1994 as a result of political disturbances. The credit in this attack was generated in the form of *tesobonos*. Suddenly, instead of *cetes*, you have *cetes* but with a forward exchange contract attached to them, in which the gains from the forward contract are payable in pesos, which would be convertible immediately into dollars.

So effectively, the Mexican government—in the form of *tesobonos*—was buying the peso forward and selling foreign exchange forward. Investors were engaged in selling the peso forward, and they found that the party on the other side was the Mexican government. So in spite of the difficulties in short-selling the peso, it ultimately could be done through the *tesobono* operation. By the time the year ended with this large sale of *tesobonos*, although there was still foreign exchange in the hands of the Banco de México, that was as a gross amount of foreign exchange, not net. The existence of the *tesobonos* created a net zero, or even negative, position even before the attacks were lodged.

Conclusion

Let me close by saying that we really have theoretical models of speculative attacks. We know how they work. They are abstract when you try to interpret any given speculative attack with the guidance of the models. One serious difficulty is that we do not know what happens in the hours or minutes that the actual attack is launched. That is a very abstract concept in these models. We need to have that knowledge in order to get a reasonable model of speculative attacks, because then we can back out what happens at the moment of the attack, the end point that determines the dynamics and the timing of what goes beforehand.

So what is necessary is some knowledge of the microactivity at the time of an attack. It is difficult to gather this information—who is selling first, what instruments are being used, what the central bank's strategy is, what is being done minute by minute. Perhaps central banks hold postmortems after they get attacked to determine what happened, but if they do, what they learn is not formally released. What we need, as academics and also as central bankers, is to have some consortium in which we, even in a secret way, combine our knowledge of the minute-by-minute operations undertaken when an attack occurred. I think that would be a valuable addition to everyone's knowledge.

Mondino:
Speculative attacks are not foreign to us in Argentina; we have experienced several of them. I'll describe how speculative attacks have worked in the case of Argentina, in particular, and, more generally, in the case of Latin America.

Before I do that, I would like to go over a couple of the issues that Peter touched on. The first is why we have speculative attacks and whether we should respond to them. The second issue involves the dynamics of the attacks.

Why do we have these attacks? I think there are basically two sets of theories, the two sets that Peter mentioned. One is the "fundamentalist" theory that something is wrong with the budget. People are concerned about either the budget or the quasi-budget deficit of the central bank or some other bank associated with the treasury. The second theory is basically associated with expectations. This theory argues that there are multiple equilibria out there, and an exogenous change in expectations—some type of a shock to the system—will trigger a move from one good equilibrium to the next.

Policymakers have to do two basic things if they want to avoid a speculative attack on their currency. The first one, and probably the less important one, is invest in reputation. They have to be very careful how they treat their customers, how they treat foreign investors and capital or asset holders. It's no surprise that the attack on the Mexican peso didn't take place when Pedro Aspe was the minister of finance. He had made a serious investment in reputation. Once he walked out and there was a new minister of finance, it was much more likely an attack would occur. The second, and key, factor in avoiding an attack is fiscal flexibility. A government should have the reflexes to look for funding to avoid the attack. This funding typically requires serious fiscal adjustment on both the expenditure and the taxation sides. Hence, the best thing any government that's under threat of an attack can do is start flexing its muscles and look for fiscal resources. In any case, given the speed of markets, a government may also need an additional source of defense because before it can have a fiscal plan to show the markets, it could be out of currency. The Mexicans learned this the hard way. It took them a long time to put together a coherent package to show the markets. It's very important that a government have the tools to undertake this defense.

What are the typical tools that are used? One, which was mentioned today, is capital controls. You can implement new capital controls once you think the currency is somewhat weak. Unfortunately, capital controls won't stop the attack. It eventually will occur unless there is also fiscal adjustment. A more efficient mechanism to stop a speculative attack is probably the use of the interest rate, which was basically what Peter was talking about.

How do speculative attacks work in practice? Even though the theories can sound complicated, speculative attacks are very simple animals. First, there is the expectation that a government is going to abandon the exchange rate regime. This abandonment typically is associated with a discrete jump in the exchange rate. Whether you fix again at the new higher level or whether you float, there typically is a jump in the exchange rate. The second important factor is that since people expect a devaluation, they will start pulling deposits out of banks. Investment houses will start betting against the currency, and everybody will start trying to liquidate their positions in the weak money and try to move into a stronger currency. When they do this, they'll do it at the defended exchange rate, of course.

Who is going to sell this defended exchange rate? Obviously, the central bank. So the central bank starts selling foreign currency through one of two mechanisms. First, it engages in a lot of forward contracts. This is the most dangerous style of defense because it doesn't get properly accounted for in a lot of countries. This is particularly true for developing countries because the governments still have their foreign reserves out there to defend the currency, but they have engaged in a lot of forward contracts that will have to be fulfilled in the future if the currency goes under. In other words, the forward contracts give room to leverage the attack.

The second practice, the most standard practice, is to sell currency in the spot market. Once the central bank reaches a certain threshold, it basically must decide what it's going to do, whether it's going to keep defending the currency, and by doing so, let interest rates go up. If they do go up, the central bank will have to decide what to do with the banking system, or it may decide to stop defending the currency and move to something else altogether.

The problem is that under certain circumstances, an interest rate defense can be the final signal the market was waiting for to clean out the central bank. Of course, when the interest rate defense works, it works because it creates a lot of illiquidity in the market; it dries up the markets. When it doesn't work, it doesn't work for other reasons. I have four scenarios about this.

In the first scenario, high interest rates will—holding everything else constant—lead to a recession. This recession will probably result in high unemployment; hence, the central bank is likely to lose its nerve and abandon the exchange rate. Speculators understand central banks are likely to abandon the exchange rate, and so they will speed up the attack.

In the second scenario, high interest rates will throw the banks out of business for two reasons. One is the recession scenario I just mentioned. The banks' loan performances will turn sour. The other reason is that there will be a liquidity squeeze in the banks, and the banking system will start experiencing serious problems. The banks will have lent at relatively low interest rates, and they will be taking deposits at much higher interest rates. They will be losing money, they will be in trouble, and the central bank will have to decide what to do. So obviously, these banks will be banging at the discount window trying to get it open, and the central bank will have to decide whether to open it.

In the third scenario, some market participants are not aware a speculative attack is brewing. When they see the interest rate going up, they suddenly wake up to what's going on and decide to pursue the attack themselves. This scenario assumes that the information is not evenly distributed, that some participants are either asleep or stupid, or that the information is really costly. This scenario assumes that interest rates will signal the collapse of the regime.

The final scenario involves mechanistic hedgers or foreign traders. This is the scenario Peter was talking about. Bankers use interest rates to read where the currency is going. The option pricing models they are using don't have a term for expectations; they read the expectations implicitly out of interest rates. Hence, when interest rates shoot up, the models basically figure out there's a devaluation coming. And if there's a devaluation coming, any model will show that you'd better get out of that currency, which is exactly what happens. People start shorting the weak currency, trying to get out of it as fast as they can. For that, they need a sucker who's going to provide them with the funds to get out of the system. The sucker in all these models is the central bank, the central bank that's willing to provide liquidity to the system. It's willing to sell the currency at a relatively low price. Of course, this scenario is basically the same as the third one. These foreign traders did not realize there was a speculative attack brewing until they saw interest rates going up. At that point, there is a very dramatic speculative attack. The only important difference in these last two scenarios, I think, is that the use of derivative instruments gives room for leveraging the attack, and hence, it can occur faster and it can be more difficult for the central bank to defend the currency.

I promised I would discuss the attack on the Argentine currency. What occurred in Argentina in 1994 was very simple. The real exchange rate appreciated dramatically in late 1993 and appreciated drastically throughout 1994. Speculators looking at the exchange rate decided that it might be overappreciated, and, therefore, why take risks?

The second important factor speculators observed was the trade balance. They saw that it had gone from a very large surplus in the very early 1990s to a large deficit in 1994. This large trade deficit was also a source of concern to speculators.

The third factor they observed was that the country ran a fiscal deficit in the last two quarters of 1994. There was the impression that it was going to be hard for the country to solve its fiscal problems because of pending elections.

The final factor was that everybody understood that banks would have to undertake some adjustment because it was the sector that was way behind in adjusting to the new rules of the game in Argentina. For example, some banks were heavily invested in bonds, and when the bonds took a nosedive, those banks were in a very difficult situation. They had huge capital losses and became dramatically undercapitalized. At the same time, there was a speculative attack on the currency, since everybody figured that the country's situation was similar to Mexico's. This triggered a dramatic loss of deposits, which was serious for a few banks.

The biggest question that arises out of all this is one that has been raised today: Suppose you manage to defend the currency. Can you defend the currency without throwing away your banking system? The answer to that is probably yes. But you need to have the flexibility to create a lender of last resort out of fiscal resources. You must have the fiscal resources to attend to the needs of the banking system. You don't need that much money, but in the event of an attack, you do need flexibility.

Savastano:
Peter's discussion of the micromechanics of trading in the last minutes of a fixed exchange rate is, I think, a perfect example of the type of insight that we have gained from the positive analyses of speculative attacks. Indeed, largely thanks to the work of Peter and a few others over the past 15 years, and contrary to what the press would like us to believe, I think that the profession has a fairly good understanding of the mechanics and dynamics of speculative attacks under different policy environments and market configurations, including those resulting from the recent expansion of international financial markets.

We no longer think of speculative attacks as market anomalies or pathologies, but rather, we tend to view them as investors' rational response to an actual or perceived inconsistency in the policies followed by the authorities in a system with a fixed or otherwise managed exchange rate. Unfortunately, that is as far as the consensus goes. As is so common in this field, considerable debate and confusion remain, in this case, in two key areas: one, the root causes of speculative attacks, and second, the implications that the existence and recurrence of these events have for the choice of exchange regime and for the use of capital controls.

I cannot pretend to settle this debate in 10 minutes, but I can offer some views on where I think the solution to this debate lies and on the type of answers I think we need to obtain before we take seriously those who argue that fixed exchange rates are no longer an option or those who call for fundamental changes in the international monetary system.

As has been mentioned, there are essentially two views with respect to the underlying causes of speculative attacks. One view is that the main cause of attacks is the adoption of policies that are essentially inconsistent with pursuing pegged or managed exchange rates. This is called the "first-generation view" or, as Peter called it, "the Federal Reserve view." The other view sees speculative attacks as being driven by the self-fulfilling expectations of rational investors who share the belief that the collapse of the exchange rate regime will trigger a fundamental change in the policy stance of the authorities. These are known as the "second-generation models."

In practice, it is very difficult to discriminate between these two views. The reason for this is that there is a fundamental observational equivalence problem. Most of the pre- and post-attack dynamics that one can obtain from collapse models with multiple equilibria can be replicated with models with a single equilibrium in which the attack is triggered by the anticipation of a change in regime. Moreover, in looking at the empirical evidence, one gets the distinct impression that the few serious studies of speculative attacks are broadly supportive of the policy-inconsistency view, or the first-generation models.

Despite these arguments and evidence, however, the debate on the causes and implications of speculative attacks seems to be more alive than ever. The collapse or near collapse of the ERM in the falls of 1992 and 1993—and, to a somewhat lesser extent, the collapse of the Mexican peso in December 1994—have fueled a new wave of interest in the self-fulfilling, or multiple equilibria, view of speculative attacks. In a way, it is as if every collapse of a highly visible exchange rate peg brings with it the temptation to revisit all we know about the subject. There is nothing wrong with revisiting old issues, but there has to be a limit to it. I have the impression that the debate on the causes of speculative attacks goes over the same ground, over and over again. I think there's an urgent need to move forward in this debate, and in my view, the only way to do so is to take a deeper and more systematic look at the fundamental driving forces that are assumed to cause a regime's collapse.

In the case of the first-generation models, this would entail addressing two crucial questions. First, why do governments follow policies that are inconsistent with the chosen exchange rate regime? And second, and more important, why do governments allow their conflicting policy objectives to collide so dramatically in a speculative attack?

The answer to the first question is rather easy. In essence, one can argue that governments follow inconsistent policies because they do not have sufficient instruments to attain their often conflicting objectives. The answer to the second question, however, is much less obvious. For example, if at some point preserving the fixed exchange rate ceases to be the primary goal of economic policy in a given country, why should the authorities wait passively for the speculative attack to occur? Why don't they undertake a preemptive strike by, say, abandoning the peg or devaluing the currency before international reserves are depleted?

There are at least three possible answers to this question. The first possibility is plain ignorance. The authorities may not have a clue that their policies are inconsistent with the exchange rate and that the whole exchange regime is headed for collapse. A second possible answer is miscalculation or imperfect information on the part of the government regarding either the timing or the cost of an attack. For example, in a highly uncertain environment, the government may believe it has an informational advantage over the private sector. And in trying to exploit this edge, it could get caught off guard by a sequence of negative shocks and a sudden attack on its international reserves.

The third possibility is that letting the speculative attack unfold represents the optimal strategy for a government that deliberately follows policies that are inconsistent with preserving the fixed exchange rate. In other words, it is possible that the net benefits of doing nothing and letting the private sector go ahead with a one-way bet on the exchange rate is the preferable course of action, all things considered.

The truth is that we really do not know which of these three options best portrays the authorities' actions and perceived trade-offs in the run-up to a collapse. The existing models and most of the policy discussion simply are not carried out in these terms. I think that we still have much to learn about this fundamental policy dimension of speculative attacks and that future research should focus squarely on this aspect of the problem.

In the second generation models, the task of looking deep into the driving forces behind a speculative attack is much more complicated. This occurs because, at least at a theoretical level, one cannot rule out the possibility that multiple equilibria will arise from several sources. Regardless of the source, however, these models typically carry two important messages. First, that an otherwise viable exchange rate regime is essentially at the mercy of speculators and might collapse even when all macroeconomic fundamentals appear to be in place. (France in the fall of 1993 seems to be the preferred example nowadays; a few years back, there were other examples.) The second message of these models is that the likelihood of a self-fulfilling attack is magnified in an environment of high capital mobility and well-developed financial markets. Some extreme supporters of this view would go as far as to say that in the current environment of globalized financial markets, it is not even technically feasible to defend a fixed exchange rate because of the implicit government guarantees on most financial liabilities (the "financial vulnerability" argument).

Although these arguments are often analytically appealing, I think that at a fundamental level, multiple equilibria models tend to raise more questions than they answer. For example, these models need to assume that there is some force out there that coordinates and pins down agents' expectations at some particular point. This by itself would, at least theoretically, give room for some sort of mechanism to abate or mitigate the seriousness of the multiple equilibria problem (for instance, designing institutions to strengthen the authorities' commitment to technology). However, it is, I think, at the empirical level that these second-generation models face their biggest challenge. In fact, I believe that no matter how analytically robust and intuitively plausible these arguments are, the supporters of these types of models still need to overcome the fundamental observational equivalence problem I mentioned earlier. Until that happens, I think that the burden of proof is bound to remain on their side of the debate, and that the first-generation models, with all their shortcomings, will continue to provide the most useful template for analyzing speculative attacks.

Appendix to Part IV

Foreign Exchange Hedging with Synthetic Options and the Interest Rate Defense of a Fixed-Exchange-Rate Regime

Peter M. Garber and Michael G. Spencer
International Monetary Fund
December 1994

Abstract

In the endgame of a fixed-exchange-rate regime, increases in interest rates to defend the currency may lead to an apparently perverse market response: further downward pressure on the exchange rate. This may result if a large proportion of investors' foreign exchange exposure is dynamically hedged. This paper describes the trading operations involved in implementing dynamic hedges and the impact of these operations on central bank policy. The success of an interest rate defense hinges on the size and timing of the funding operations of those who are being squeezed relative to those engaged in dynamic hedging.

Summary

The usual prescription for the defense of a fixed exchange rate during a speculative attack is the combination of aggressive sales of foreign currency on the spot and forward markets and increases in short-term interest rates of a sufficient magnitude to squeeze speculators who are short in the currency. Two developments in international financial markets in recent years may have reduced the effectiveness of this advice. First, institutional and other large investors have diversified their portfolios internationally. Consequently, the potential exposures to currency risk are growing and therefore, too, the potential selling pressure if the ability of the authorities to maintain a fixed exchange rate comes into question. Second, the growth in the markets for foreign exchange derivatives has both improved the ability of investors to hedge their exposures and provided instruments through which speculators can take highly leveraged positions against weak currencies.

This paper discusses the possibility that the operations of banks and nonbanks to hedge their currency exposures may weaken the effectiveness of the classic interest rate defense. The focus is on market and central bank behavior in the last moments of a fixed-exchange-rate regime. In addition to providing powerful tools for speculation, option pricing models can be used by banks and investors to construct synthetic currency put options by trading regularly in the cash markets. These synthetic options provide a hedge against exchange rate changes if the positions can be adjusted continually. In the presence of this dynamic hedging, an increase in interest rates to defend against a speculative attack may automatically trigger even more selling of the currency that is under attack. The interaction between the timing of different trading strategies—fixed-exchange-rate regime dynamic hedging programs and the reaction of speculators who are caught by the interest rate increase—is crucial to the outcome of the central bank's policy. If the volume of selling motivated by dynamic hedging overwhelms that of the purchases by speculators seeking to close out their positions, the central bank may reach its credit limits with commercial banks or its own position limits, forcing it to abandon the fixed exchange rate.

Foreign Exchange Hedging with Synthetic Options and the Interest Rate Defense of a Fixed-Exchange-Rate Regime

Coincident with the internationalization of portfolios and the interlinking of money markets across currencies has been the expanded use of methods to hedge currency risk. While basic hedging instruments such as forward exchange contracts have a long history, the use of newer instruments such as exchange-traded options and futures contracts and over-the-counter (OTC) options and currency swaps has grown dramatically in the past decade. In addition, option pricing methods have been used in dynamic hedging strategies to construct tailor-made synthetic derivative products—a transplantation to currency markets of the portfolio insurance methods used to hedge equity market exposure.

The crash of 1987 led to justifiable skepticism about the ability of mechanistic trading strategies like dynamic hedging actually to deliver the intended hedge protection when markets are illiquid.[1] In addition, these strategies have been criticized for their tendency to exacerbate price trends. Such criticisms carry over to the use of dynamic hedging in currency markets, although currency markets are usually among the most liquid of financial markets.

In this paper, we examine the impact of dynamic hedging strategies on foreign exchange markets during those crisis periods when even the exchange markets can become illiquid. Though we place some emphasis on the well-known inability of these strategies to perform well for the hedger when a discontinuity in the exchange rate or an upsurge of volatility occurs, we are concerned primarily with the impact of hedging strategies on the efficacy of the classic central bank interest rate defense of a fixed exchange rate. It is generally believed that a central bank can defend an exchange rate if it is willing to raise short-term interest rates sufficiently high to squeeze speculators who are short in its currency. In the presence of dynamic hedging, however, mechanistic selling of the domestic currency may arise in the endgame of the interest rate defense, and this may overwhelm the credit lines available to the central bank for intervention in the exchange market before those squeezed by the interest rate increase start to buy. Thus, our ultimate focus is on market and central bank behavior in the crucial last moments of a fixed exchange rate, the boundary point toward which the collapsing system converges.

The essay is organized as follows. In the next section, we outline the growth of the foreign exchange markets in general and the markets for currency derivatives in particular. Following that, we consider the hedging operations of nonbanks and the techniques in general use. We next examine the theory and practice of dynamic hedging and the hedging operations of banks in particular. We then examine the mechanics of central bank currency intervention and the effect of interest rate defenses on market liquidity, focusing particularly on the response of dynamic hedging programs to interest rate increases. We also consider how the interaction between the timing of different trading programs—dynamic hedging versus closing positions to avoid a squeeze—and the credit lines of the central bank may force the central bank to abandon a fixed exchange rate if it is driven either to the limit of its credit lines with commercial banks or to its self-imposed position limit before buyers of the currency arrive. The last section of the paper contains some concluding remarks.

Markets for Foreign Exchange Products

The foreign exchange market is the largest financial market in the world, with average daily turnover in April 1992 estimated at $880 billion, compared with $620 billion in April 1989.[2] The largest market segment is that for spot delivery —generally two days later—which accounted for just under half of the turnover in 1992, followed by the market for foreign exchange swaps, which accounted for 40 percent of turnover. The proportions of turnover due to outright forward deals, options, and futures were 7 percent, 5 percent, and 1 percent, respectively.

The market is largely an interdealer market: 84 percent of transactions were made among financial institutions and other foreign exchange brokers and dealers in 1992. This characteristic is reflected in the average deal size, which for the U.S. dollar was approximately $6 million overall. Deals were relatively smaller in the spot market, in which the proportion of transactions with end users was higher, while in the derivatives markets deals tended to be higher. For example, the average size of an over-the-counter (OTC) Deutsche mark-pound sterling option was $32 million.

The bulk of foreign exchange market activity still involves the U.S. dollar on one side of the transaction. The dollar was involved in 83 percent of all deals in 1992—including 72 percent of spot trades and 95 percent of swaps contracts —although this proportion had fallen since the previous survey conducted by the Bank for International Settlements (BIS) in 1989. Transactions between currencies in the European exchange rate mechanism (ERM) accounted for only 7 percent of aggregate turnover.

The 1992 survey results indicate how rapidly the use of financial derivatives has grown in recent years. While spot turnover increased only 14 percent between 1989 and 1992, forward transactions increased 60 percent, as did turnover in currency futures. Swaps trading increased 50 percent, and options trading increased by 124 percent.

The notional value of outstanding exchange-traded and OTC financial derivative contracts—including futures, forwards, forward rate agreements, swaps, options, caps, floors, and collars—grew from approximately $7.2 trillion at end-1989 to $17.6 trillion at end-1992.[3] The 1992 notional amounts are comprised of $4.8 trillion in exchange-traded contracts, $4.7 trillion in swaps, and $8.1 trillion in OTC options and forward contracts. By expanding the opportunities for borrowers and lenders to change the risk characteristics—such as maturity or currency denomination—of their portfolios, the growth in these markets has dramatically altered the nature of international finance and the behavior of market participants.

Exchange-traded derivative products—futures and options—are standardized, retail-sized products. Though they are retail in nature, they are frequently used by the dealers in OTC markets to balance positions when credit lines with other financial institutions are filled or when wholesale counterparties are hard to find. Because the exchange's clearinghouse is the counterparty to each contract and because positions are usually well-collateralized through margin requirements, the evaluation of creditworthiness is less of an issue on organized exchanges than in the OTC market.[4] The most actively traded financial derivatives on organized exchanges are futures on interest rates, primarily U.S. Treasury bond rates,

Eurodollars, French government bonds (OAT), German bonds, and Japanese government bonds.

The OTC markets in derivative products are concentrated in a small number of large banks and securities firms in the major financial centers. For example, bank holding companies with more than $10 billion in assets hold between 98 percent and 100 percent of all OTC derivative positions taken by U.S. banks.[5] OTC contracts are often designed specifically for the needs of particular end users and therefore have tailor-made features such as maturity, currency denomination, and notional principal, and are frequently combined with other derivatives and sold as a package. Many OTC trades are interdealer trades in which dealers seek to balance their positions.

Foreign exchange derivatives are important components of these markets, particularly the OTC markets. While the notional principal of outstanding exchange-traded foreign exchange derivatives at the end of 1992 was only $105 billion, there were $860 billion in currency swaps and $5.5 trillion in foreign exchange forwards and OTC options outstanding. In contrast, the notional principal of outstanding interest rate products were $4.4 trillion in exchange-traded contracts, $3.9 trillion in swaps, $634 billion in OTC options, and $2 trillion in forward rate agreements. Stock index derivatives totaled $245 billion.

The Markets for Currency Options

The market segment of particular interest in this paper is the market for options. The options market is divided into two parts: the market for exchange-traded options and the OTC market. Currency options are listed on six exchanges in Europe and North America, but most trading takes place on the Philadelphia Stock Exchange (PHLX) and the Chicago Mercantile Exchange's International Monetary Market (IMM). PHLX lists options on spot currency, while most of the contracts on the IMM are options on currency futures. Most listed options are available with a limited choice of maturities up to one year and have American exercise characteristics.[6] In the OTC market, contract specifications are in principle negotiable, although there is considerable standardization. Furthermore, OTC options are options on currency rather than options on futures, and the European exercise convention is the norm. OTC options are also contracted in much higher amounts. While an individual Deutsche mark contract on PHLX provides an option to buy or sell DM 62,500, options in the OTC market are written for amounts of at least $1 million.

The BIS data show that activity in the OTC market segment dominates total trading in currency options, accounting for 85 percent of turnover in April 1992. As with the bulk of foreign exchange trading, the U.S. dollar dominates the options markets: 98 percent of exchange trading and 74 percent of the OTC market's turnover involved the dollar on one side of the transaction. Assuming that the currency composition of Deutsche mark OTC options trading is representative of that for the other ERM currencies, only an estimated 10 percent of the OTC options market involves intra-ERM transactions. Moreover, two-thirds of the banks' options transactions, measured by notional principal, had other banks or dealers as counterparties.

While the BIS (1993) does not provide data on the maturity structure of the options market, it does provide it for forward contracts. These show that maturities are heavily concentrated in the near term: 64 percent of contracts mature within seven days, and only 1 percent have a maturity of longer than one year.

The Demand for Hedging in Foreign Exchange Markets

Open positions denominated in foreign currencies expose market participants to losses from exchange rate changes. Accounting for such risk is vital for portfolio managers with foreign currency exposure, corporates with foreign-currency-denominated assets or liabilities such as receivables or payables, or banks with currency exposure. These risks can be reduced by taking an offsetting position in the foreign currency. For example, a long position is hedged by shorting the currency in some fashion. This may consist of a spot sale with borrowing in the foreign currency to cover settlement, the purchase of a forward or future contract that locks in the level of the exchange rate for future payment, or the acquisition of a put option or the sale of a call option on the currency. Access to these instruments differs across types of hedgers: exchange-traded futures or options are retail products with little credit risk but with relatively high margin requirements; OTC products provided by banks and nonbank dealers are typically offered in much larger notional values and require a credit line from the bank to the customer along with a bank's assessment of its exposure to a given client. Options generally provide a partial hedge. For example, a portfolio manager may buy a put option to ensure a floor to the domestic currency value of the foreign currency component of its portfolio, but the portfolio remains subject to risk of currency fluctuations while the portfolio value is above the floor.[7]

At the end of 1991, institutional investors—mutual funds, pension funds, and insurance companies—in OECD countries had total assets of approximately $11.7 trillion, compared with the assets of commercial banks, which totaled $19.6 trillion.[8] The sizes of their foreign currency exposures in absolute terms and even in relation to their total assets can be quite large. For example, U.S. mutual funds and pension funds held $214 billion in foreign assets, or 5 percent of their combined end-1991 assets of $4.1 trillion. In contrast, U.K. mutual funds and pension funds invested $151 billion abroad, 23 percent of their total assets. Institutional investors in Germany, Japan, and the Netherlands also invest sizable proportions of their assets abroad. More significant perhaps, there are few restrictions on the foreign investments of institutional investors in industrial countries, and the trend appears to be toward relaxing those constraints that do exist. Banks, in contrast, often have well-defined position limits—either statutory or self-imposed—on their foreign exchange exposures.

Managers of pension funds, mutual funds, and bank trust accounts generally hedge their currency risk, often using dynamic hedging operations to create synthetic securities. For fixed-interest holdings of pension funds with obligations denominated in a given currency, the hedge reflects the desire by fund management to place a floor on the long-term value of foreign-currency-denominated holdings. For funds investing in foreign equities, the long-term reasons for establishing currency hedges is not as obvious because of the long-run tendency for exchange rates to conform with purchasing power parity. Nevertheless, in the short term—on a quarterly or annual basis—fund managers' performance, and therefore their compensation, often is compared to a benchmark. Moreover, fund managers seek to protect short-term performance from significant declines to prevent an increase in redemptions. Similarly, for pension funds, underfunding of liabilities may force an injection of securities into the fund that tests the liquidity of the parent entity. For these reasons, fund managers are sensitive in the short term to exchange rate movements and will wish to hedge positions. In the simplest hedging operation, fund directors may establish currency risk targets or limits to which management must adhere by following agreed hedging strategies. To place an absolute ceiling on losses from currency fluctuations, fund directors may mandate the acquisition of a put option to cover the entire foreign exchange position of the fund.

If they are willing to bear more risk from volatility changes, fund directors may instruct management to replicate a put dynamically.[9] This method has become typical for fund management. As indicated below, this buy-high, sell-low strategy will, ex post, have been less costly than an actual put if volatility declines and more costly if volatility increases. Finally, many portfolio managers follow a constant-percentage portfolio insurance strategy: this is a buy-high, sell-low dynamic strategy that does not replicate a put option.[10] Rather, it is driven entirely by price movements. For example, one realization of this strategy may aim at outperforming a 50-percent hedged position and would begin with a 50-percent hedge. A 1-percent move in the exchange rate would trigger an x-percent change in the hedge ratio. If the foreign currency appreciated by 10 percent, the hedge ratio would fall to $50 - 10x$ percent. Currency depreciations would be met with opposite adjustments in the hedge ratio. The strategy tends to work well when exchange rate changes come in trends but fails with a jump in volatility.[11]

Dynamic strategies are often implemented through cross-hedges—that is, a hedge may be implemented through shorting a currency whose exchange rate is highly correlated with the currency in which the fund holds securities. The purpose is to take advantage of greater liquidity in the exchange market or an interest rate premium in the currency used for the cross-hedge.

Individual firms and portfolio managers ultimately must turn to banks to engage in foreign exchange hedging since banks are the principal dealers in the foreign exchange spot and derivatives markets. By taking the opposite side of a transaction undertaken by a customer, a bank will acquire foreign exchange exposure that it will then attempt to eliminate. For those exposures that do not net out in the course of a day's trading with other customers—for example, currency or value-date mismatches in forward contract long and short positions or different features of options contracts—the bank must actively seek coverage by initiating its own transactions in the same OTC and exchange-traded derivatives markets or in the underlying markets.

Because of internal risk-control operations and regulations on foreign exchange risk, banks are active in using dynamic hedging techniques. Typically, they will hedge the net exposure to exchange rate changes acquired through transactions with clients, but they may leverage exchange risk when trading for proprietary accounts.

Regulation on banks' net foreign exchange positions varies widely across industrial countries.[12] In some countries, such as the United States, banks' exposures and internal controls are monitored on a regular basis, although there are no specified limits. Elsewhere, as in, for example, Germany, Japan, and the United Kingdom, guidelines or stronger constraints limit open positions to a specified ratio to total capital. Banks' internal risk management controls include the separation of dealing operations—in which buy/sell orders are taken—and back-office activities where contracts are confirmed and settled, the imposition of open position limits on the dealing book, and limits on the extension of credit to individual counterparties.

A bank that writes an option becomes exposed to the possibility that the option will be exercised and it will have to buy or sell foreign currency (depending upon whether it has written a put or a call). The simplest hedge in this case would be to acquire a perfectly offsetting contract. For a bank that maintains a large options book, many of its options contracts will indeed offset each other. However, to hedge the remaining options exposure, banks will generally turn to the more liquid underlying markets and hedge their exposures by creating synthetic options. Dynamic hedging strategies provide a simple means by which complicated options books can be hedged by constructing synthetic options.

As the earlier discussion indicates, trading in options is only a small part of the foreign exchange market. Most of banks' foreign exchange exposure comes from dealing in the spot and forward (including swaps) markets. As with their options-based exposures, banks will actively hedge their net exposure arising from these other transactions. Moreover, not all options (or other) transactions entered into by banks are derived from hedging operations. Unlike transactions in the underlying markets, options provide tools for taking positions in the volatility of spot exchange rates or exchange rate futures, instead of or in addition to speculating on the future direction of these underlying assets. Banks both sell packages of options to their customers that allow them to choose their own degree of exposure to the level, direction of change, and volatility of the underlying asset, and enter into transactions with other dealers to do the same for their own account.

Mechanics of Option Pricing and Dynamic Hedging

Pricing Put Options on Foreign Currency

Because option pricing theory is at the heart of dynamic hedging, it is helpful at this point to review the basic option pricing formula for foreign exchange—the Garman–Kohlhagen formula—before describing how dynamic hedging works.[13] Although banks and other wholesale traders may use more sophisticated pricing methods that account for varying interest rates and exchange rate volatility, the Garman–Kohlhagen formula is in general operational use by pension fund and other portfolio managers, and it is pedagogically useful for illustrating the management of risk in a bank's foreign exchange book.[14]

Suppose that a customer buys a European put option to deliver Deutsche marks for dollars after T periods for an exercise price of $\$X$ per Deutsche mark. The value of the put option, P_t, is

$$P_t = -[1 - N(d_1)]\exp[-r_{DM}T]S + [1 - N(d_2)]\exp[-r_{\$}T]X, \tag{1}$$

where r_{DM} and $r_{\$}$ are the (constant) risk-free instantaneous Deutsche mark and dollar interest rates, S is the current dollar–Deutsche mark spot exchange rate, and X is the exercise or strike exchange rate of the option.[15] $N(d_1)$ is the value of the normal distribution function evaluated at the argument

$$d_1 = \{\ln(S/X) + [r_{\$} - r_{DM} + \sigma^2/2]T\}/\sigma\sqrt{T}, \tag{2}$$

where σ is the (constant) instantaneous standard deviation or volatility of the exchange rate S. Finally, $d_2 = d_1 - \sigma\sqrt{T}$. The put price, or premium, is graphed against the spot exchange rate in Figure IVA–1. The premium is a downward-sloping, convex function of the exchange rate and lies closer to the option's intrinsic value, max $[0, X - S]$ (depicted as the dashed 45-degree line, which

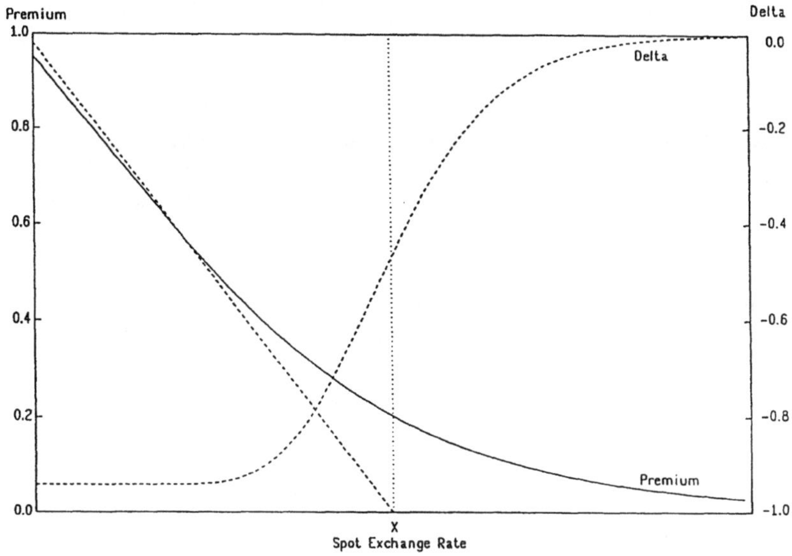

Figure IVA–1. Currency put option premium and delta.

coincides with the horizontal axis to the right of X) the shorter the time to maturity. Note that it is possible for the price of the option to be less than its intrinsic value for deep in-the-money puts.

Implementing the Dynamic Hedge

The put pricing formula is determined by finding the short position in Deutsche mark loans and the long position in dollar loans such that a portfolio with these positions and also short a put is riskless with respect to small exchange rate movements.

Thus, an investor that wants to hedge its exposure to fluctuations in the dollar–Deutsche mark exchange rate can either hedge a long Deutsche mark position by buying a put option or use equation 1 to determine positions in Deutsche mark and dollar loans that mimic the value of a put—that is, to create a synthetic put. The basic security in the first half of the formula is a loan promising to deliver 1 Deutsche mark in T periods; this has a Deutsche mark present value of $exp[-r_{DM}T]$ and a dollar value of $exp[-r_{DM}T]S$. The coefficient $-[1 - N(d_1)]$ indicates that the mimicking portfolio should consist of a short position of a fraction of such a Deutsche mark loan—that is, a short Deutsche mark position. Similarly, the dollar position is long a fraction $[1 - N(d_2)]$ of a loan promising to pay X dollars in T periods with a present dollar value of $exp[-r_\$ T]X$. However, since d_1 and d_2 constantly move with the exchange rate, the interest rate differential, and the standard deviation projected for exchange rate movements, the positions must be adjusted constantly—hence the term *dynamic hedging*—to maintain the equivalence of the position to a put option.[16]

The foreign exchange exposure of the bank that sells the put is to the *possibility* of having to buy deutsche marks at the exercise price at date T. Under the assumptions behind the pricing formula, it is not necessary to hedge the total face value of the contract prior to the exercise date. How much of the face value to hedge, which in turn determines the hedge ratio, is provided by the option's delta, the change in the value of the option with respect to a movement in the exchange rate. From the pricing formula developed above, the delta of a currency put option is

$$-[1 - N(d_1)]exp(-r_{DM}T).$$

Thus, a rise in the dollar value of the Deutsche mark makes it less likely that the option will be exercised and reduces the value of the put. The put delta takes values between −1, for a deep-in-the-money option that would almost certainly be exercised, to 0, for a deep-out-of-the-money option that would never be exercised (see Figure IVA–1). The negative of delta, therefore, provides a proxy for the probability of exercise. Delta multiplied by the number of units of foreign currency provides an estimate of the expected foreign exchange that is sold short at any point in time to hedge against possible exercise of the option.

A writer of a put option may, therefore, hedge the option dynamically according to the prescriptions of the put pricing formula. First, it must establish the portfolio that mimics the value of the option—for example, by shorting $[1 - N(d_1)]$ Deutsche mark forward for dollars and buying $[1 - N(d_2)]\ exp[-r_\$ T]X$ in U.S. Treasury bills. As the exchange rate fluctuates, the now-hedged writer of the option must adjust the short Deutsche mark and long dollar positions according to the formula to continue to mimic the option. Typically, the adjustments will not be continuous; instead, to avoid transactions costs, adjustments to the mimicking portfolio will be made as part of a regular rebalancing exercise.[17]

Among other assumptions, the put pricing formula is based on assuming that exchange rate volatility will remain constant during the life of the contract. Because volatility typically is not constant, the mimicking portfolio will never perfectly track the actual option's value—gains or losses relative to the initial option premium will always occur—and so the portfolio must constantly be adjusted to changes in volatilities as measured, frequently, by implied volatilities in options prices. If volatility jumps above the value implicit in the price of the actual put option, the writer of the put who engages in dynamic hedging will take a loss and the buyer of the put will gain. It is well known that strategies to create synthetic options to hedge actual options through the use of dynamic trading, designed to be delta neutral, can be used to take positions on volatility in underlying prices and in interest rates.[18]

The loss to the writer is immediately apparent if the portfolio is marked to market. A volatility increase will, ceteris paribus, increase the value of the actual option (a liability) and leave unchanged the value of the hedging portfolio (the supposedly balancing asset). Alternatively, if the option value is not marked to market, the loss will be booked through the dynamic adjustment of Deutsche mark and dollar positions until the exercise date. According to the hedging strategy, a rise in the exchange rate will cause the writer of the put to reduce the short Deutsche mark position: the writer of the option will buy Deutsche marks when the Deutsche mark appreciates and sell when it depreciates. This "buy dear-sell cheap" strategy generates a foreseeable loss to the writer of the put, or indeed of any other option, for which it is compensated by the put premium. If volatility jumps, however, the premium will be insufficient to cover the now greater-than-expected realized loss on these hedging trades.

To hedge the risks acquired from their OTC options transactions with other dealers, banks generally construct a dynamic hedge by purchasing or selling currency in the spot market to close the currency exposure and entering into a swap contract to shift the exposure to coincide with the maturity date of the option. Indeed, such transactions have become part of banks' normal operating procedures (Walmsley 1992).

To monitor its overall exposure, a bank must have a method to break down each option in its book into its implied foreign exchange position. It can then determine its global net position in each currency by adding its net position from trading in other foreign exchange products to its net position implied in its options book, and then hedge the combined exposure. The foreign exchange equivalent into which a bank will decompose its options will depend on the currency-options-pricing formula used by the bank, but it will usually be based on delta hedging methods. The bank calculates the delta for all the contracts it has written or bought and multiplies these by the face values of the contracts. These are then added up for each currency to estimate the expected net foreign currency delivery requirement. For European-style options, in which exercise is only possible at maturity, the hedge portfolio will include futures or forward contracts that offset these amounts, while for American-style options, the hedge will include cash positions because the exercise date is uncertain. Because the management of the foreign exchange book is global, the amounts required to hedge the options will be netted against spot and forward net positions.

For example, suppose that the global position in the currency option book of a bank making a market in derivatives is short one OTC European Deutsche

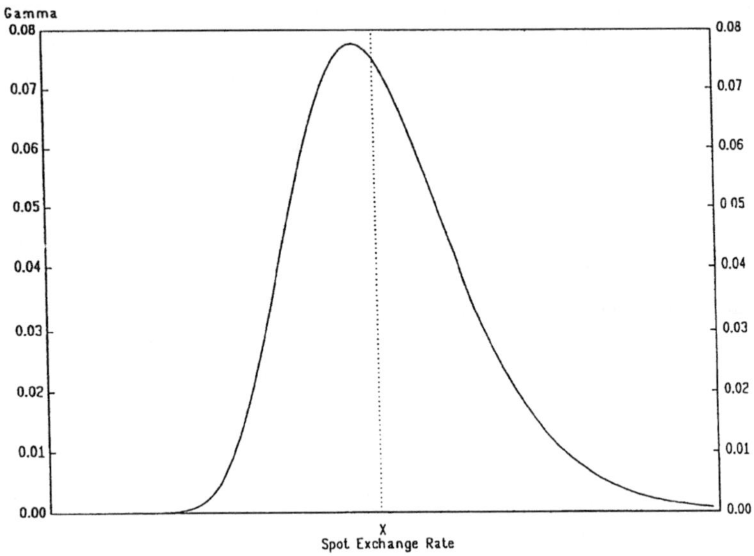

Figure IVA–2. Currency put option gamma.

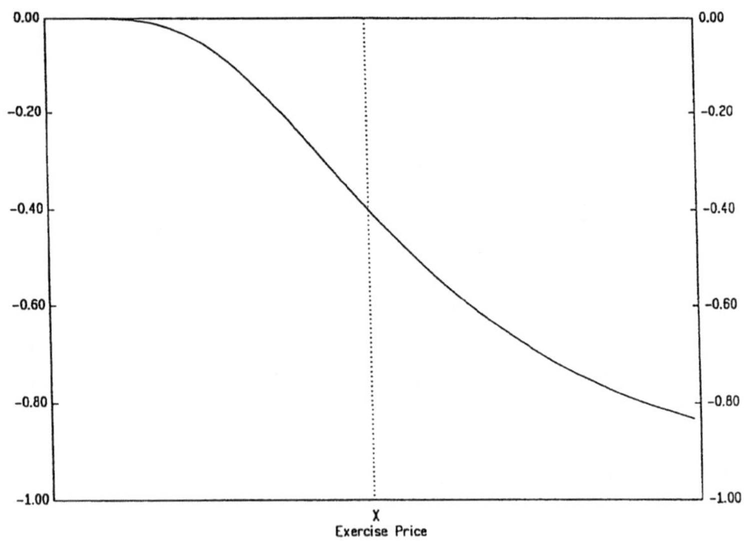

Figure IVA–3. Sensitivity of put delta to the exercise price.

mark put option that allows the holder to sell DM 1 for \$$X$ at time T and long one European put option to sell DM 1 for French francs at T^*. If the bank uses the Garman–Kohlhagen formula, its Deutsche mark position from its options book is

Option	DM Position
1. Short 1 Put DM/\$	$[1 - N(d_1)] \exp[-r_{DM}T]$
2. Long 1 Put DM/FF	$-[1 - N(d_1^*)] \exp[-r_{DM}T^*]$

In these formulas, d_1 and d_1^* are defined as above, with the appropriate volatilities and exercise prices substituted for each option. If the bank is also long Deutsche mark in its forward and spot trading, it can determine its global foreign exchange exposure in Deutsche marks by adding these three quantities. The bank can then hedge the foreign exchange risk by taking the opposite position in the forward market. Because the implied delivery dates across its Deutsche mark contracts may differ, this still leaves the bank with an interest rate risk that can be hedged through appropriate Deutsche mark forwards or swaps.

Properties of the Put Option Delta

Given the centrality of delta to the construction of the hedge portfolio, it is worth considering its properties. In particular, we are interested in identifying the response of delta to changes in the parameters of the model. Unfortunately, these relationships are often not monotonic.

The partial derivative of delta with respect to the exchange rate is the option's gamma, or convexity. For a put option, this is always positive, as portrayed in Figure IVA–2. Thus, an increase in the exchange rate makes the option less likely to be exercised and lowers the absolute value of delta. Note that the put delta is most sensitive to changes in the exchange rate when the option is close to being at-the-money. Conversely, an increase in the exercise price, X, increases the value of the option, raising the probability of exercise and the short position needed to hedge it. Thus, delta is a decreasing function of X, as shown in Figure IVA–3. The only other partial derivative of delta that is unambiguous is that with respect to $r_\$$, which is positive. An increase in this rate lowers the present value of the dollars that will be received if the option is exercised. This lowers the likelihood that the option will be exercised, and so delta is an increasing function of $r_\$$, as in Figure IVA–4.

The remaining derivatives, with respect to the volatility, time to maturity, and r_{DM}, are all of ambiguous sign. Figure IVA–5 shows the effect of changes in volatility on the put option delta. For at-the-money options, there is little change in the delta. For out-of-the-money options, delta is a decreasing function of

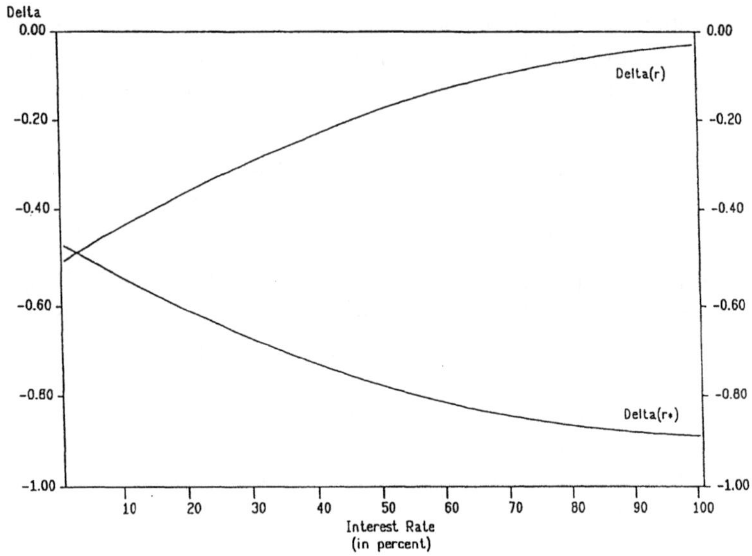

Figure IVA–4. Sensitivity of put delta to domestic and foreign interest rates.

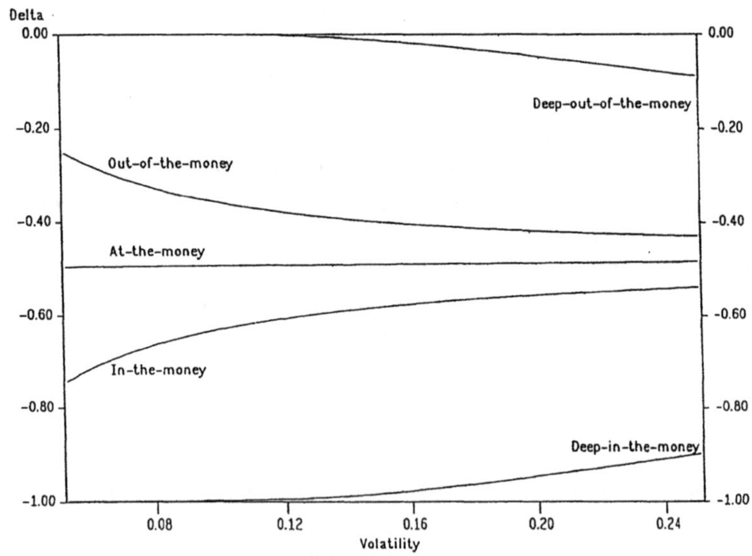

Figure IVA–5. Sensitivity of put delta to volatility.

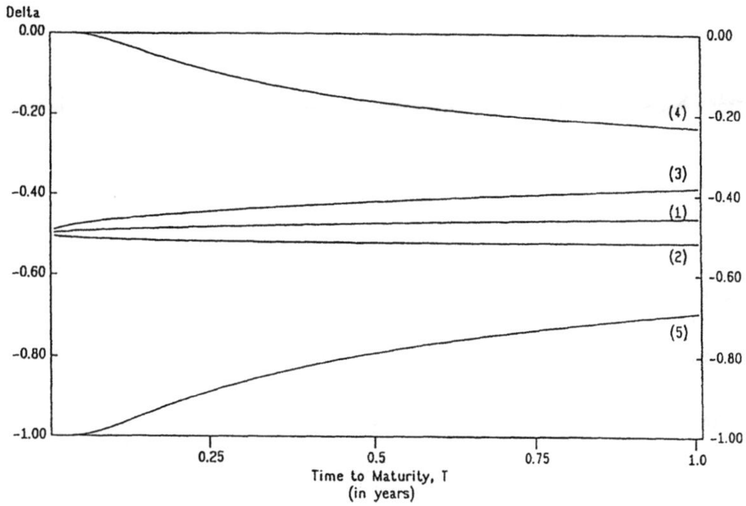

Figure IVA–6. Sensitivity of put delta to the expiration date.

exchange rate volatility: an increase in volatility increases the probability that the exchange rate will fall far enough that the option will move in-the-money, and so the probability of exercise increases. For in-the-money options, delta increases with volatility since an increase in the latter only increases the probability that the exchange rate will rise above X by the time the option expires. Clearly, for very deep in- or out-of-the-money options, a very large increase in volatility is necessary for there to be an appreciable change in delta.

An increase in the time to maturity has a similar effect on the option delta, as does an increase in volatility.[19] Figure IVA–6 shows that for in-the-money options, a longer time to maturity increases the probability that the option will move out-of-the-money before expiration, and so the delta decreases, and conversely for out-of-the-money options. For at-the-money options, the effect on delta is sensitive to the sign of the interest rate differential. Some intuition about the effect of changing time to maturity is obtained from Figure IVA–1. As the time to maturity falls, the options price function, P, collapses onto the intrinsic value function. Thus, reversing the process, as the time to maturity increases, the price function moves upward and to the right, away from the intrinsic value function. Hence, for out-of-the-money options, delta, which is the slope of the price function, falls from zero to some negative value, while for in-the-money options the slope rises from –1. For at-the-money options (and possibly for

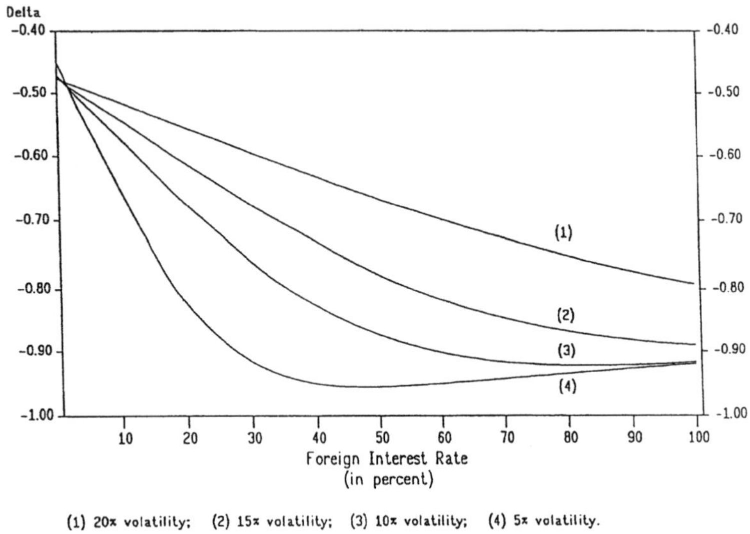

Figure IVA–7. Sensitivity of put delta to the foreign interest rate and to volatility.

options for which the spot price and the exercise price are very close), the change in slope depends on the convexity of the price function, which in turn depends upon, inter alia, the interest rate differential.

The most important partial derivative for the purposes of the discussion in the next section is the effect of changes in r_{DM} on the put option delta. Under most circumstances, the relationship is as it is depicted in Figure IVA–4—downward sloping. However, since the derivative is of ambiguous sign, and given the importance of this relationship, Figures IVA–7 through IVA–9 show how this derivative varies with values of the other parameters. Figure IVA–7 shows that for most common values of the volatility parameter, the relationship is always negative. However, if the exchange rate's annualized volatility falls below 5 percent, the curve slopes upward after r_{DM} rises above approximately 45 percent. Figure IVA–8 shows that as the intrinsic value of the option, $X - S$, rises, a similar reversal in slope is possible. Indeed, for deep-in-the-money options, delta is everywhere increasing in r_{DM}. Finally, Figure IVA–9 shows that as the time to maturity of the option increases, further increases in r_{DM} can lead to an increase in delta (a fall in the short foreign exchange position).

The inference that can be drawn from these last three figures is that, for the most commonly observed parameter values, delta declines with increases in the foreign interest rate. However, for options that have long terms to maturity or that are in-the-money or written on very low volatility options—or, more likely,

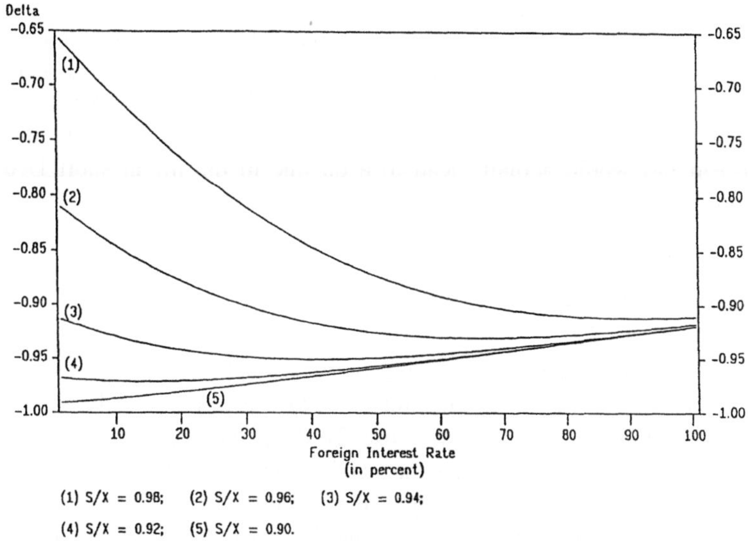

Figure IVA–8. Sensitivity of put delta to the foreign interest rate and to the intrinsic value.

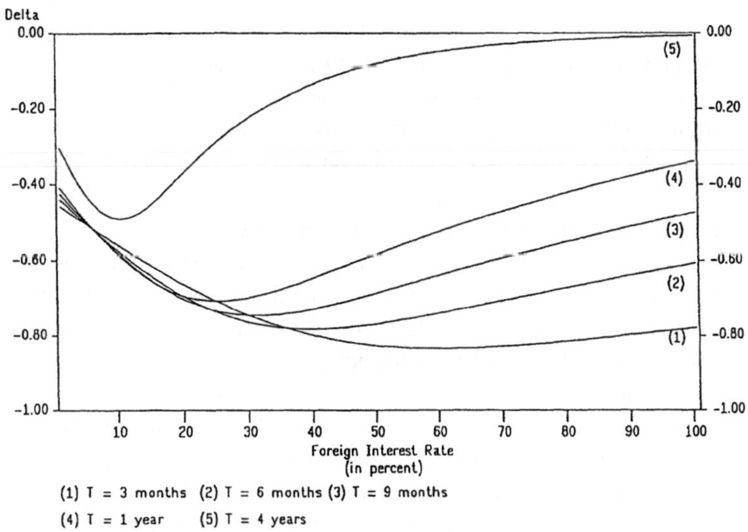

Figure IVA–9. Sensitivity of put delta to the foreign interest rate and to the contract maturity.

a combination of these characteristics—it is possible that for a sufficiently large increase in r_{DM}, the relationship between delta and r_{DM} could actually become positive. Subsequent increases in r_{DM} would then lower the short Deutsche mark position held to hedge the short put position. Note, however, that except for multiyear options—which are extremely rare—it is highly unlikely that any increase in r_{DM} would actually lead to a decline in the initial short Deutsche mark position.

Hedging in a Crisis

Dynamic hedging strategies are not an entirely new activity; stop-loss trading has always been triggered by price movements beyond a certain threshold. Dynamic hedging simply mechanizes this response. To the extent, however, that the technique has been adopted by large segments of the financial intermediation industry and can be implemented more rapidly than previous techniques, dynamic hedging strategies have added to trading volume and have accentuated price movements by contributing to momentary illiquidity. In this section, we consider how the widespread use of dynamic hedging techniques may interact with central bank exchange rate and liquidity policies to undermine a defense of a fixed-exchange-rate system.

When a fixed-exchange-rate regime moves toward a crisis, speculation against the currency is generally channeled through forward sales of the currency to the banking system. Some margin is required by counterparty banks, but this can be leveraged up by a factor of 10 or more by the speculator. In a crisis, these sales will generally not be matched by other customers' forward purchases of the currency. The central bank defending the currency may intervene with forward purchases, but the extent of such an operation is limited by the unwillingness of a central bank to risk large capital losses on negative net foreign exchange positions and by limits on credit lines to the central bank made available by the major dealing banks.[20] Once the central bank ceases to buy its currency in the forward market, banks must balance their forward purchases with spot sales of the currency (to balance the net currency position) and by currency swaps (to balance maturities).

Once again, during a crisis, the central bank will be the most important buyer on the spot market through its intervention to maintain the fixed exchange rate. At the same time, it provides its currency through the discount window to the banks that need to sell currency in order to match their forward and spot foreign exchange positions, as discussed in the previous paragraph. By providing liquidity to banks through this kind of facility, the central bank is effectively financing the attack on its own reserves. To settle its spot transactions, the central bank must deliver its own foreign exchange reserves or draw down lines of credit from other central banks or multilateral entities. As its short foreign exchange position mounts during the intervention, the central bank must act by raising the discount rate. This increases the cost to speculators who speculate against the currency by borrowing from the central bank. The central bank may also impose a squeeze on short sellers by channeling available credit away from identified speculators.

This final operation is the classic interest rate defense of a fixed exchange rate. It works though a liquidity effect in the money market—domestic credit grows less rapidly than central bank net reserves decline, thereby producing a decline in the supply of the domestic settlement medium. If large short positions in the currency are due for settlement, holders of short positions may sell foreign exchange to the central bank rather than face the high interest costs of rolling over overnight loans in the weak currency. The costs to holders of short positions are further accentuated if, in addition, they are caught in a squeeze so that they have to pay more than the discount rate to obtain funds.

The market's acquisition of foreign exchange from the central bank does not arise exclusively from forward sales by nonbank speculators. Speculators and hedgers may also buy put options on the weak currency from the banks. Again, in a crisis, the banking system will likely be unable to find nonbank sellers of puts to balance these positions.[21] To hedge, the bank that writes the put may create a long position in a synthetic put by selling the weak currency forward, by selling on the futures market, or by selling spot and entering a swap contract. Any of these operations will trigger a spot sale of the weak currency to the central bank, as described above.

A common hedging strategy employed by customers is the implementation of a range forward, depicted in Figure IVA–10.[22] An investor wanting to hold a lire position might buy a put option and sell a call with a higher exercise price chosen so that the revenue from the sale of the call equals the price of the put. In addition, the investor would purchase lire in a forward contract (which has zero cost at inception). In such a strategy, the investor bears the risk of exchange rate depreciation in the range, $\bar{X}-\underline{X}$, but is protected from very large depreciations, as demonstrated by the payoff function RF. The bank that sells the range forward is short a put option and long a call option with similar strike prices. The bank may choose to hedge these exposures by creating synthetic options. The hedge portfolio for both of these option positions requires a short lira position.[23]

The Effect of Interest Rate Changes on Dynamic Hedging

Once a central bank raises interest rates in defense of the fixed exchange rate, hedging operations may trigger further sales of the currency rather than the

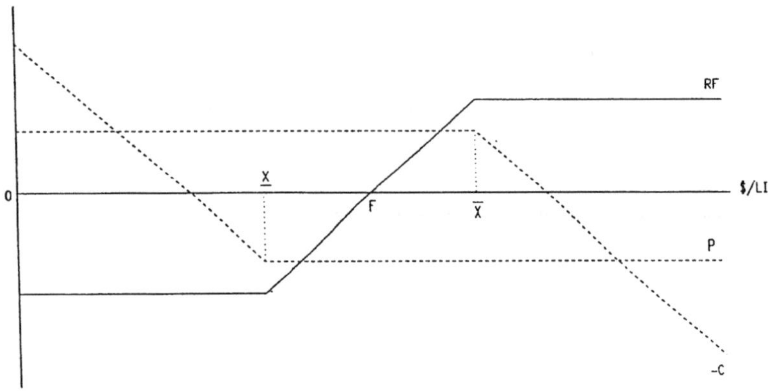

P: Payoff to long put with exercise price $\overline{X}$

-C: Payoff to short call with exercise price $\underline{X}$

F: Contracted forward exchange rate

RF: Payoff to range forward strategy

Figure IVA–10. Range forward payoff diagram.

purchases anticipated from the squeeze. This result follows from the relation between interest rate movements and the hedging portfolio in equation 1.

Intuitively, the interest rate differential between the two currencies reflects the expected rate of depreciation of the exchange rate plus a risk premium. Unless volatility increases or attitudes toward risk change, a rise in the differential between deutsche mark and dollar interest rates means that the Deutsche mark is expected to depreciate more rapidly against the dollar—that is, the hedge ratio increases.[24]

With an unchanged current exchange rate, exercise price, and exchange rate volatility, the put option is much more likely to finish in-the-money when the foreign interest rate jumps upward. That the option is more likely to be exercised means that it provides a higher effective hedge to a portfolio manager covering a deutsche mark exposure. The manager of the bank's portfolio who uses a synthetic put in a dynamic hedging operation must likewise provide an increased hedge ratio in response to the greater probability that the option will be exercised. This means that the manager must short-sell more Deutsche marks so that the synthetic put continues to mimic an actual put. Taken to an extreme, if Deutsche mark interest rates rise so high that, according to the underlying theory, it is almost certain that a put option will be exercised, the put then provides the equivalent of a 100-percent hedge ratio. The bank's portfolio manager using a synthetic put must similarly sell sufficient Deutsche marks to cover his entire Deutsche mark position to provide the same coverage as an actual put.

How important will the dynamic hedging response be? Figure IVA–8 provides some indication of the response of dynamic hedging programs during the final days of a managed- or fixed-exchange-rate regime. In the days leading up to the collapse of an exchange rate band regime, the gradual depreciation in the spot exchange rate will have a significant effect on the hedge ratio, necessitating a gradual increase in the short foreign currency position. However, in the final hours or minutes of such a regime or of an absolutely fixed exchange rate, the use of large interest rate increases to defend the fixed exchange rate can result in increases in the hedge ratio of a similar magnitude. What makes this effect important is that in a fixed-exchange-rate regime, or a quasi-fixed system such as the ERM, the boundary values for the nominal exchange rate become focal points for speculation about the direction of change of the exchange rate. Not only will more investors begin to hedge their exposures as the risk of realignment or a change in the parity increases, but the options that are written for customers will all tend to have similar exercise prices, so that they will tend to react similarly to changes in the foreign interest rate. Moreover, as the spot foreign exchange rate falls toward the lower boundary value—a natural value for the put option's exercise price—the option's delta will become more sensitive to changes in the foreign interest rate (Figure IVA–8).

For example, in the United Kingdom on September 16, 1992, the Bank of England increased the base lending rate twice, from 10 percent to 12 percent and then again to 15 percent (effective the next day).[25] The one-month London interbank offer rate increased from 10.4 percent at the end of the previous day to 28.9 percent at the end of September 16. According to equation 1, such an interest rate increase would have resulted in a 22 percent decrease in the delta (or increase in the hedge ratio) of an at-the-money put—from –0.54 to –0.66—a larger change than would have been obtained from a 1.5-percent depreciation at the initial interest rate.[26] In the Swedish market, the increase in the marginal lending rate from 75 percent to 500 percent on September 16 led to an increase in the one-month STIBOR rate from 25 percent to 70 percent. An increase of this magnitude implies a 14-percent decrease in delta.[27] On November 19, the eve of the Swedish devaluation, the one-month STIBOR rate rose from 13.9 percent to 28 percent, implying an 18-percent increase in the hedge ratio.[28]

Industry sources indicate that, indeed, when there is an increase in the interest rate spread with no movement in the exchange rate, the forward rate discount will trigger a sell-off in the currency through dynamic hedging. During the ERM crisis of September 1992, for example, industry sources estimate that dynamic hedging sales to adjust positions because of increases in interest rate spreads, exchange rate movements, and increases in volatility accounted for 20–30 percent of the selling in the crisis.[29] It apparently was a major factor in the lira market one week after the first devaluation and also in the Swedish krona market later in 1992. Up to 10 percent of the sales were due to increases in interest rate spreads. In the case of the United Kingdom, on September 16, 1992, the dramatic increase in forward discounts triggered sales of pounds. When interest rates rose and nothing happened to the exchange rates, the selling programs were turned on. The lack of movement (appreciation) in the exchange rate meant that the forward rate fell farther below the floor. Thus, the full force of programmed sales triggered by interest rate movements was not offset by exchange rate improvement. Another source of the sales volumes at this moment was the rising perceived volatility resulting from the suddenly larger movement of the forward rate below the floor. The effect of dynamic hedging sales may also have been a source of some of the selling pressure observed on August 12, 1994, when the Italian lira depreciated sharply after the Banca D'Italia raised the discount rate by 50 basis points, though the consensus view is that markets reacted mostly in the belief that the interest rate increases were fiscally unsustainable.

In an exchange crisis, therefore, a large defensive rise in the interest rate aimed at imposing a squeeze on speculators will instantaneously trigger hedging programs to order sales of the weak currency.[30] The experiments conducted using the actual data on interest rates and historical volatility suggest that the selling triggered by dynamic hedging programs during an interest rate defense can be significant. The existence of a large amount of such programs in the market would undermine the use of an interest rate defense of a weak currency—the moment that a central bank raises interest rates, it might face an avalanche of sales of its currency rather than the purchases of the squeezed shorts that it had anticipated. In effect, the hedging programs make the hedgers insensitive to the added costs of funding their weak currency sales.

If the central bank has a credit line limit in foreign exchange or a self-imposed negative net reserve position, the upsurge of selling brought about by the interest rate increase might cause a sudden jump to its limit and force it to cease intervention in defense of the exchange rate. Whether this counterintuitive result occurs depends on the weight of these mechanistic traders relative to those caught in the short squeeze.

In one scenario, the hedging operation may in, any case, far exceed the amount of the weak currency demanded by those caught in the squeeze. In this case, the timing of the hedging sales—the prearranged rule for awakening the selling programs—relative to the time at which those caught in the short squeeze appear on the market is immaterial to the survival of the fixed exchange rate. Dominance by the mechanistic hedgers will defeat the interest rate defense.

In the scenario in which the amounts of these opposite transactions are roughly balanced or even where those caught in the short squeeze dominate, the timing of transactions is key. If the selling programs switch on instantly, but the buying operations to cover short positions occur with some lag, the central bank's net short foreign exchange limit may be exceeded prior to the appearance of the buyers of its currency, causing the abandonment of the fixed exchange rate. Buyers might have appeared by the end of the day to offset the sellers, but the initial selling may unnerve the central bank and force devaluation. The devaluation will ratify both the actions of the sellers and of those caught in the squeeze who hesitated. Sellers will have sold prior to the devaluation of the exchange rate, and those caught in the squeeze can buy back into the weak currency at a lower price. If the central bank simultaneously relaxes the high interest rates, overnight borrowing will cease to be a problem for those caught short, and the squeeze will be suspended.

Conclusion

In their impact on the viability of the interest rate defense of a fixed exchange rate, dynamic hedging programs can be interpreted as a new wrinkle on an old phenomenon. Skeptical participants in the foreign exchange market have sometimes interpreted a defensive increase in the interest rate as the last rearguard action preparatory to the abandonment of a fixed rate. In this light, the suddenly higher interest rate differential signals only the extent of the impending depreciation of the exchange rate and certainly not a drastic and extended tightening of liquidity in the weak currency's money markets. Interpreting the interest rate increase in this way dictates that a speculative selling program should be begun. Dynamic hedging programs automatically place this interpretation on an interest rate increase; thus, they are a mechanization of the previously informal skepticism that occasionally arose about exchange rate defenses. To the extent that such programs are present in generating large selling volumes, they signal a major shift toward skepticism about the strength of the central bank's adherence to the policy of defending the exchange rate, thereby undermining the efficacy of a previously useful defensive tool.

The scenario that we depict here is a technical story about the character of minute-by-minute trading in the death throes of a fixed exchange rate. A dramatic interest rate increase in a last ditch defense triggers dramatic selling pressure. If this technical feature of the market is important in the last moments of a fixed exchange rate, it is necessary to implement a defense operation that takes it into account. For example, it is often argued that a resolute defense of a fixed-exchange-rate regime requires that at an early date interest rates be raised gradually, though ultimately to high levels.[31] Such a policy would trigger daily selling of the currency by dynamic hedgers, but not in quantities that would overwhelm the central bank's net reserve limits before the appearance as buyers by the end of the day of those caught short in the currency. Thus, raising rates gradually in an interest rate defense may immunize the central bank against being pushed beyond its position limits.

Notes

We thank Philippe Jorion, Paolo Kind, Richard Lyons, John Montgomery, Victor Ng, David Ordoobadi, and Thierry Pujol for helpful comments. The conclusions of this paper are those of the authors and are not necessarily those of the International Monetary Fund.

1. See, for example, the Brady Commission (1988) and Securities and Exchange Commission (1988) reports. Grossman (1988) forecast this problem. Gennotte and Leland (1990) model the relationship between hedging operations and market liquidity and show how a relatively small volume of transactions initiated by hedgers can lead to a large price change.

2. Bank for International Settlements (1993).

3. These estimates are derived in General Accounting Office (1994). The notional value of a contract is the nominal amount used as a base to calculate a transfer of payments according to a contractual formula. For example, an interest rate swap may have a notional value of $10 million. This notional value is not delivered as principal. Rather, counterparties deliver or receive the net between fixed interest on $10 million and floating interest on $10 million, so the claims that counterparties might have on each other are far smaller than the notional value.

4. OTC derivatives dominate exchange-traded products with limited liquidity, such as longer dated contracts or options that are not at- or near-the-money.

5. Estimates reported in Board of Governors of the Federal Reserve System, Federal Deposit Insurance Corporation, and Office of the Comptroller of the Currency (1993). See also Bank of England (1993), Bank for International Settlements (1992), Deutsche Bundesbank (1993), Commodity Futures Trading Commission (1993), General Accounting Office (1994), Group of Thirty (1993), Goldstein et al. (1993), and Office of the Comptroller of the Currency (1993) for discussions of the activities of banks in OTC derivatives markets.

6. That is, the option can be exercised at any time prior to maturity. Under the European exercise convention, the option may only be exercised at maturity.

7. In addition, portfolios will be subject to basis risk when the security underlying the hedge instrument is not identical to the security whose return is being hedged so that the returns on the two securities are not perfectly correlated. A hedge constructed with a related, but not identical, instrument to the one whose value is being hedged is called a *cross-hedge*.

8. See Goldstein et al. (1993) for a discussion of the foreign holdings of institutional investors in industrial countries.

9. Using real put contracts to hedge long positions is not entirely free of volatility risk, of course, since changes in volatility can result in losses when put contracts are rolled over if the maturity of the contracts is shorter than the horizon of the hedging operation.

10. This strategy is referred to by Leland, O'Brien, and Rubinstein and Associates as a perpetual protection policy.

11. A constant percentage portfolio insurance strategy has an advantage over an option replication strategy in that at the end of the period, a renewal of the hedge does not require a large trading operation. For an option replication strategy, at expiration the portfolio is either 100 percent hedged or completely unhedged. Renewal of the strategy for another period then requires a large jump in the hedge ratio.

12. See Goldstein et al. (1993) for a discussion on the regulatory and internal constraints on banks' foreign exchange trading.

13. See Garman and Kohlhagen (1983) for the development of this formula. For pricing formulas taking account of stochastic volatility, see Chiang and Okunev (1993), Kroner and Sultan (1993), Melino and Turnbull (1990), Naik (1993), and Perraudin and Sorenson (1992). Dumas, Jennergren, and Näslund (1993) derive options-pricing formulas for currencies restricted by target zones, as in the European exchange rate mechanism. However, as the data above indicate, the majority of OTC and exchange-traded options contracts are written for dollar exchange.

14. Most exchange-traded currency options, except those traded on the Philadelphia Stock Exchange, are options on futures, for which the Garman–Kohlhagen formula for spot exchange options is inapplicable. In the standard formula for pricing options on futures, the foreign interest rate does not appear. The effect of foreign interest rate changes is felt through their impact on the futures price. Moreover, in the OTC market it is more common to price options with respect to the forward exchange rate rather than the spot rate (see DeRosa 1992, 109).

15. This equation is identical in form to the Merton adaptation of the Black–Scholes put formula for a stock that pays a continuous, constant dividend. This formula is constructed on the assumption that the percentage change in the price of the underlying security, in this case the dollar–Deutsche mark exchange rate, follows a Wiener process, that the instantaneous interest rates in both countries and the standard deviation of the percentage exchange rate change are fixed parameters for the life of the option. Such a simple formula does not exist for American put options; these must be evaluated by numerical methods (see DeRosa 1992).

16. Note that the ability to maintain a dynamic hedge depends critically on the existence of a liquid spot foreign exchange market in which the rebalancing trades can be executed. If, as happens during a crisis, markets become illiquid, investors that rely on dynamic hedging may not be able to adjust their portfolios and will be exposed to further exchange rate changes.

17. Since the hedge is not adjusted continuously, the bank will incur losses between rebalancing exercises. Leong (1990–1991) argues that the option premium charged by a bank will, in equilibrium, equal the expected value of this hedge slippage.

18. See, for example, Cookson (1993) or DeRosa (1992).

19. This is the negative of the change in delta with respect to the remaining time to maturity of the option, which is sometimes called *charm* (see Garman 1992).

20. The ability of the central bank to enter forward contracts with its own nationally chartered banks is circumscribed by credit line limits imposed by banks elsewhere on these banks.

21. Even if nonbank sellers of puts exist somewhere in the financial system, the selling bank seeking cover may not find them through the banking system. In a crisis, gross trading volumes surge, thereby causing many banks to reach their credit ceilings with other banks. As the banking system becomes illiquid in this way, transactions that passed through the banking system on a credit basis now must seek a cash market. To hedge, the selling bank will place an order to buy a put onto the organized currency options market, where credit risk is not an issue, and will find the potential seller in this market. As the crisis progresses and more interbank credit lines fill, volume will tend to move to the more secure organized exchanges.

22. We are grateful to Paolo Kind for suggesting this example.

23. Intuitively, a short put position is a contingent long position in the foreign currency (here lire), as is a long call position. Hence, both are hedged by going short in lire.

24. A central bank squeeze generally operates through overnight interest rates, which are not the interest rates used to value longer dated options. Nevertheless, in a squeeze, a jump in overnight rates will usually have a strong impact on short- and medium-term interest rates, which are relevant to option pricing.

25. See Goldstein et al. (1993) and Group of Ten (1993) for descriptions of the European currency crisis of 1992–1993.

26. On September 15, the one-month LIBOR rate for dollars closed at 3.0625 percent and the historical volatility of the $/£ exchange rate, estimated over the previous month, was 15.8 percent per annum. As Figure IVA–7 shows, if the banks sold options with volatilities higher than their historical levels, which during a speculative attack is very likely, the change in the hedge ratio may have been smaller.

27. Based on a historical volatility, calculated over the previous month, of 6.08 percent.

28. With an estimated volatility of 12.9 percent.

29. These estimates were obtained during confidential interviews with market participants in October 1992 (see Goldstein et al. 1993).

30. Who is actually squeezed in such a defense? All borrowers in the weak currency whose debts are due for settlement or rollover soon (after two days) will find that their costs and risks have suddenly jumped as they now have to pay high and volatile yields to the money market scalpers unleashed by the squeeze. This group could conceivably include even those who have constructed synthetic puts if they have established their short currency position by borrowing on overnight rollover credit, as Richard Lyons has pointed out to us. Typically, however, a synthetic option is constructed by establishing a short forward position whose expiration date coincides with the expiration date of the option. If many of the existing hedges were constructed within a one or three month period before the speculative attack and with a relatively long maturity, they would have locked in longer term finance and the position would be immune from a short squeeze.

31. *Early* is relative to the time of outbreak of the next speculative attack. How to recognize when an attack will come in order to implement this early defense is problematic.

References

Bank of England (1993), *Derivatives: Report of an Internal Working Group* (London: Bank of England, April).

Bank for International Settlements (1993), *Central Bank Survey of Foreign Exchange Market Activity in April 1992* (Basle: Bank for International Settlements, March).

Bank for International Settlements (1992), *Recent Developments in International Interbank Relations* (Basle: Bank for International Settlements, October).

Board of Governors of the Federal Reserve System, Federal Deposit Insurance Corporation, and Office of the Comptroller of the Currency (1993), "Derivative Product Activities of Commercial Banks," Joint Study Conducted in Response to Questions Posed by Senator Riegle on Derivative Products, mimeo. (Washington, D.C.: January 27).

Brady Commission (1988), *Report of the Presidential Task Force on Market Mechanisms* (Washington, D.C.: Government Printing Office, January).

Chiang, Raymond, and John Okunev (1993), "An Alternative Formulation on the Pricing of Foreign Currency Options," *The Journal of Futures Markets* 13(8), 903–907.

Commodity Futures Trading Commission (1993), *OTC Derivative Markets and Their Regulation* (Washington, D.C.: Commodity Futures Trading Commission, October).

Cookson, Richard (1993), "Moving in the Right Direction," *Risk* 6 (October): 22–26.

DeRosa, David F. (1992), *Options on Foreign Exchange* (Chicago: Probus Publishing).

Deutsche Bundesbank (1993), "Off-Balance-Sheet Activities of German Banks," *Monthly Report of the Deutsche Bundesbank* 45 (October): 45–67.

Dumas, Bernard, L. Peter Jennergren, and Bertil Näslund (1993), "Realignment Risk and Currency Option Pricing in Target Zones," NBER Working Paper Series, no. 4458 (Cambridge, Mass.: National Bureau of Economic Research).

Feiger, George, and Bertrand Jacquillat (1979), "Currency Option Bonds, Puts and Calls on Spot Exchange and the Hedging of Contingent Foreign Earnings," *Journal of Finance* 34 (December): 1129–1139.

Garman, Mark (1992), "Charm School," *Risk* 5 (July–August): 53–55.

Garman, Mark, and Steven Kohlhagen (1983), "Foreign Currency Option Values," *Journal of International Money and Finance* 2 (December): 231–237.

General Accounting Office (1994), *Financial Derivatives: Actions Needed to Protect the Financial System* (Washington, D.C.: Government Accounting Office, May).

Gennotte, Gerard, and Hayne Leland (1990), "Market Liquidity, Hedging and Crashes," *American Economic Review* 80 (December): 999–1021.

Goldstein, Morris, David Folkerts-Landau, Peter Garber, Liliana Rojas-Suarez, and Michael Spencer (1993), *International Capital Markets: Part I. Exchange Rate Management and International Capital Flows* (April), World Economic and Financial Surveys (Washington, D.C.: International Monetary Fund).

Grabbe, O. (1983), "Exchange," *Journal of International Money and Finance* 2 (December): 239–253.

Grossman, Sanford J. (1988), "An Analysis of the Implications for Stock and Futures Price Volatility of Program Trading and Dynamic Hedging Strategies," *Journal of Business* 61(3): 275–298.

Group of Ten (1993), "International Capital Movements and Foreign Exchange Markets," mimeo., April.

Group of Thirty (1993), *Derivatives: Practices and Principles* (Washington, D.C.: Group of Thirty, July).

Hull, John C. (1993), *Options, Futures, and Other Derivative Securities*, 2nd ed. (Englewood Cliffs, N.J.: Prentice Hall).

Kat, Harry M. 1993, "Portfolio Insurance: A Comparison of Alternative Strategies," *Journal of Financial Engineering* 2(4): 415–442.

Kroner, Kenneth, and Jahangir Sultan (1993), "Time-Varying Distributions and Dynamic Hedging with Foreign Currency Futures," *Journal of Financial and Quantitative Analysis* 28 (December): 535–550.

Leong, Kenneth (1990–1991), "Solving the Mystery," *Risk* 4 (December–January).

Melino, Angelo, and Stuart Turnbull (1990), "Pricing Foreign Currency Options with Stochastic Volatility," *Journal of Econometrics* 45, 239–265.

Naik, Vasanttilak (1993), "Option Valuation and Hedging Strategies with Jumps in the Volatility of Asset Returns," *Journal of Finance* 98 (December): 1969–1983.

Perraudin, William R., and Bent E. Sorenson (1992), "Foreign Exchange Option Pricing in a Continuous Time Arbitrage Pricing Model with Stochastic Volatility and Jumps," mimeo., June.

Securities and Exchange Commission (1988), *The October 1987 Market Break* (Washington, D.C.: Government Printing Office, February).

Walmsley, Julian (1992), *The Foreign Exchange and Money Markets Guide* (New York: John Wiley and Sons).

Part V THE ROLE OF THE DOLLAR AS AN INTERNATIONAL CURRENCY

What role should the United States play in a world where financial and goods markets are increasingly integrated? Is U.S. monetary policy becoming less effective?

Alan S. Blinder
Professor of Economics
Princeton University

My subject is of interest to the Federal Reserve, to other central banks, and, I hope, to you: the role of the dollar as an international currency.

There is much talk these days about the current or prospective decline of the dollar as a reserve currency. But much of this talk is remarkably undisciplined by facts. So I'd like to explore with you what we do and do not know about the dollar's role as the linchpin of international transactions. Is it really declining? And what are the implications of such a decline for the United States?

Before you measure a phenomenon, you must define it. But there is no clear definition of what it means to be the world's central international currency. I would suggest that the tacit working definition is a blend of four characteristics, which among them encompass the three classic roles of money as a store of value, medium of exchange, and unit of account.

First, an international currency should constitute a preponderant share of the official reserves of central banks. This, of course, is the narrow definition of an international reserve currency. Second, the currency should be used extensively as hand-to-hand currency in foreign countries. Third, it should be used to denominate a disproportionate share of international trade. Fourth, it should have a dominant role as the currency of choice in international financial markets.

Note that the last three characteristics are the results of millions of private economic decisions—about what currency to hold, about how to invoice trade, and about the currency denomination of securities. The first characteristic results from government decisions. But these are, in turn, probably guided by market realities.

On all four counts, there is really only one serious contender for the title of principal international currency today: the U.S. dollar. But is the dollar's role declining? As we shall see, the answer is probably yes, but slowly.

But before getting enmeshed in the facts, a bit of historical perspective may be useful. A glance back over the centuries suggests that the international use of a country's currency is strongly linked to the centrality of that country in world trade. International trade in Europe initially was centered on regional fairs where merchants and local buyers gathered. By the 12th century, Italian bankers were playing a pivotal role in serving these merchants with coins, credit, and what we would now call a payments mechanism. Later, especially after the discovery of the New World, the Spanish joined in.

However, it would be a stretch to claim that Italian or Spanish cities provided the first international currency. That honor probably belongs to the Dutch guilder. As commercial activity and trade shifted northward in Europe in the 17th century, deposits at and notes issued by the Bank of Amsterdam—denominated in guilders—became the means of payment for much trade in the Western world. This dominance lasted until the end of the 18th century, when Napoleon's army occupied Amsterdam—an event that, I imagine, caused some severe disruptions to the guilder payments system!

The action then shifted to Paris and, especially, to London as Britain (a) went on the gold standard in 1816 and (b) became the world's biggest exporter of manufactured goods and biggest importer of raw materials. British banks and financial institutions came to dominate the financing not only of intra-European trade, but also of trade with the Orient. Soon foreign banks began settling transactions in pounds.

The outbreak of World War I knocked Britain off the gold standard and somewhat diminished London's role as the world's preeminent financial center. Its upstart rival, of course, was New York. The period from 1914 to 1931 saw the dollar gradually gain on sterling as the principal international currency—a process that was greatly accelerated when Britain suspended convertibility in 1931 and then war ravaged Europe. But sterling continued to play a large international role for years after Bretton Woods, and London remains a major international financial center to this day. There is a good deal of inertia in these matters.

The period of dollar dominance probably began with World War II. The question, of course, is when and how it will end. History suggests, first, that the honor of being the world's premier currency moves around the globe as patterns of trade change. But, second, that these things evolve slowly, although major events like wars can certainly hurry things along or even change their direction. The guilder dominated world markets for almost two centuries; the pound for about a century. The dollar has now had a run of about a half-century. Are our days numbered?

Don't count the dollar out too soon. Part of the reason is that institutional inertia that I have just mentioned. Another part is the fact that the successor currency is far from clear. By most measures, the Deutsche mark is in second place now and is gaining on us. But with monetary union somewhere on the European horizon, the long-run future of the mark itself is in question. Will the Euro become the next international reserve currency? The only other rival at present appears to be the Japanese yen, and the nexus of world trade does indeed seem to be shifting toward Asia. But, as we shall see, the yen's international role is quite limited now, and if we peer into the distant future, one may legitimately wonder whether Asia's dominant trading nation will be Japan or China.

The Facts: The Dollar as Official Reserve Currency

Let me now turn to some facts, beginning with the dollar's role in official reserve holdings. The number of dollars held as official reserves has grown rapidly, and with minimal interruptions, since the collapse of the Bretton Woods system. Since 1986 alone, dollar reserves have roughly tripled (Figure V–1). But, of course, official reserves in other currencies have also risen (Figures V–2 through V–4). The dollar's share of total reserves rose irregularly from about 55 percent in the mid-1960s to nearly 80 percent in the mid- to late 1970s and then declined in stages back to about 56 percent in 1990. Since then, however, it has risen again to about 63 percent (Figure V–5). Focusing on the past 15 years, for which we have the best data, the total net decline in the dollar's share is only about 7 percentage points. That's something, but not much.

Which countries gained at the dollar's expense? The unsurprising part of the answer is the yen, which rose from 4.3 percent of reserves in 1980 to 8.5 percent

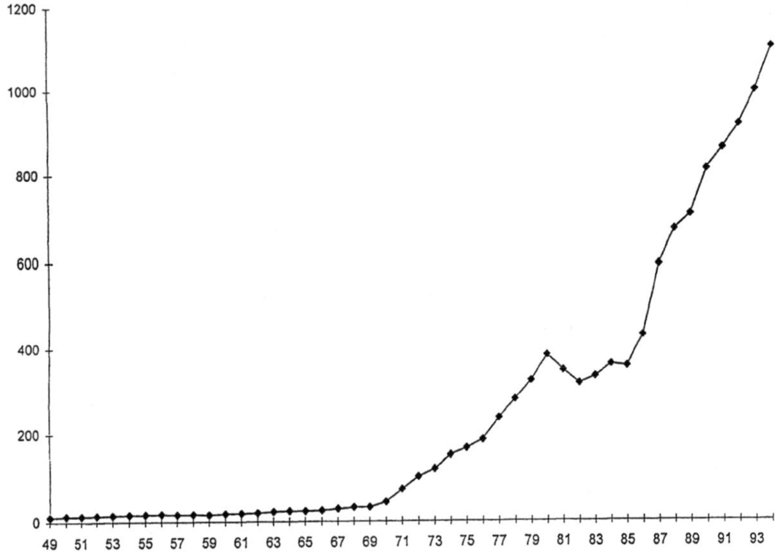

Figure V–1. U.S. dollar reserves.

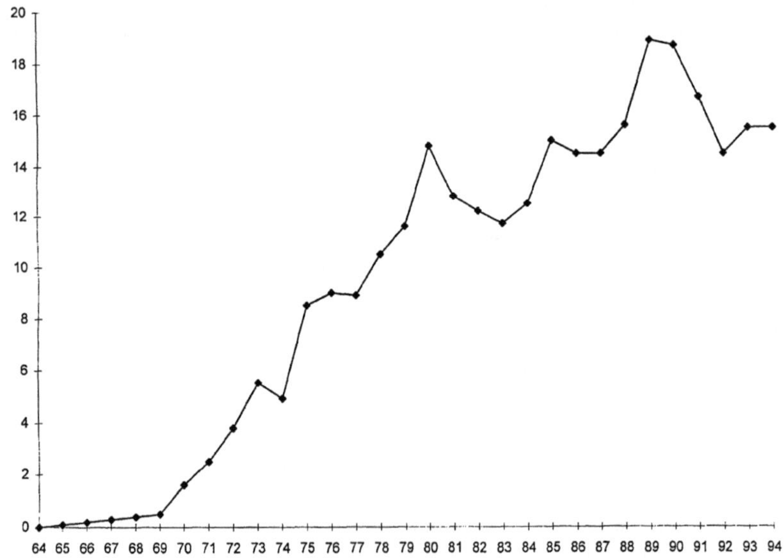

Figure V–2. Reserve currency—the German mark.

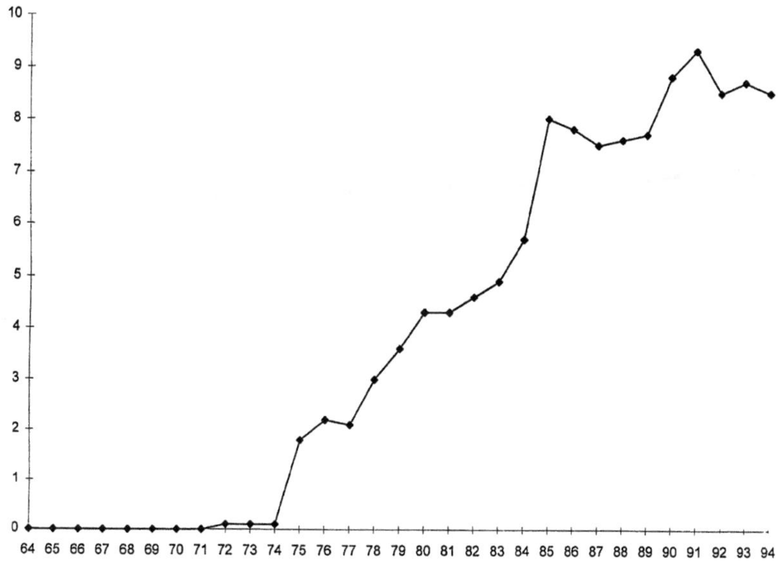

Figure V–3. Reserve currency—the Japanese yen.

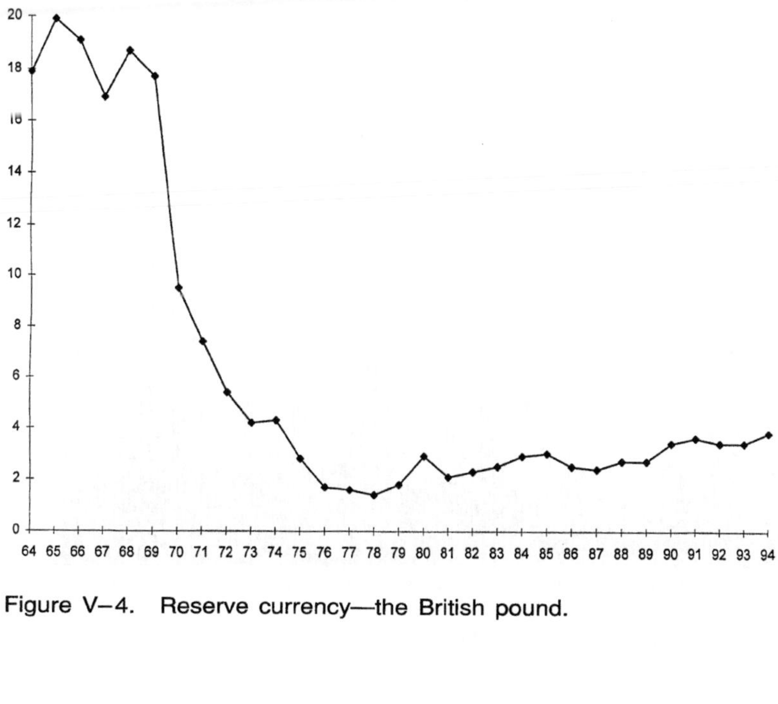

Figure V–4. Reserve currency—the British pound.

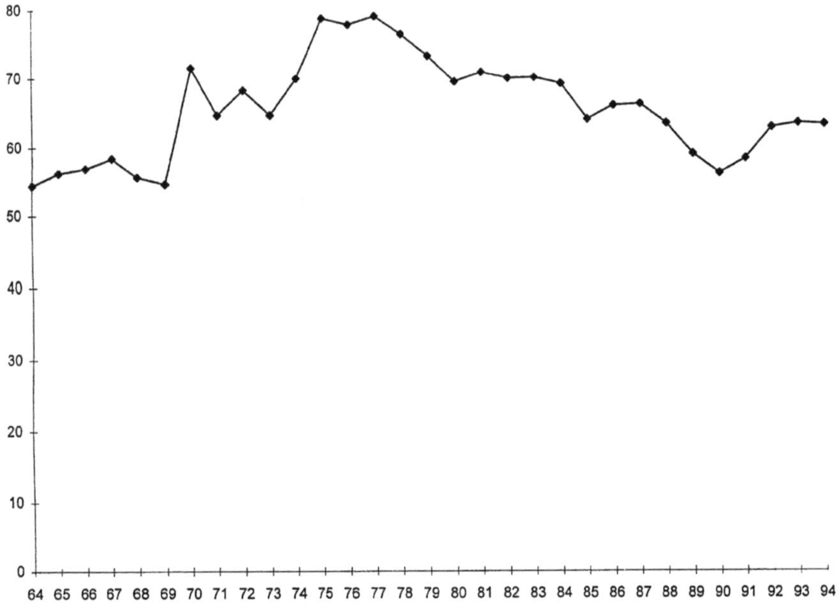

Figure V–5. The U.S. dollar's share of total reserves.

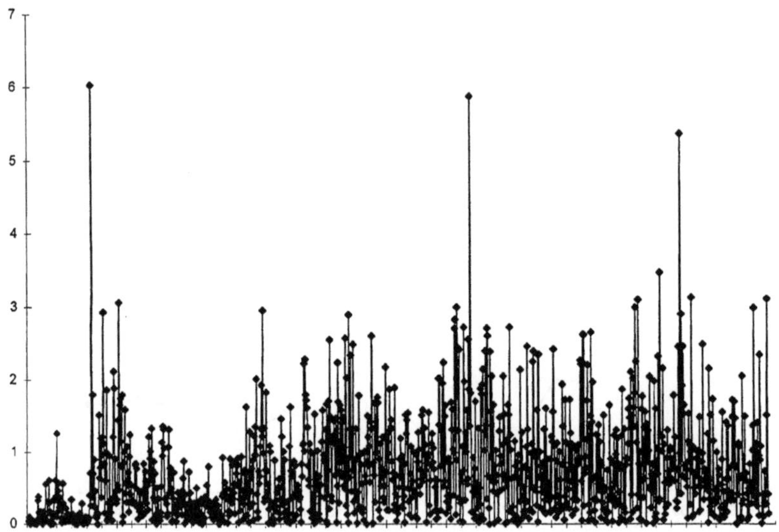

Figure V–6. Volatility of the U.S. dollar.

in 1994. The surprising part of the answer is that the share of the Deutsche mark in world reserves has not increased. It has instead fluctuated in the 12 to 19 percent range since 1980 without much trend.

Earlier this year, there were scare stories in the media about central banks, especially Asian central banks, diversifying away from the dollar. As best we can tell, these rumors were mostly unfounded. For the region as a whole, the share of the dollar in official foreign exchange holdings has been quite stable at around 60 percent. It is true that some nations, like Taiwan, have reduced their dollar share in recent years, but others, like Hong Kong, have raised theirs.

To the extent that the dollar's share in central bank portfolios has declined, what is the reason? One argument is that the increased volatility of our exchange rate has diminished the dollar's attractiveness as a reserve currency. Here we should start and can finish the debate with George Stiger's old question, Is this fact in fact a fact? The answer is no, volatility has not increased in recent years (Figure V–6). I am more inclined toward a simpler hypothesis: the share of world trade and finance denominated in dollars has declined (more on this below), and central banks are just adjusting to a changing reality.

Facts: The Dollar as Hand-to-Hand Currency

The statistical basis becomes a good deal thinner when we turn to the next aspect of the dollar's international role: as a medium of exchange for cash transactions in foreign countries. An almost overwhelming collection of casual observations and anecdotes tells us that the dollar is the currency of choice in Latin America, Asia, Russia, the Middle East, and elsewhere. But accurate, or even systematic, data are not available.

Federal Reserve staff estimate that 50 percent to 70 percent of U.S. currency —a total now of $185 billion to $260 billion—is held outside the United States. The methods we use are, of necessity, indirect. For example, one technique is based on shipments of $100 bills by the Federal Reserve Bank of New York. But the fact that different methods, using different data, all point toward the same range gives us some confidence in the estimate—which is, of course, a pretty rough one.

Seignorage earnings on these foreign-held dollars are not trivial. Using the current interest rate on Treasury securities of maturity equal to the average of the Fed's portfolio to impute interest, they amount to a hefty $11 billion to $15 billion per year. That is a considerable fraction of our total earnings.

Is this highly profitable role of the dollar diminishing? We know that currency shipments abroad are growing faster in the 1990s than they did in the 1980s. And we believe that the share of new currency flowing abroad exceeds the share of the stock, meaning that the share of our currency held abroad appears to be rising. But what about the dollar's share in the burgeoning market for paper money circulating in foreign countries?

Anecdotal evidence says that the yen's share is quite small, but the Deutsche mark's share is not. One recent German study estimates that 30 percent to 40 percent of German currency is held outside Germany. If correct, that would amount to roughly $35 billion to $55 billion—a large sum, but less than 20 percent of the volume of dollars circulating abroad. Overall, it seems safe to assume that the dollar comprises the lion's share of foreign currencies in hand-to-hand circulation outside their native lands. But we know literally nothing about whether the dollar's market share is rising or falling.

Facts: The Dollar's Role in World Trade

The third aspect of the dollar's role as an international currency is its use as the currency for pricing goods and services in world trade—as the international unit of account, so to speak. It is well known that a great deal of international trade is conducted in dollars. The latest available data pertain to 1992, so I will use that year for comparisons and hope that things have not changed much since.

Taking U.S. trade first, one of the more amazing statistics to me is that roughly 80 percent of American imports—largely the products of foreign companies—are invoiced in dollars. Such a large share is quite atypical, presumably because our domestic market is so large. Among the other major industrial countries, the fraction of imports invoiced in destination currency ranges from a low of 17 percent (Japan) to a high of 56 percent (Germany). On the export side, of course, invoicing in your own currency is much more common—ranging from 40 percent to 77 percent for other countries, and 92 percent for the United States.

But dollar prices are also common in trade that does not involve the Untied States as either buyer or seller. Overall, almost 50 percent of total world trade is denominated in dollars. Since U.S. exports and imports denominated in dollars account for only about 23 percent of trade, roughly 25 percent of world trade does not involve the United States but is nonetheless priced in dollars. We have no real competitor in this regard. The mark is the currency for invoicing about 15 percent of world trade. But all this is either German exports or imports.

Has the dollar's role as the international unit of account been declining? Superficially, it appears to have fallen—from 56 percent of world trade in 1980 to 48 percent in 1992. But this decline was entirely due to the declining relative importance of oil, which is, of course, priced in dollars, in world trade. In non-oil trade, the dollar's share has been fairly stable for years.

The Facts: The Dollar's Role in International Finance

Historically, as I noted at the outset, the market's choice of international reserve currency has followed patterns of trade—with Italy, Holland, Britain, and the United States dominant in their turn. But, in the modern world, financial considerations may overwhelm trade considerations. For example, the vast majority of foreign exchange transactions today stem from trade in assets rather than trade in goods. So we need to consider the dollar's role in international financial markets.

Let us start with foreign exchange transactions. According to the 1992 Bank for International Settlements (BIS) survey, fully 83 percent of reported foreign exchange turnover involved the dollar on one side of the transaction. The two closest competitors were the mark at 38 percent and the yen at 24 percent. (In case you are wondering why these shares already exceed 100 percent, there are two sides to every foreign exchange transaction, so shares measured this way must add up to 200 percent.) A similar survey in 1989 found that the dollar was involved in 90 percent of foreign exchange transactions. So the dollar's role in this regard, while still dominant, appears to be declining.

Turning to other financial markets, we find that in 1994 about 43 percent of banks' cross-border claims were denominated in dollars. The closest competitors were the mark and the yen, each with about 14 percent to 15 percent. Similarly, about 47 percent of Eurocurrency deposits were Eurodollars, versus about 17 percent for Euromarks and only about 5.5 percent for Euroyen. In both of these cases, however, the dollar's market share has declined rapidly and substantially from peaks that were 20 to 25 percentage points higher about 15 years ago.

In international bond markets (defined roughly as bonds floated outside the borrower's country), about 35 percent of the outstanding issues are presently denominated in dollars—versus 16 percent in yen and 11 percent in Deutsche marks. But here, too, the dollar's franchise has been eroded substantially in the past 10 to 15 years. Its market share was about 53 percent in 1981.

Thus, it is in world capital markets that the dollar's dominance has eroded most. Surprisingly, at least to me, none of this erosion can be attributed to the diminishing share of the United States in world gross domestic product. That share has not, in fact, declined since 1980. So we must look elsewhere for an explanation.

One candidate is the fact that, while the United States went first and probably furthest, many foreign countries have followed our lead in liberalizing and deregulating their financial systems. Financial innovation naturally follows in the wake of liberalization. And some of this deregulation and innovation, such as easing restrictions on foreign participation in foreign markets and domestic participation in foreign markets, particularly impacts cross-border transactions.

We believe that these developments have, on the whole, been salutary for the world financial system and for the global economy more generally. But, as a side effect, they have diminished the dollar's preeminence in international finance.

Implications: What Does It All Mean?

In sum, wherever we have data, the message seems to be more or less the same: the dollar is still unquestionably the world's dominant international currency by any conceivable definition. But its preeminent position is eroding slowly, as mainly the Deutsche mark and, secondarily, the yen move up on the pecking order. What, then, are the implications for the United States? Let me repeat the list of four characteristics, focusing now on possible implications rather than bare facts.

Central bank use of the U.S. dollar as official reserves presumably raises the demand for the assets that serve as reserves—mostly, Treasury securities. That, in turn, should lead to lower interest rates on those securities relative to comparable private securities. To look for such evidence, Board staff compared yield spreads between government and private securities in the United States, United Kingdom, Canada, Germany, and Japan. It turns out that the yield spread in the United States is not unusually large. Similarly, a decline in the demand for dollars as central bank reserves should reduce this spread, but, in fact, the spread seems to have widened slightly in recent years.

In brief, it is not clear that the dollar's role as an official reserve currency gives the United States Treasury any bonus in the form of lower borrowing costs. But, if it does, there is no evidence that this bonus is diminishing.

The chief implication of the use of paper dollars as a hand-to-hand medium of exchange in foreign countries is that the U.S. government earns considerable seignorage profits. In essence, the Fed borrows interest-free from foreign holders of our currency, invests the proceeds in U.S. government securities, and turns over the profits to the Treasury. As noted earlier, this seignorage revenue amounts to perhaps $11 billion to $15 billion per year.

Should demand for U.S. currency decline, this revenue source would, of course, decline proportionately. I mentioned earlier that we do not know whether the dollar's share of the world currency market is increasing or decreasing. But we are fairly sure that the absolute volume of foreign holdings of U.S. currency is growing faster than our GDP, the federal budget, or almost any other indicator of the size of our domestic economy. Thus, seignorage is becoming a relatively more important source of financing for the U.S. government. For example, it is now roughly the same size as federal receipts from estate and gift taxes.

The third aspect of the dollar's role as an international currency is its use in invoicing trade. The interesting question here is whether the fact that most of our imports are denominated in dollars affects the pass-through of exchange rate changes into domestic prices—either in the short run or the long run.

The short-run case is easier to make. Suppose the dollar depreciates. If foreign goods sold to American importers are priced in foreign currency, their dollar prices rise immediately and automatically—unless foreign suppliers decide to cut their home-currency prices. But there is no such automaticity if these same goods are invoiced in U.S. dollars, as most of them are. Instead, dollar prices rise only if foreign exporters make affirmative decisions to raise them. From a strictly neoclassical view of the world, currency denomination should be an institutional detail of no importance to pricing. But in a world with both nominal and bureaucratic rigidities, it might matter.

I suspect that dollar invoicing may help explain the relative immunity of U.S. domestic prices from exchange rate influences. But this is just a conjecture, neither supported nor refuted by research, despite the best efforts of Board staff. The data we need to test it are simply not readily available.

Last, but certainly not least, comes the dollar's role in world financial markets. Here, two plausible implications spring to mind.

First, just as was the case for official reserves, a worldwide portfolio preference to hold dollar-based assets should lead to lower dollar interest rates, other things being equal. And, of course, any decline in this preference should erode that interest rate advantage. But many other factors—especially expected changes in exchange rates—influence interest rate differentials between dollar and nondollar assets. So looking for this (presumably small) effect in the data seems a bit like looking for a needle in a haystack.

Second, it is at least believable, though by no means certain, that the dominant role of the dollar in world financial markets gives U.S. financial institutions a competitive edge over their foreign rivals. For example, U.S. banks have access to the Federal Reserve as lender of last resort. And U.S. financial institutions may have a comparative advantage in dollar-based financing. After all, the dollar markets are our home turf. If hysteresis matters in these markets, as it probably does, American firms acquired a durable competitive advantage simply by being there first.

Do American firms really have such an advantage? We simply do not know. I can offer only one suggestive piece of evidence. In the Eurobond market, American companies lead in underwriting dollar-denominated debt issues, Japanese companies lead in Euroyen financing, German banks lead in Euromarks, the French lead in Eurofrancs, and so on. That's hardly proof, but it does point toward a home-court advantage.

Conclusion

One final, and very general, implication is worth mentioning. A shift away from dollars for any reason—including international diversification—should, other things being equal, lead to a decline in the dollar's value. Indeed, worries that the shrinking international role of the dollar is putting downward pressure on the exchange rate seem to underlie recent concerns about the dollar's preeminence in world markets.

But what is declining is our international market share, not the absolute demand for dollars in world markets, which is growing rapidly. Furthermore, any influence of these developments on the exchange rate must be swamped by other more fundamental factors like actual and prospective monetary and fiscal policy. So it seems unlikely that the dollar is being weighed down by its loss of market share.

It would be going too far to say that the recent concern over the declining role of the dollar as the world's preeminent currency is much ado about nothing. Rather, it is a bit too much ado about relatively little. The dollar's dominance has, in fact, declined, but only a little bit—and rather slowly. Furthermore, the costs of this decline to the United States are hard to assess and look to be fairly minor. Of course, I might have a different assessment if the dollar was being rapidly dethroned and relegated to secondary status in world markets. But that, fortunately, is most emphatically not the case.

Part VI INTERNATIONAL CAPITAL FLOWS: DIRECT VS. PORTFOLIO INVESTMENT

The growth of international capital flows, especially portfolio investment, has provided an unprecedented pool of funds for developing countries. Moreover, the speed at which funds can travel between countries is much more rapid than ever before. Are international capital flows a blessing or a curse?

Presenter:
Michael P. Dooley
Professor of Economics
University of California at Santa Cruz

Moderator:
John Duca
Research Officer
Federal Reserve Bank of Dallas

Discussants:
Agustín Carstens
General Director of Economic Research
Bank of Mexico

Edwin M. Truman
Staff Director—International Finance
Board of Governors, Federal Reserve System

Dooley:
I have distributed two papers to conference participants. The survey paper on capital controls (Appendix VI–A) would be excellent to put by your nightstand if you suffer from insomnia because it will, without question, put you to sleep. It is a survey paper on what everybody has written for the last 30 years on capital controls and their effectiveness. It's a long survey. I wouldn't go so far as to call it tedious, but it's not meant to be entertaining.

The other paper, on capital inflows (Appendix VI–B), is more exciting and is what I'm going to focus on today. It challenges the conventional wisdom about capital flows and, by implication, about the control of capital flows and what countries might hope to accomplish with capital controls.

Let me start with a couple of quotes that express two views about capital controls that I think we have to address. The first quote is an old one: "We lend to countries whose condition we do not know and whose want of civilization we do not consider, and therefore we lose our money."

Was that the Treasury secretary in 1995? No. That was Walter Bagehot, 1867. So some things don't change.

From the other side:

> A serious but manageable recession has turned into a major development crisis unprecedented since the early 1930s mainly because of the breakdown of international financial markets and an abrupt change in conditions and rules for international lending (Carlos Diaz-Alejandro, 1984).

I think both these quotes are relevant today. Both lenders and borrowers often see international capital flows as a welfare-reducing phenomenon. The lenders' view is that there are big losses involved, that people put their money into emerging markets naively, and then they systematically lose it.

The recipient countries' view is that bouts of capital inflow lead to a brief period of prosperity, followed by long periods of very costly depressed economic activity. Certainly, the brief periods of prosperity before 1982, before the first debt crisis, and the brief period of prosperity before 1994, what I'll call the second debt crisis, were not worth the economic pain—the recessions, slow growth, low investments rates, and so on and so forth—that followed.

The question, then, is, do we need these capital flows? Do international investors need the access to these markets? Is it in the interest of the recipient markets to accept these capital inflows? These issues, which have been aired in the press and even in academic circles in the past year or so, have led to a reconsideration of capital controls and the conjecture that they might even be welfare-enhancing.

Today, I think we need to address three general issues before we can answer this question about whether we need capital inflows. The first is the motivation for the capital flows. The second is the consequences of a reversal in those capital flows. And the third is available solutions. So the three things we have to understand are why the money goes there in the first place, the consequences both for the inflow and for subsequent reversals, and, finally, what solutions are optimal from the point of view of the recipient countries. In discussing this third topic, I will take up the issue of capital controls.

Motivation for Capital Flows

First, motivation. It was remarkable yesterday that in all the papers that analyzed the macroeconomic effects of capital inflows, whether they supported investment, consumption booms, overvaluation of exchange rates, and so on and so forth, there was very little discussion of why the private sector was doing this in the first place. If capital inflows into Mexico before 1994, for example, supported a consumption boom, why did private investors make those investments? Why didn't they look ahead and see that this was a foolish use of their money that was unlikely to provide the basis for prompt repayment? Did they care?

Well, there are two basic ideas about motivation, I think. One is that investors are dumb. Not only are they dumb, but they are dumb repeatedly, in the same way, time after time. They were dumb in 1982, they were dumb in 1930, they were dumb in 1867, they were dumb in 1793, and they presumably will be dumb again in a few years. This is an important issue to address because, if true, it has substantial policy implications. If the problem is that investors refuse, for some reason, to look out for their own interests, then the presumption, I assume, is that government interference with these markets is warranted.

The argument I prefer, which is in my paper on capital inflows, is that investors are not dumb, but they are taking advantage of government-guaranteed programs.

Why did people put their money into emerging markets uncritically in recent years? Undoubtedly, one reason is that the fall in U.S. interest rates generated a desire to regain income and to look for alternative investment outlets. So I have no doubt that the interest rate cycle in the United States is a dominant consideration. But note that if it is a dominant consideration, that interest rates that go down will almost certainly come back up again, and therefore, these flows are, by definition, reversible.

But why go into an emerging market? I think there are two reasons, and they both come down to an insurance policy. The first insurance policy was the exchange rate. As we heard yesterday, it became very popular—to me, astonishingly popular—to argue that fixing the exchange rate was a good way to generate a credible anti-inflationary policy. This became popular at the International Monetary Fund (IMF). The IMF was advocating fixed exchange rates as a part of a disinflationary process. I can find no evidence that this was a good thing to do, but it became firmly entrenched that this was a good policy.

This meant that the foreign investor didn't have to worry about the exchange rate, at least as long as the country had ample reserves and as long as it had access to borrowing. Any return in a peso-denominated or nondollar-denominated currency would also be a dollar rate of return, so the investor didn't have to worry about it. There's credit risk, but the credit risk also can be ignored if the investor believes that the government will step in to stop any financial panic in the recipient country.

The easiest way to see this is by looking at investing in a foreign bank deposit. If foreign banks are too big to fail, or if the government has a history of supporting the country's domestic credit market, then just as a depositor in a Texas savings and loan in the 1980s didn't care what the S&L did with the money, an investor in a bank in an emerging market didn't really care what the bank did with the money as long as the insurance policy was credible.

Were these insurance contracts credible, and did they extend just to the banks or to other assets as well? I would argue that they were credible for a long period of time. Why is that? Ironically, it's because of the good policies put in place by these governments. Yesterday, we heard several convincing reports that fiscal reform in these countries was effective and that privatization generated lasting improvements in the governments' ability to raise money. Ironically, I think this makes insurance offered by these governments credible. That, in turn, generates a capital inflow.

We always think of capital inflows as a balance-of-payments phenomenon, as transfers of wealth from one country to another. In fact, there was a big capital inflow to Texas in the 1980s. It came—the way I like to put it—from the Chicago Federal Reserve District. People pulled their money out of the Chicago Federal Reserve District and put it in Texas savings and loans. I know this because I did it, and my mother lived in Texas, and so she did it, too. And my brother did it, and my brother-in-law did it. Everybody did it. Why? Well, Texas savings and loans were offering higher rates of return, and they were insured. Did we care what they were buying? No, we didn't care. We were getting a high rate of return; it was an insured deposit. They could have bought anything, and they did buy anything. My point is that this is not a south of the border, north of the border thing. In the case of the S&Ls, we just move the border up between

Chicago and Texas, and we have the same phenomenon going on here. This was a capital flow with clear motivation. We did not worry about our investments because there was a fund of money there, the FSLIC.

There was a fund of money in the case of the emerging markets, too. It's called international reserves. Mexico had what? $10 billion? $12 billion? That's money in the bank. That's collateral. In the event of trouble, there was $12 billion we could identify. More important, Mexico had access to credit. Just as the FSLIC has access to credit from the U.S. Congress, the government of Mexico had access to credit from the Federal Reserve, from the International Monetary Fund. That, in turn, is the government's borrowing power. The government's borrowing power in both private markets and official markets—the IMF, the U.S. government—depends in part on its fiscal track record. I think the policy reforms in Mexico and other emerging markets made those government guarantees much more credible.

So there was a large capital inflow, a private capital inflow, but I think it was basically an insured private capital inflow. Therefore, the investors were not dumb; they were simply responding to the incentives as they saw them. Even though it was an international capital transaction, it really was more in the nature of a financial substitution. Let me go a step further. We don't even need the United States in this argument.

If we look at the capital flight from Mexico and other emerging markets from 1982 or, say, 1980 to 1992, it's more than sufficient to explain the capital inflows to emerging markets, particularly in Latin America from, say, 1989 to 1994. I don't have any evidence of this and nobody else does either, but the stock of unrecorded capital positions of residents of emerging markets that existed in 1989 was more than sufficient to account for the entire flow back into these markets between 1989 and 1994. It's probably not true that it was all resident money going back, but it could have been. There was enough resident money out there. I think, therefore, that all discussions of the different motivations of residents are misplaced. I don't think the people in the Dallas Federal Reserve District behaved much differently than the people in the Chicago Federal Reserve District. I think they put their money into the savings and loans here.

Okay. So we get a big capital inflow. What happens to the money? I think that depends entirely on the local banking system and the local financial markets. Why do those people lend? What kind of microdecisions do they make? Who actually gets the money? I think that a local system of regulation, of incentives, and so on and so forth, is important, but I don't think it's important to the international investor.

Let's compare this with an earlier round of large capital inflows that was, in fact, met with large capital controls. In the early 1970s, there were massive capital inflows into Germany and Switzerland and the other so-called strong-currency countries. But it's hard to imagine a much different set of historical precedents. Germany was a low-inflation country. It had chronic balance-of-payments surpluses. People were betting on the revaluation. And they were right. They won. They made lots of money in 1973 and 1974 when the dollar was devalued against the mark.

In this case, it's hard to imagine a more different scenario. The money is going in, the currency is strong, but the country has a big balance-of-payments deficit. It's a relatively high-inflation country with a fixed exchange rate. How do you make sense of that? I think you can only make sense of it by arguing that it was a temporary inflow and everybody knew it, that people were betting on the high yields. They were betting they could get out before the trouble came. But the trouble was a part of the inflow; it wasn't a surprise that came later. The size of the inflow was roughly equal to the insurance policy, the reserves plus the borrowing policy, and the investors planned to get out when the insurance fund was exhausted. The only people who got caught were the real slow ones.

The policy implications of this view are quite different. In this view, it's not the inevitable stupidity of investors that's the problem. If I dare say so, and with apologies, it's the inevitable stupidity of policymakers that is the problem. They offer insurance contracts, people respond to them, and then they pick up the pieces. I've never really met a rich naive investor. I've met a lot of dentists who have lost a lot of money, but the pros on Wall Street are generally pretty good, and they look for government guarantees. It stands to reason, if you are going to play a game, if you are going to play against other smart people, other private people, that's going to be hard. So you find a government. And the government hires lots of smart people, but not always enough. And they aren't always listened to.

Consequences of a Reversal in Capital Flows

Next, the consequences. The consequences are less amusing. The consequences of the reversal in 1982, I've argued in another paper, were 10 years of depressed growth and, as Diaz-Alejandro said, a development disaster. An important question that hasn't received nearly the attention it should is why these financial crises, these reversals, these capital outflows, are propagated so long in terms of economic activity in the recipient countries. Why don't we just have the financial crisis, get it over with, and get on with our business? Stock markets go up and down all the time. Why do these particular kinds of financial crises seem to be so damaging for so long in terms of the economic development of the recipient countries?

I think the answer to that in the 1982 crisis was that the prolonged bargaining between U.S. banks and basically the U.S. government—or, more generally, the industrial country banks and industrial country governments—about who would take the loss or how the loss would be allocated made it difficult to invest in these countries for a long time. That's a controversial argument, but it's one I have been making for 10 years so I'm not going to change my mind now.

I think there's a disturbing counterpart in the most recent exchange rate crisis or financial crisis. This time, of course, U.S. banks were not involved. This time the capital inflows generally took the form of direct investment, portfolio investment, not banks from the industrial countries lending to residents of the emerging markets. And so the long negotiation between U.S. banks, for example, and the U.S. government will not be a feature of this workout. However, much of the risk was shifted to firms, nonfinancial firms and financial firms, in the emerging markets, which has led to a banking crisis of massive or large proportions in many of the emerging markets. This includes, by the way, Argentina, which has not had the foreign exchange crisis, and Mexico, which has. In both countries, I would argue, the crisis is real and is measured by a loss on the books of the domestic banks that has not been allocated yet. We know, from our experience in the United States, that when banks are in trouble, when banks have weak balance sheets, that it leads to credit crunches, it leads to misallocation of credit over time, and it depresses economic activity.

My fear—and this is just pure conjecture—is that if you look for a mechanism by which the financial crisis will be propagated over time and that will limit the recovery of the emerging markets, in this case, it would be the problems in their domestic banking systems. The domestic banks' assets took a big hit in terms of market value. Their liabilities are still out there. As in general in banks, the nominal value of the liabilities has not been adjusted; therefore, the banks have negative net worth. We know two things about negative net worth banks or negative net worth banking systems. One is the problem grows. One way of putting it is that if you have 100 banks that are in a loss position, they'll make bets with each other so that 50 become big winners and 50 become even bigger losers. This is called derivative trading. I think that generally, when you put people in a position where they have nothing left to lose, human nature says they'll take a big bet. When there are lots of such people in an economy, they'll bet with each other. The ones who lose will go to the central bank and say, "I'm very sorry, but here is your loss." The ones who win will say, "I'm a hero," and they'll actually hire the people that lost. So the idea that the losers are punished, I think, is wrong.

In any case, it seems at least possible that there is another mechanism for propagating this financial crisis over time into a real economic crisis in the recipient countries. And I worry about that a lot. I think it's a number one policy issue, and, if I could just propagandize a little bit, the policy issue is that the loss has to be taken off the books. You can't just look at it and say it's not hurting anything because it affects the behavior of the bankers. It gets bigger, and it has to be taken off. How is it taken off? There are only two ways, basically: inflation and government expenditure to buy the bad paper. Government expenditure to buy the bad paper is tough in countries that have fiscal constraint. Inflation, of course, is tough on everybody. But the threat of those two things—that is, fiscal problems in bailing out the banks or the temptation to inflate the problem away—will, I'm afraid, constrain new investment in these countries, maybe for a long time.

Solutions

For solutions, we have to go back a step. The solution is to stop the insurance chain in the first place. The problem is not the capital outflow. It's the capital inflow. The problem with the savings and loan crisis was not that people eventually decided they ought to pull their money out and declare the end of the game; the problem was the money went in in the first place.

How do we stop it? Here, hard economics comes back into play. For a long time I have argued that the only really effective way to break the insurance chain is with the exchange rate. The only way to do it is to say that private investors take the risk of exchange rate changes when they invest in an emerging market. That means that there has to be exchange rate flexibility; that's the only way to do it. There are alternatives, of course, but they won't work. One alternative is to say there is no credit guarantee: "I don't care what happens to my banks. If you put a lot of money in and you come to get it out and our banks have made bad investments, tough for you." That's the currency board solution. Has anybody ever done it? No. Will anybody ever do it in the future? No. Does it make sense? No. Is it credible? No. Forget it; it's not going to happen. Governments can't repudiate their own financial systems. This is axiomatic.

The second alternative is to put your banks out of the banking business—100-percent reserve requirements. I wish I had a dollar for every conference I've been to in my career where 100-percent reserve requirements in Chicago banking have been offered as a solution to all our problems. Has that ever happened? No. Will it ever happen? No. Why not? Well, there are huge incentives for banks to make loans. You've got a guy sitting around with lots of money and you say, "Well, I'm sorry; you can't be a banker anymore. Put all your money into non-interest-bearing reserves and charge for deposits, and we'll take you out of the payments mechanism." This solution has the huge advantage of logical consistency and the huge disadvantage that it can never happen because bankers are a powerful lobby everywhere, and they like what they do. They like making money. If you make them warehouses where they can't make any money, you are going to have a lot of angry bankers, and bankers spend lots of money in Congress. So that's not going to happen.

Another possibility, and I think a very good one, is to really beef up the prudential regulation of the banking system, to have the central bank and maybe the treasury much more active in monitoring and controlling and limiting what depository institutions invest in. Some countries have the capacity to do this and some do not. This is a very country-specific idea, and I think it's one of the reasons that in Southeast Asia, for example, capital inflows have not led to consumption booms. If you look at the domestic markets in Southeast Asia, we may not like the efficiency of those markets, but I can tell you that the central bank regulators and the central bank presidents know exactly for what their banks are lending. If they don't like it, they tell the banks not to do that anymore. And it works. It only works in a tightly controlled banking system, and in Latin America, that sort of thing probably doesn't work very well. But, certainly, prudential regulation would help.

The final alternative is capital controls. Can we just stop the investment in the first place? In other words (and this makes perfect economic sense) if we set up a market imperfection—that is, an insurance contract—then it's always important for the government to limit the moral hazard behavior that that insurance contract generates. This is a clear second-best argument. If the government generates a market imperfection, which it has with the fixed exchange rate and the insurance guarantee, then it is clearly welfare-improving if it can be done to regulate the capital inflow. For example, it would have been optimal for the government to limit the inflow of funds into savings and loans in Texas. We would have gotten a much smaller loss; we wouldn't have had the damaging property boom. That's an administrative action that would, in theory at least, work.

So is there a theoretical basis once you've set up this crazy system to control capital inflows? I think the answer is clearly yes. If you have done three crazy things, you are already over the edge. You might as well go all the way. And, in fact, you can perhaps limit the loss of doing that.

What should the controls seek to do? Well, they should seek to stop or slow the capital inflow in the first place. How do you do that? Well, you tax it. There are lots of different ways to do that. There are interest equalization taxes, differential reserve requirements, and outright prohibitions on certain kinds of transactions.

The logic that lies behind some capital control programs is that some kinds of capital inflows go in and come out but others don't. Others stay there. They are stuck. This is wrong. This is just wrong. Direct investment is a financial transaction, not bricks and mortar. All direct investors hedge. You can always borrow and get your money out. You can short the stock index in the domestic market. There's nothing that keeps direct investors in a country when trouble comes. In fact, I would argue that direct investors are likely to be the most sensitive to the need to pull their money out because they're the better informed. They have lunch with the finance minister, for example, so they know when there's trouble because he doesn't show up for lunch. They say, "Ah, the finance minister didn't show up for lunch; I'm getting out. Sell."

Now, there's no empirical content to this. In a paper I did with Stijn Claessens and Andy Warner about a year ago, we looked at different categories of capital flows. For example, we asked whether short-term capital flows are more likely to be reversed than long-term capital flows or direct investment capital flows. We found that there is no correspondence at all. In Mexico, for example, short-term capital flows are the most stable over time. If there's an increase in short-term capital flows, the next quarter they are more likely to be followed by another short-term capital inflow than, say, direct investment.

If you talk to direct investors, they are always puzzled by the academic view that they are stuck in the country. They are not. So capital controls that try to channel foreign investment into certain categories (for example, direct investment or long-term capital) actually seem to work, in some sense. If you look at the data, there are many examples where a capital control program has changed the composition of the capital inflow.

Unfortunately, this doesn't have anything to do with the policy objective, which is to stop the reversibility of the flow in the first place, since, as far as I can tell, all these flows are equally likely to be reversed and will be reversed when trouble comes. So we are left, then, with the unfortunate problem that the only way to stop capital inflows is to stop all of them. And that requires a very comprehensive program, a very administratively expensive program, and one that has to be adapted almost daily to catch the new kind of capital flow.

One of my first jobs at the Federal Reserve was as an assistant to the person who administered the mandatory control program, the Voluntary Foreign Credit Restraint (VFCR) program. The United States established a voluntary program in 1965 to discourage direct investment by U.S. firms abroad. The program became mandatory in 1968 and was administered by the Fed. I had the misfortune of being the most junior member of the international finance division, so I was the person that went to these interagency meetings when the regular staff person was unable to. The first thing I noticed was that the law was in a loose-leaf binder, a big fat one. "Do I have to learn all that?"

They said, "No, don't worry. Just go to the meeting and don't say anything," which I did.

But I did ask, "Why is it in a loose-leaf binder?"

They said, "Well, we keep adding to it."

I said, "You keep adding to it?"

They said, "Well, yeah. See, we tell the corporations not to do something and they agree, but then they do something else and we find out about it about a month later so we write a new part of the law; we stick it in the binder, and that's why it's getting so fat."

I said, "What happens when you run out of space?"

"We'll get another binder."

This is the problem with a control program: it has to be adapted constantly to blunt the incentives. After all, what the government is trying to do with these programs is to stop people from taking advantage of clear profit opportunities, and that's very difficult. I think governments that say, as a matter of principle, we don't want to get into that business, are probably correct.

My survey paper on capital controls (Appendix VI–A) goes through the evidence, but I think a fair representation is as follows: Capital control programs have generated interest differentials, so they have worked in some sense. It is possible for a government to control the rate of return that nonresidents earn in that country's economy, maybe as much as 2 to 4 percentage points annually. So this massive capital control program, this bureaucracy, can generate yield differentials that last for years. On the other hand, has it stopped speculative attacks, the kind of speculative attack scenario that Peter Garber talked about yesterday? The answer to that is clearly no. Why? If the currency is going to be devalued over the weekend, that's a pretty big annual rate of return. A capital control program that depresses yields a little bit or raises yields a little bit, depending on the program, is not going to stop a speculative attack.

Finally, there is some evidence that capital control programs become captured by the industry. Strangely enough, sometimes bankers are big fans of capital control programs. Why? Because they've learned to live with them, and they limit competition for other kinds of financial transactions. And it wouldn't surprise me too much if, after being frustrated a bit by the private sector's getting around the controls, the government asks the private sector how the program can be more effectively administered. The private sector will be glad to help. They'll even help you write the regs. This makes some people very angry, and it can be a serious public policy problem.

Conclusion

Let me close with just a brief review of my three points. What is the motivation for capital flows? I think the motivation derives pretty closely and pretty clearly from government policy. An interesting empirical implication of that is that the size of the capital inflow will be a function of the credibility of the insurance fund. So policy reforms, particularly fiscal reforms, will, ironically, generate capital inflows, but the size of the capital inflow will be just sufficient to exhaust the insurance fund. It doesn't have anything to do with people's perception of the profitability of investment in the emerging market.

Consequences are serious. Not for the investors. For my dentist friends, it's serious, but for most of the investors, they got the insurance, they got the *tesobonos*, they got the reserves, they got out. Consequences for the recipient countries are serious because financial crises can be propagated for a long time in terms of economic crises, development crises in the countries. This to me is a serious problem, the only serious problem in all this.

As for solutions, a government can't repudiate its domestic financial system, and, therefore, it cannot revoke the credit guarantee. Regulation and supervision can help, but that's a limited option for many countries. Capital controls might work, but they have significant administrative costs.

What's left? The exchange rate. The only way, in my view, to break the insurance chain and discourage these kinds of capital inflows is to introduce uncertainty in the exchange rate and make the private investor bear the risk when he makes a bet on a country and in a currency. Make the private sector investor bear the risk of that investment.

Carstens:

Before going to the topic at hand, I want to pose a question that Professor Dooley might want to answer later. When you have a floating-exchange-rate regime, you will also, in a sense, be providing some guarantees because any central bank that has a floating-exchange-rate regime will, by a monetary policy rule, try to guarantee stable nominal variables such as stable interest rates. Therefore, an application of Professor Dooley's theory is that a stable monetary policy rule may provide stable interest rates and a type of guarantee. But at some point you might have a shock, and somebody who invested long term might be wiped out. Therefore, the problem is that you might not be able to escape the supposed guarantees.

I think that this is a simplistic way of looking at the issue of investment returns. For investors there are risks, and there are returns. I think that what a central bank needs to do is follow a clear policy that helps people determine their expectations. That can be interpreted as a way of providing guarantees. So is there a way out of providing guarantees? Or do we have to close the central banks? I would ask. I don't know.

I would like to comment on the issue of capital inflows, especially from the point of view of Mexico, which has been in the spotlight for a while on this particular topic. I think for countries like Mexico, the real issue is how can you depend less on capital inflows in the future. This issue ties directly to the topic of last year's Dallas Fed conference, which was how to promote internal saving. This is not a trivial issue. Certainly, you have to address the issue of providing a stable financial environment, but I think you also have to address the issue of institutions. Chile has provided us with a very good example of how to promote financial savings through institutional changes, such as through pension funds and social security reform. Fiscal discipline and the provision of financial instruments to eliminate risks to investors can also be quite appropriate.

I think that a way to avoid many of these problems related to capital inflows, particularly in less developed countries, is to insist more on the creation of internal savings. I think the issue of efficiency in savings is very important and, in my view, has not been sufficiently addressed.

A question posed to us in this conference is whether something should be done about portfolio versus direct investment. My own view, and I agree here with Professor Dooley, is that both portfolio and direct investment can be volatile. Countries like Mexico want capital inflows because they need foreign capital, but these, to be helpful, should be stable inflows. To attain stability, three basic things need to be achieved. One is a consistent macroeconomic program. I think that in all instances in which there was a financial collapse, there was a problem that wasn't addressed in time. Second is the dissemination of adequate information to investors. And third, there have to be an appropriate legal system and property rights allocation. These will provide the framework that will attract stable, reliable capital inflows into countries. I agree with Professor Dooley that it doesn't make sense—or is a waste of time, I would say—to look into capital controls because most of the time this is only an excuse to avoid making serious decisions about, for example, providing a consistent macroeconomic framework.

Now, what have we learned in Mexico about volatility in short-term capital inflows? What we have learned is that it's very important to distinguish between the types of capital inflows. Something that surprised us, and, I imagine, the whole financial community, was how new institutional innovations speed up markets' reactions to macroeconomic inconsistencies. Mexico's macroeconomic position before the collapse, from a historical point of view, could be considered not that bad. To correct Professor Dooley a bit, at one point last year Mexico had $30 billion in reserves, and the day before the devaluation, we had more than $12 billion. Many years ago, that would have been considered a quite stable and relatively sustainable situation.

What happened is that new institutional innovations had made previous precautionary measures insufficient. Here, I want to underscore one particular innovation, derivatives trading, which can multiply traders' opportunities to shorten their positions. When those who have a short position in the local currency try to hedge their positions, it puts massive pressures on the exchange rate. Therefore, if a country wants to have a fixed exchange rate, it certainly needs to take into account the attacks it can suffer as a result of derivatives.

The other issue involves other types of institutional innovations: hedge funds and large pension funds. We were accustomed to having atomized economic agents with limited speculative capacity. Something really needed to be wrong for them to get together and produce a currency collapse. Now we face situations where eight or 10 hedge funds and pension funds can just collude and attack a currency and make it collapse. We certainly experienced some of this is Mexico, and I am sure this also has occurred in other countries, such as some that were part of the European Monetary System (EMS). Therefore, it is extremely important for a country to consider these institutional innovations when deciding upon its exchange rate regime.

My last point is that the importance of having a solid banking system cannot be stressed enough. In the case of Mexico, certainly, our capacity to defend the exchange rate regime was weakened by the fact that we had a very weak banking system. In many regime collapses—in Chile in 1982, in Scandinavia, and now in Mexico—this has been a factor. Therefore, this microeconomic aspect, the state of the banking system, is an essential consideration when deciding which exchange rate regime to adopt and how to treat capital inflows and outflows.

Truman:
The first question is, Are capital flows a blessing or a curse? My answer, somewhat in contrast to Mike Dooley's, is that they are both because we live in an uncertain world and therefore don't always know the long-run implications of capital inflows. And, as Mike stressed, they are driven at least in part by what might be called nonsystematic and nonfundamental factors.

Now, based on my 23 years of experience with Mike, there are two things you have to know about him. One is that he is very entertaining; I think you've learned that already. The other is that he is very convincing, but he is only right about 15 percent of the time. Let me be quick to explain that 15 percent of the time is a much better batting average than anybody in this room probably has, myself included; therefore, you are forced to listen to him and figure out which 85 percent to throw out.

When you address this issue about whether capital flows are a blessing or a curse, it seems to me you do have to have a bias in the direction of evaluating them in the context of the general competitive model, which Mike nicely lays out in his survey paper, which concludes that on balance, capital flows are a net benefit and that restrictions on capital flows—like restrictions on trade flows—are welfare-reducing. This is not to say that we live in such a world, but it is to say that the distortions in our world, our second-best world, are not very easily specified. And as Mike has entertainingly illustrated in talking about the VFCR program, those distortions don't provide much guidance for putting together a program for controlling inflows.

The next question is, of course, whether the existence of these flows is significantly affected by the existence of an explicit or implicit guarantee that may be the source of the distortion. We do know that governmental interference, in almost every form, does create distortions. The question is whether, on balance, you want to pay for that distortion. I think in the case of capital controls, the answer is no, but in the case of some other forms of insurance, if you want to call restrictions *insurance*, the answer is yes. However, I think it is important, particularly in thinking about the savings and loan analogy, to distinguish between explicit and implicit guarantees. Explicit guarantees should be honored, in part, because they are a contract between the government and its citizens, or the citizens of the world, if you want to put it that way. In the case of the savings and loan crisis, had the government not honored those guarantees, there would have been a big problem. There would have been a huge deflationary contraction. On the other hand, one should be much more careful about honoring implicit guarantees. This does not mean it should never be done, because sometimes the cost of honoring them is less than the cost of not honoring them. But there is a distinction, I think, between explicit and implicit guarantees.

It seems to me that Dooley's indictment of the implicit guarantees in the Mexican case is somewhat extreme. I would submit, contrary to what Mike said, that no portfolio investor cares what the borrower does with his money. Do you care when you buy U.S. Treasury securities what the U.S. government does with that money? No. Do you care when you buy corporate bonds what they do with that money? The answer is no. Do you even care when you buy corporate stocks what is actually done with that money? The answer is no. What you care about is whether you are going to be repaid or whether you are going to get the kind of return on your investment that you expect. So the notion that people investing in emerging markets don't care and people investing in other markets do care, or that it's normal for investors to care, strikes me as a little exaggerated. What investors do is make as assessment based on judgments of the fundamentals, including the capacity of the borrower or the borrower's country to repay or to produce an adequate return. Clearly, policies and performance are part of that assessment, as Mike would agree, but I don't think you can get around that. This is a matter of making judgments and making investments and about being right and being wrong.

Finally, in the Mexican case, it is not at all true that all or even a substantial amount of the capital inflows were either in domestic currency or took the form of bank debt, government bonds, or equities, or corporate debt. Moreover, in those four categories of obligations, most of the holders lost. The corporate debt holders lost; equity holders lost. Some holders of bank claims won, and some holders of bank claims lost. As far as the holders of government bonds are concerned, at least those *tesobonos* that are linked to dollars, they didn't lose, but the holders, and there were some, of government bonds denominated in Mexican currency certainly lost.

Moreover, to address Mike's concern about the future, I think it's incorrect to say that the losses are principally lodged in the Mexican banking system. The Mexican banking system had losses, and those losses were exacerbated by the peso's devaluation. But this was a consequence of the borrowing mechanisms operating principally through the Mexican banking system. Moreover, inflation is not the way to solve the problems of a domestic banking system, since, generally, domestic banking systems make long-term fixed-interest loans and pay short-term variable rates for their obligations. Increasing inflation is a sure way to bust the banking system even further.

This brings me to whether there is a case for limiting capital inflows and what the costs and benefits of doing so are. I agree with Mike here. Mike's survey, which I do recommend to you, does not offer much theoretical or empirical support for the proposition that controls are good or effective. In the long term, the controls don't work, and in the short term, it's very difficult to tell what you should be using because if you stick your finger in one hole in the dike, then you end up with lots of other holes in the dike.

I think one of the failures in this area is to draw a distinction between industrial countries and developing countries. Somehow, it's all right to have capital controls in developing countries and not so good to have capital controls in industrial countries. First, the distinctions between countries are breaking down. And second, they probably shouldn't have been made to begin with. Everybody is disadvantaged in the process.

There is, however, this current fascination with the capital control programs in Chile and Colombia and the few other countries that have them. I think there are three points that should be made about this. One is that the controls in these countries apply to a very limited range of short-term capital inflows, so not all capital inflows are prevented in either Colombia or Chile. In particular, capital flows into the stock exchange or in the form of trade credits are not covered. Second, if you believe these controls are effective in reducing capital inflows and impose them, then there is a price to pay. The government pays the price. Although I suspect it is a reasonable price to pay, there is a price in terms of interfering with the market mechanisms. Third, if they are not effective, then what you are saying is that in a crisis, you will have the same problems with capital outflows that every other country has, which I think is one of the points that Mike was implicitly making.

As Mike has said, countries do face difficult choices. But along with Agustín, I don't agree that the right way to solve this problem is merely to cut the exchange rate anchor. Actually, in his paper, Mike has four components to the insurance chain: access to capital markets, the exchange rate anchor, guarantee of the banking system, and sterilization policy. He has four links to his chain. I don't think that just cutting the exchange rate anchor will solve the problem.

To illustrate this, I would point out data in Mike's paper (Appendix VI–B) that show that in the period 1990 to 1993, private capital inflows to Chile, which didn't have an exchange rate anchor, and Mexico, which did, in a manner of speaking, were essentially the same, scaled by GDP. In one case, it's 5.9 percent of GDP; in the other case, it's 6.1 percent of GDP. The swing, in fact, from the 1984 to 1989 period was larger in the case of Chile than in the case of Mexico. I pick on Chile because I'm confident that it's not going to become a problem in the next 12 months. Now, Mike should have come back and said, "But remember, back in the early 1980s, Chile had this huge government guarantee program, so it clearly had an implicit guarantee system as well."

I would agree, however, that countries should take great care with their exchange rate anchors. That does not mean don't use them. It does mean don't overuse them and recognize the conditions required for their extended use.

The last point I am going to cover is the issue of foreign direct investment versus portfolio investment because I have had the benefit of reading Mike's other papers on this subject in which he says there aren't any differences, and, therefore, there's no great advantage to one over the other. They all present the same kind of problems; some even present the same kind of opportunities. But I think one thing that he didn't cover is that if you get in the business of favoring one form of capital inflow over another, through various mechanisms and inducements and so forth, you then have additional problems. I think many people would argue that countries that have become more relaxed about foreign direct investment are probably doing themselves a favor because there are some advantages associated with those flows. But if you disproportionately favor foreign direct investment, you are confronted with potential political problems.

Dooley:
I'd like to thank both discussants for very thoughtful and thorough comments. The only factual thing I'd like to dispute is that on questions that can be answered either yes or no, I'm right 50 percent of the time, considerably higher than the 15 percent that Ted [Truman] mentioned.

On the substantive points, I find little to disagree with the disagreements. The one point that I think should be clarified is that once the government leads investors onto a certain path or sets up the incentives to make certain investments, to then not honor the implicit insurance is, I think, a policy mistake. People often think this is an inconsistent position, and maybe it is. But I think once the damage has been done with the implicit insurance contracts, for the government then to stall or withhold clearing the situation up is what propagates the real costs of the crisis. So I think the solution is not to be ex post tough but to be ex ante tough. How to do that? I think the exchange rate is the most important part of the equation, but I also agree with both discussants that monitoring the credit system, the domestic banking system—in other words, what people are doing with the money—is very important. It's interesting that in a banking system that has been around for a long time, there is a system of control, of monitoring what that banking system is doing. Why do international transactions have to be any different? I don't think they do qualitatively, but quantitatively they do. For most emerging markets, the only source of very large, per unit of time, increases in the liabilities of the commercial banks happens to be nonresidents. It may even involve residents, but it usually involves an international capital flow. People move money across borders. The fact that it happens to show up in a balance-of-payments account is an accident of history. Balance of payments is a flow-of-funds account. It records a subset of transactions that happen to involve people who claim that they're residents of different countries. There are several problems with this data set. One, it's probably not even true that they are residents of different countries. The second is that the real distinction in those accounts is between official and private. So while I agree that monitoring the domestic system is important, I also continue to believe that the exchange rate is the dominant part of the story.

Agustín had an interesting challenge: Should central banks do anything? Should we close them? Well, no. Where would I have gotten a job if we had closed all the central banks? This is an employment argument if nothing else. It would be very bad for international economists if they closed central banks. But I think the lesson is quite general. The central banks should not peg the domestic interest rate. They should never set a price for people to shoot at, and they should never say that they're going to keep the federal funds rate at 4.6932 percent for the next 15 years. That would be a bad policy, one that generates instability. Having an exchange rate target is the same. It is a price that everybody can shoot at and that is never supposed to change, and I think that's not credible.

Questions and Comments from the Floor

Question:
I have read in the press that the IMF recently made some proposals on controlling capital inflows. All I have been able to do is read the press reports. First question is, What do the panelists think the IMF was aiming to say? Second question, What do they think of what the IMF was aiming to say?

Dooley:
I think the Fund's view, which has come out in a number of different places, is that the question of controls over capital flows is not a theological one, that there

may be circumstances under which a set of incentives has been put in place that for some reason cannot be removed in the short run. The countries have the right to think hard about what their commercial banking systems, in particular, are doing with capital inflows and to have some influence over that. I interpret what the Fund is saying as, it's an open question and it's one given. The part of it with which I agree is that given the apparent costs in terms of long recessions that these episodes have generated, we should think very seriously about all of the policy options. There may even be a country where capital controls are appropriate.

Truman:
I think the source of the information you refer to was not the IMF itself but the IMF's capital market report, which made some favorable comments on some countries' experiences with the use of capital controls in certain circumstances. I would remind you that, of course, the IMF does have, constitutionally, a bias in this direction. And in light of recent developments, there is a reopened debate about whether that bias should be maintained or should be eliminated. As I said earlier, saying that capital controls are good for developing countries and not good for industrial countries is not doing the countries a service. Countries can adopt controls, and one probably should have some degree of open mind about such choices. But the chances are—as Mike has said, and I agree with him—they are only going to be marginally effective, and there is a big chance that they will have serious unattended consequences over time.

Carstens:
I think that there is a set of alternatives, as has been outlined in Mr. Dooley's papers, to control some types of capital inflows. It is possible to avoid some macroeconomic problems through sterilization.

I think that some countries have not experimented sufficiently with the idea of just letting the market work. I think there is an intrinsic fear of allowing capital inflows to appreciate the exchange rate. In most cases, you end up having a very appreciated real exchange rate anyway, and controlling capital flows might generate more problems. So my view is that we probably should experiment more with market forces and interfere less with capital flows.

My final point is that capital controls are very, very hard to impose. Mexico, for example, will probably have $160 billion of trade with the United States this year. Even when we had the most closed economy after the 1982 crisis, it was very difficult to control capital.

Question:
I want to commend Professor Dooley on his challenging paper. I think that there's another link that can be broken, and it's the very one that you think can't

be. I mean, the notion of governments being blanket ex ante guarantors of the financial system is really a modern contrivance. If you just look at our country, government guarantees didn't exist in the 19th century in any systematic way. The Federal Reserve was instituted in large part to do that. It failed after 20 years, and we got the FDIC. For 50 years, people thought that was a costless solution. The savings and loan crisis pointed out the costs, and, indeed, we've had several major laws passed that amend that public guarantee and in essence say that the depositors are guaranteed, but the ultimate payer is, for now, going to be the equity holders of financial institutions because they will be closed while there's still some equity. There hasn't been a very long test on this, but the evidence so far is that the cost to the public has gone down significantly. So I think we can at least, if not break the link, twist it a little bit.

Dooley:
I agree with that, and I think it's important for the government to try to establish in people's minds that they will suffer the consequences of their decisions. The problem is that it's hard to do that convincingly. I think if you are in the room on the Sunday night when the market is going to open the next morning, and the policymaker asks you, "What's the worst thing that can happen if I'm tough?"

You say, "1930."

"What's the worst thing that can happen if I'm easy?"

"Your successor will have a tougher time."

Most people will go for easy, but I agree with you 100 percent. It's better public policy to be tough, to twist, as you put it.

Question:
As an equity markets portfolio manager, I found the conference and, in particular, this panel very interesting. I want to make a statement and ask a general question. Mr. Truman said that we, as investors, do not care what a company does with the proceeds of its bond or stock issue. We may be in the minority, but we care very, very much what a company does. And, in fact, that's an integral part of any investment decision. If you are referring to a transaction in a secondary market, I would say we still care very much what the company does with its funds because that affects the viability of the company, the efficiency of its production, and the efficiency of its marketing and distribution plans. So we do care very much. We look at it in every deal we are involved in.

The question I have revolves on how you look at the psychological, or the human, the nonrational, impact of people's feelings about the markets. When we look at emerging markets in particular, we think that the multilaterals are, in general, staffed with very good people and have the best of intentions but that the guarantees that are out there are really more guarantees of intention than something that can be backed up. In other words, there is a limit to the pain that any multilateral can and will go through. When we look out at the investors in our universe, we in general think that many of them are very naive. They make decisions based more on fear and greed than they do on rational economic expectations. I think part of that is because unlike economists, many people do not have a sense of history and realize that this cycle of emerging markets has come and gone several times in the last couple hundred years. So I'm curious to hear, when you factor in these psychological, as I said, or philosophical aspects as opposed to a more rational approach to investing, how you see it.

Truman:
I knew when I said what I said that I was falling into a trap of being a little bit more glib than I should be, especially since I'm still working for the central bank. What I meant to say was that, sure, I think, for investors as well as investment advisors, the basic issue is whether they are going to get their money back and whether it's going to be a sound investment or a profitable investment. To answer that question, depending on the nature of the investment, they have to know, more or less, how the money is going to be used. But I think it is only in terms of getting their money back or getting a reasonable return that those questions are asked. Obviously, you have to ask those questions somewhat more when you are building a factory directly than when you are buying U.S. Treasury bills. But it seems to me the basic processes and the amount of information needed is the same. That's all I was trying to capture; you are dealing with a continuum. Maybe this is my own bias as an economist, but I don't think a lot of final investors in equities pay much attention to what the money is actually going to be used for. They make a judgment as to whether it's going to be a good investment or not, not precisely as to what each dollar is going to be used for. I think Mike probably signs on to the fear and greed element. As an economist, I have a little trouble with this because I really like to believe that fundamentals matter. But there are psychological elements in the market, and the real trick for public policy is how to deal with those elements. To what extent do you encourage them, try to structure incentives or disincentives, or structure implicit guarantees so that the system works, more or less efficiently, while all this froth, as Arthur Burns used to call it, goes on but doesn't do great damage to the system as a whole? But the truth of the matter is that in making policy, you need to try the best you can to anticipate these kinds of things. My problem as a professional economist has always been that you say, "Now, let's consider the psychological implications of all that and then figure out what the market is anticipating or what the people in the market are anticipating is going to be anticipated," by which time you not only end up being a two-handed economist but an octopus.

Dooley:
I think the critical issue is whether that kind of behavior dominates the market always, sometimes, or never. And I think economists sometimes foolishly argue never; I guess I would argue sometimes. I agree with Ted that you should try to deal with that. I remember Arthur Burns, when I was at the Fed, refused to publish money supply data weekly because he though it would be bad for the speculators. They would overreact to it. I think he took it a little far. I think that the psychological part is at times important, but I think as economists, our job is to try to look behind it for other things. These same irrational people also buy carrots, but we don't use that as a reason to interfere in the carrot market.

Carstens:
The issue of having investors being very well informed is a relevant one. In the case of Mexico, we have recently substantially improved the information we provide to the market. This has come about precisely because the market or market participants have been demanding it. The IMF, in its international capital markets report, said that Mexicans have more access to information than foreign investors, which is completely wrong. As a matter of fact, Mexico has its own information system, similar to Reuters, and there are almost the same number of terminals in New York as in Mexico City. I think that the spillover effect that the financial investment has had in Mexico is that it has forced institutions in the Mexican financial markets to acquire international standards. And I think one of the most important issues is precisely how to handle and how to analyze information. So I think that the point of view of the gentleman is very, very valid.

Question:
First, I think the capital controls in Chile have not worked. A recent paper by one of my colleagues shows they don't work. They don't have any effect on the capital inflow. The central bank thinks they work, but they don't. They just changed the composition of the flow. They don't have any impact on the total amount; they don't affect the real exchange rate. Chile is doing very well not because of capital controls but because there has been a very responsible macroeconomic policy for 10 years. One aspect of that policy requires that the current account deficit be not more than 4 percent of GDP. When the current account deficit comes close to that percentage, the government generates a fiscal contraction and a monetary contraction to keep the current account deficit under 4 percent of GDP. This year, we are going to have a surplus in the current account of around 1 percent of GDP. What I'm saying is that it's the macroeconomic fundamentals that explain why Chile is doing so well; the capital controls have had nothing to do with it. There's no way that in a country doing so well, that's growing 7 percent per year, inflation is coming down. So there's no way to keep capital out.

I liked Michael's paper. I think that he covered all the bases. I have just one more point. I think that an essential part of the story is the incentives that come from the domestic financial system. Michael was saying that the way to protect against the problem that could arise out of that is to have better supervision. I don't think that this works sufficiently in many countries. We need to have the law, the supervision, the regulation, but we need something else. Maybe we need to increase the incentive for bank owners to do a better job. Perhaps the 8-percent capitalization that is used by industrial countries is good for industrial countries but not good for developing countries. Maybe we need 15 percent. Maybe banking is not a sector in which there should be free entry because there has to be some value to having the license so that people mind the store. Perhaps you would elaborate more on this point.

Dooley:
I think that your last point is particularly interesting, that the capitalization of banks in emerging markets should be even higher than in industrial countries. I think that's right because there's typically less diversification in domestic portfolios. So generating incentives along those lines is very important. But I would also say that just requiring increased capitalization doesn't get it. A part of supervision is making sure the capital is actually there and in a form that is actually at risk. And that's hard.

I probably spent too much time in Washington, but I think the central bank and the government have to be involved with the financial institutions and have to be very aware of what's going on.

Question:
A very brief comment on capital controls. In Colombia, we do believe that to some extent they work. But I think Mr. Carstens is right; it's very different in Mexico. If you haven't had capital controls and you have the Mexican situation in which you had a closed economy but you had an open capital account for many decades, it's probably not a very good idea. However, most Latin American countries are in a different situation. They've had capital controls for 40 years, and they are loosening them. The question is how quickly they should do it. I think this is very clearly the case in Colombia and, to some extent, in Chile. Also, these capital controls are limited. They are controls for incoming, not for outgoing, capital. Controlling outgoing capital is pretty difficult because nationals know how to get around the regulations. However, controlling incoming money has the advantage that large international banks are not willing to make very many illegal bets. So there is a limit to the amount of bypassing that the international market will do, and that's where the big money is. So I think to some extent they may be effective. They won't be effective for too long.

The second point I want to make concerns the circumstances under which capital controls should be used. I think that in the case of Latin America, most of these countries were undergoing significant reforms, which meant that there would be very large capital inflows. Most of the reforms would mean a lot of capital repatriation, so they knew that the money was going to come in and affect the real exchange rate, revaluate it in a rather dramatic way. Second, they were loosening up their trade regimes, and for the first time in decades, people were going to be able to buy consumer goods, and people abroad were going to finance that consumption. So these countries knew there was going to be a consumption boom financed from abroad. That, also, would lead to revaluation. Under these circumstances, it would seem rather logical that in the transition period between the start of the reforms and a couple of years down the road, these countries wouldn't want an awful lot of additional international money because the impact on their exchange rates would be substantial, and they would have a serious problem with "Dutch disease."

So again, whether the controls are useful and how long they should be left on depends on a country's situation. If what you are trying to do is manage a transition, they're okay, but you shouldn't think that they can be left on for a long time. So, I think there are special circumstances under which some of these capital controls may be justified. In Colombia, controls have worked. Capital inflows did not decrease, but without the capital controls, they would have increased more. How can we tell? The interest rate in Colombia, without a major change in monetary policy, increased.

Dooley:
I think that in my survey paper I deal with the transition case, where you anticipate a consumption boom capital inflow that's a kind of once-and-for-all event in which some markets might benefit from controlling the capital inflows for a while. The thing that we generally talk about is where a policy regime, which is an ongoing thing, is protected by capital controls; that doesn't work. But a transition is one of those cases in which it might make sense.

Question:
Mr. Dooley, I think your results on the volatility of different types of capital flows are important, but I think there are other questions to be answered about short-term and long-term capital flows. We found, in work corresponding to your own, that short-term capital flows tend to lead or cause growth across the spectrum of countries, and that growth, in turn, causes long-term capital flows. In other words, the maturity structure of liabilities of countries tends to be endogenous.

I guess the policy conclusion goes to what Mr. Truman was saying about the cost of capital controls. In other words, it says that short-term capital flows for countries are good in terms of growth. The hard part is transforming that into long-term capital flows. And in that particular case, an entry tax or some other type of mechanism that keeps short-term capital flows out may be more detrimental than helpful.

Dooley:
That goes way beyond what I found, but it's interesting research. I would like to see it.

Appendix A to Part VI

A Survey of Academic Literature on Controls Over International Capital Transactions

Michael P. Dooley
International Monetary Fund
July 1995

Abstract

This paper reviews recent theoretical and empirical work on controls over international capital movements. Theoretical contributions reviewed focus on second-best arguments for capital market restrictions, as well as arguments based on multiple equilibria. The empirical literature suggests that controls have been effective in the narrow sense of influencing yield differentials. But there is little evidence that controls have helped governments meet policy objectives, with the exception of reduction in the governments' debt service costs, and no evidence that controls have enhanced economic welfare in a manner suggested by theory.

This paper was prepared while the author was a consultant, Monetary and Exchange Affairs Department, Exchange Regime and Market Operations Division.

The volume of international private capital transactions has increased dramatically in recent years, both for developed and developing countries. The forces that have pushed private investors and borrowers into international markets include technological improvements that have reduced the cost of international financial intermediation as well as a reduction in government interference with such transactions.

The opening of international markets has also presented important challenges for policymakers. Recent examples include the series of crises that have beset the European exchange rate mehanism (ERM) since 1992, widespread capital inflows to emerging markets through early 1994, and, most recently, the turbulence in some developing-country exchange and capital markets in late 1994 and early 1995 as these inflows were partly reversed. These events have raised questions concerning the social costs and benefits of private capital flows and government programs designed to limit or modify the composition of such transactions.

The private benefit from access to international capital markets for both savers and borrowers is a basic conclusion of welfare economics. Free capital movements tend to allocate capital to its most productive uses across countries and allow residents of different countries to engage in welfare-improving intertemporal consumption smoothing. In a competitive model with perfect foresight and complete markets, the welfare benefit from intertemporal trade is identical to the welfare benefit from international trade in goods and services. This general conclusion is not sensitive to the exchange rate regime (Helpman 1981).

While this general result imposes considerable discipline upon the search for optimal limits on capital mobility, economic theory also suggests that exceptions to this general rule are possible in cases where preexisting distortions violate the assumptions necessary to support a first-best competitive equilibrium. Such second-best arguments are dealt with in an extensive literature, reviewed below. The basic idea is quite simple. If the economy is assumed to suffer from one distortion, it is possible to improve welfare through the judicious introduction of another distortion.

The theoretical literature that is the raw material for a survey of second-best policy regimes naturally focuses on models in which government programs might generate welfare-improving interventions in international capital markets. Since there are, in principle, an infinite number of possible market failures, there are an infinite number of welfare-enhancing second-best capital control regimes.

Many of the disagreements about the desirability of capital flows can be traced to different assumptions concerning the efficiency of private intertemporal decisions. While most economists argue that markets work well for static allocation of resources, there is a strong tradition of mistrusting so-called speculative behavior as being contrary to the collective interests of the community. This has led to proposals that range from "throwing sand in the wheels" of international capital movements to complete prohibition of such transactions.

An equally strong tradition that has influenced the literature is the view that government interventions in capital markets seldom accomplish their stated objectives. While there is a well-developed literature dealing with the economic effects of capital control programs, there has been very little work that attempts to relate observed capital control programs to specific government objectives.

The conclusion drawn here from this literature is that an ideal government dealing with one clear distortion could, in principle, improve welfare by intervening in international capital markets. This is not a policy recommendation, however, since the actual effectiveness of such a program is an empirical question. An easy, and perhaps wise, way to avoid the empirical issue is to point out that it would be better to remove the existing distortion rather than introduce another to mitigate the damage inflicted by the first. The present paper will refrain from repeating this, even in cases where this seems to be the obvious answer.

Not all arguments for government intervention in international capital markets are based on second-best considerations. A quite different exception to the general rule that government constraints on capital mobility are welfare-reducing arises in cases where stable, multiple equilibria are predicted. If multiple equilibria are possible, it follows that the first-best equilibrium might be attained or maintained through government intervention in capital markets. This is a much more recent contribution to the debate concerning capital controls, and it is emphasized by proponents of capital controls to protect a fixed-exchange-rate regime during a transition to a monetary union. In reviewing these arguments below, this paper aims to clarify the very special circumstances under which such theoretical arguments are valid. The paper also reviews recent attempts to relate these models to recent experience in Europe.

The first step in determining whether capital controls have been used effectively is to see if data support the proposition that controls have had a measurable effect on economic variables. There is an extensive literature on this issue, and recent contributions are reviewed below. It is concluded from this literature that both developed and developing countries have succeeded in driving wedges between domestic and international interest rates. Moreover, governments seem to have used controls in concert with various forms of financial repression to generate revenue and limit debt service payments on domestic government debt. The power of control programs to affect other important economic variables such as the volume or composition of private capital flows, changes in international reserves, or the level of the exchange rate is, however, generally not supported by the data.

One important lesson that can be drawn from this work is that there is considerable evidence that capital control systems have not prevented successful speculative attacks on fixed-exchange-rate systems. The obvious problem here is that in cases where a discrete parity change is expected, the yield differentials that can be generated by control programs are quite small as compared with the capital gains available to private investors that correctly anticipate a parity change. This is fully consistent with a variety of theoretical models of speculative attacks surveyed below. There is some evidence that controls prolong the life of the regime. Unfortunately, very little is known about the timing of speculative attacks with or without control programs, so it is difficult to evaluate the view that control programs buy time while the government comes to grips with its policy conflicts.

The literature has generally not focused on the question of whether observed capital control programs actually mitigate the effects of well-defined distortions. Giavazzi and Giovannini (1989, 162), for example, conclude that,

> The widespread use of capital controls is not clearly justified by any widely agreed-upon economic theory; indeed to our knowledge, there have only been a very few attempts to study capital controls using explicit second best arguments.

Some very recent work on the political economy of capital controls has begun to ask the question of what types of distortions seem to motivate existing control programs. Preliminary findings reviewed below suggest that governments have used controls over extended periods to limit the cost of debt service and to maintain a tax base for inflation and financial repression.

The more important question of whether the costs of the distortions generated by controls outweigh potential benefits has not yet been addressed. A very informal test of this proposition is that enthusiasm for such programs seems to be inversely related to the observer's experience with trying to formulate and enforce a set of administrative rules that have as their objective preventing participants in financial markets from maximizing private returns.

A familiar analogy drawn from international trade theory is an optimal tariff that might exploit a country's market power over production of its exports. Such arguments for government intervention are clearly correct given the assumptions. Nevertheless, no one in recent memory has suggested that government could or should attempt to adopt such a tariff. All of the standard arguments against the practical usefulness of an optimal tariff on exports apply with equal force to taxes or quantitative controls on intertemporal trade—that is, trade in financial assets. These include the possibility of retaliation by other countries, evasion, administrative costs, inability to quantify the distortion, and therefore the appropriate tariff, the political temptation to intensify the preexisting distortion, and, finally, the possibility that the protected industry will "capture" the political machinery that sets the tariff.

A topic that deserves more attention is what might be called the public-choice approach to controls. The idea here is that control systems, once established, are likely to take on a life of their own as the control bureaucracy and its constituency attempt to maximize their own power and wealth. Thus, controls designed to mitigate a temporary distortion might outlive the economic rationale on which they were established. Further, private investors that have invested heavily in avoiding the control mechanisms are likely to welcome the protection from other investors that have not done so. Cairncross (1973), for example, argues that the British capital control system that evolved from a comprehensive system of exchange controls during World War II survived long after the original rationale was relevant. Moreover, he argues that by the early 1970s, the bite of controls was very uneven across investors because certain types of transactions were exempt from controls. Dornbusch (1986) argues in favor of controls under some circumstances but points to an example where the control system had outlived its usefulness and had become the problem rather than the solution.

There is a very large academic literature dealing with the economic effects of legal restrictions on private capital flows. This survey organizes this body of work according to the apparent objectives that might justify such restrictions. First, the survey examines models that relate controls to the ability of monetary and fiscal policy to stabilize output, prices, or the real exchange rate. The implicit assumption in this literature is that governments have good reasons for using these policy tools and that they do so in a welfare-improving manner.

The survey next considers a variety of distortions to a competitive equilibrium that might make a control program optimal. These include provision of a tax base in an optimal fiscal regime, a means to counteract distortions that limit domestic capital formation, and a means to insulate the economy from destabilizing capital flows.

The next part of the paper considers a very different rationale for restrictions on capital flows. In these models, multiple competition equilibria are possible, and controls might be useful in maintaining a good equilibrium or in moving from a low to a high welfare equilibrium.

Finally, the paper considers the empirical evidence on the effectiveness of controls. It also examines recent work that relates the use of controls to characteristics of individual countries.

Stabilization

Short-Run Stabilization of Output and Relative Prices

The classic framework for evaluating the implications of capital mobility and the effects of limiting capital mobility is the Mundell–Fleming model of a small open economy. In commenting on Williamson's (1993) review of the policy issues associated with recent private capital inflows, Branson (1993) notes that while a description of the stylized facts is useful and interesting, it is difficult to evaluate the policy options in the absence of a generally agreed upon theoretical framework. The framework suggested by Branson is the familiar Mundell–Fleming model. This paper shares the view that lessons about capital mobility drawn from simple versions of the model have proven remarkably robust to subsequent theoretical refinements and empirical evidence. In the remainder of this paper, it is argued that the role of capital controls in stabilization policy is only part of the story, but it is a potentially important part. It follows that this is a good place to start an evaluation of what the academic literature has to offer in evaluating policies that affect international capital movements.

The Mundell–Fleming tradition starts from the implicit assumption that policies designed to stabilize economic activity are useful and welfare-enhancing.

The working assumption is that the government values the ability to "distort" domestic spending decisions by manipulating the real interest rate in order to influence the growth in output and perhaps the rate of inflation. In this literature, the primary existing distortion is slow adjustment of nominal wages and prices. It follows that the assumption of flexible nominal prices (nominal prices, wages, exchange rates, and interest rates) eliminates the distortion and the rationale for welfare-improving capital controls. Such a model is considered in the next section.

If capital is free to move across national borders and the nominal exchange rate is fixed or heavily managed, the government loses control over domestic monetary conditions. If the exchange rate is not managed, monetary policy might still be constrained by incipient capital movements, since changes in domestic interest rates can generate large changes in nominal and real exchange rates. While this ensures a powerful transmission mechanism for monetary policy, governments might consider the resulting large changes in relative prices as a constraint on monetary policy. Flexible exchange rate models are reviewed below.

In contrast, fiscal policy is a powerful tool for stabilizing domestic output even if capital markets are highly integrated. It follows that if stabilization policy is welfare-improving, increased capital mobility generated by a relaxation of capital controls should be followed by assigning fiscal policy to domestic stabilization.

This framework provides a simple criterion for the optimality of capital account restrictions. If another policy tool is available for assignment to domestic stabilization, it might be optimal to open the capital account. Thus, Branson (1993) argues that existing capital controls imply that the government faces constraints on the exercise of fiscal policy for stabilization. It follows that removal of capital controls may not be optimal unless the constraints on the effective utilization of fiscal policy are first eliminated.

The well-known arguments reviewed above start from the proposition that wages and prices fail to clear markets and that this generates the rationale for stabilization policy. In an early attempt to better understand the nature of the sticky price distortion, Flood and Marion (1982) develop a model in which labor contracts generate inertia in wages. They then see if capital controls in the form of a dual foreign exchange market can minimize the variance of employment in the face of a variety of shocks to the system. They also show that the labor contracts chosen by the private sector depend upon the policy regime in place, including the controls on capital flows. It follows that a full evaluation of the welfare implications of capital controls should consider the private reaction to the removal of controls. In some cases, the preexisting distortion may be an endogenous response to the controls themselves. This is one of a very few attempts offered in the literature to deal with the well-known Lucas critique of analyses that attempt to predict the economic effects of policy changes without explicit consideration of how the private sector's behavior is likely to change in response to the regime change.

Long-Run Stability of the Regime: Speculative Attack Models

Early contributions to analysis of capital controls using the Mundell–Fleming model focused on dual exchange rate regimes (Argy and Porter 1972, Fleming 1974, Lanyi 1975). These models show that effective segregation of financial and current account transactions, with no official intervention in the financial exchange market, is equivalent to the prohibition of net private capital flows. These authors suggested that such a control might be only partially effective, but even if fully effective, the Mundell–Fleming model does not predict that controls over capital flows can sustain an inconsistent policy regime forever. Effective capital controls alter the channels through which the private sector responds to changes in the economic environment. Thus, effective controls alter the mechanism through which an inconsistent regime is forced to collapse but not the eventual result. A straightforward extension of the Mundell–Fleming framework allows a better understanding of the process by which an inconsistent policy regime comes to an end with or without capital mobility.

Regime Changes with Perfect Capital Mobility

Krugman (1979) and Flood and Garber (1984) provide models of speculative attacks against inconsistent policy regimes.[1] The inconsistency is that the government sets a rate of growth for the domestic assets of the central bank in order to finance a fiscal deficit that is inconsistent with the fixed nominal exchange rate and the growth in the demand for money. With perfect capital mobility and purchasing power parity, the demand for real money balances is predetermined so that increases in the domestic part of the monetary base are instantly offset by changes in international reserves. When the central bank's international reserves fall to a certain level, it is known that the central bank will withdraw from the foreign exchange market and the currency will float freely.

This regime comes to an end when speculators calculate that a successful attack will generate a discrete depreciation of the currency. Competition among the speculators will force the speculative attack to occur at a point where no expected profit is possible. While quite simple, the model has the important feature that no apparent change in the fundamentals occurs at the time of collapse.

Nevertheless, the private capital flows that generate the collapse are driven by fully rational interpretation of the fundamentals.

Regime Changes with Capital Controls

The key feature of capital controls in the context of a speculative attack model is that the private sector can no longer trade private debt for foreign exchange and, in turn, trade the foreign exchange for domestic money. With capital controls, the private sector can adjust its money holdings, but only through net transfers of goods and services to the rest of the world. A more complete evaluation of the effects of capital controls therefore requires a model of the current account. Because the private sector's willingness to distort its consumption over time is probably limited, effective capital controls might considerably extend the life of an inconsistent regime.

Several authors have incorporated a partial equilibrium model of the current account into the monetary models discussed above in order to study the long-run effects of capital controls. If changes in domestic absorption are assumed to be a fraction of changes in output (an implication of a simple Keynesian consumption function), any permanent (temporary) increase in demand causes a permanent (temporary) increase in the trade deficit. Moreover, if the Marshall–Lerner conditions are satisfied, a real depreciation of the exchange rate causes a reduction in the trade balance. Using these partial equilibrium assumptions, it is straightforward to determine the long-run response of the system to a shock such as an increase in the money stock or government spending.

Delbecque (1993) develops a model of a dual exchange rate system that captures these interactions. In this model, all private capital transactions are effectively limited to the financial exchange market. Since the government does not participate in this market, net private capital flows are necessarily zero. Current account transactions are permitted in the commercial exchange market. The government intervenes to fix the exchange rate in this market.

An important implication of this model is that private net intertemporal trade in goods and services is matched by a secular change in the government's net international reserves. The general point is that the government acts as a type of financial intermediary for the private sector in a system with capital controls. Thus, the model is closed by an assumption that the government cares about its stock of net international reserves. The inconsistent policy settings cause a deterioration of the current account that eventually exhausts the government's stock of international reserves.

Gros (1992) also models speculative attacks but points out that while capital controls can limit private-sector speculation in most cases, governments are forced to augment the capital controls program with domestic interest rates that are much higher or lower than would be the case in the absence of speculative pressure. An important aspect of this framework is that controls are effective but can be overcome at some cost to the speculator. In this setup, the government's commitment to maintain the peg can be easily monitored by the private sector since it is revealed in interest rate policy. When the government reveals that it is unwilling to sacrifice control over domestic interest rates, the private sector will know that a small speculative attack, and the associated low costs of avoiding the capital control program, will be successful.

The welfare effects of controls are not well-defined in these models. The intuition, however, is clear. If the additional time during which the regime survives is used wisely, in the sense that consistent policies are introduced, the measure of policy independence generated by the control program might be welfare-improving.

The models reviewed above are designed to clarify the dynamics of a speculative attack on an inconsistent regime but do not provide insight as to why a rational government would pursue such a policy. Wyplosz (1986) develops a similar model and argues that capital controls that are only temporarily effective nevertheless make an adjustable peg regime viable. In this framework, the authorities operate a monetary policy that is inconsistent with permanently fixed exchange rates but overcome this potential inconsistency with discrete changes in the exchange rate peg. Wyplosz points out that capital controls play a crucial role in making such an adjustable peg system work.

The key to the argument is that the volume of private capital flows in response to an expected profit opportunity is limited by the capital control system. In this model, controls are modeled so that residents of the country cannot change their holdings of foreign assets or their financial liabilities to nonresidents. Nonresidents are assumed to hold domestic money, for transactions purposes, and are free to sell it against foreign currency at the commercial exchange rate.

The crisis in this model comes when nonresidents believe that selling off all their holdings of domestic money will trigger a devaluation or revaluation of the nominal exchange rate. At this point, the central bank announces a discrete change in the parity. Wyplosz does not attempt to assess the optimality of such a system, although the desire to reduce the short-run variance of exchange rates, discussed below, would provide a rationale.

Regime Changes with Maximizing Models of the Current Account

The partial equilibrium approach to modeling the current account described in the previous section clarified the important point that capital controls shift private adjustment from capital flows to the current account. A weakness is that the private sector is rearranging its intertemporal consumption in response to incentives created by the government policy, but there is no forward-looking theory for why this might be optimal.

Econometric evidence does support the view that over a time horizon of a year or so, movements in the current account are dominated by relative rates of income growth and relative prices. But over longer time horizons, the outstanding stock of debt begins to play a dominant role. In general, the simple model is not well suited to dealing with issues associated with increases in indebtedness over time.

The modern literature on the macroeconomic effects of capital controls focuses on these long-run effects.[2] Moreover, by including expectations about the long run as determinants of current economic behavior, the modern literature provides a link between capital mobility and observed short-run behavior of the economy and how it is affected by controls over capital flows.

Calvo (1987) develops a model that addresses the issue of the behavior of the private sector in a regime that is known to be inconsistent and where it is known that the regime will be abandoned when the government exhausts its international reserves. The model has the same building blocks as the speculative attack models discussed above except that the current account is explicitly modeled. The model predicts, in cases where a successful speculative attack is expected, that the public will increase its consumption (a current account deficit) until the date of the regime change and then will decrease consumption (a current account surplus) thereafter. The financial counterpart of this leading up to the regime change is, of course, a decline in the government's net international reserve assets.

The key to this result is the condition that after the attack, revenue from inflation must rise to balance the fiscal budget. As the higher rate of actual and expected inflation optimal real money demand falls, the real marginal utility of money balances falls, and so the marginal utility of consumption just before the crisis must also be less than the marginal utility of consumption just after the crisis. The model is also extended to consider the effects of anticipated real exchange rate changes.

This type of model clarifies the fact that a distortion in the time profile of consumption is suboptimal, and so there must be some offsetting benefit of prolonging the life of the inconsistent regime.

Park (1994) provides a maximizing model in which households adjust their intertemporal consumption of goods and real money balances in order to maximize expected utility over an infinite planning horizon. He asks if a liberalization of the capital account can generate an immediate speculative attack on a fixed-exchange-rate regime. The model suggests that initial conditions are crucial to the answer. If the domestic real interest rate is initially below the world interest rate, the initial result of liberalization is an incipient net capital outflow and a rise in the domestic real interest rate. The increase in debt service cost of the government's domestic debt is assumed to be met by an increase in the growth of domestic assets in order to finance the resulting fiscal deficit.

If the liberalization is a surprise, foreign and domestic expected yields equalize immediately, and if a speculative attack is expected to be successful, the private sector reduces its demand for real money balances because of the higher rate of inflation that follows the successful attack. The resulting sale of domestic assets to the central bank might exhaust its reserves and generate an immediate attack and regime change. If the fixed exchange rate is initially sustainable, a secular fall in reserves is anticipated and, eventually, a successful speculative attack similar to those discussed in the previous section.

Auernheimer (1987) compares the breakdown of inconsistent regimes in a maximizing model with and without capital controls. The model suggests that with capital mobility, it makes no difference if the government chooses an inconsistent exchange rate or monetary rule in the onset of the crisis. However, like Calvo, he shows that with capital controls the inconsistent regime generates lasting suboptimal real effects on the current account.

In general, these models reinforce the lessons from the partial equilibrium model discussed above. Even perfectly effective controls on private capital transactions can at best extend the life of an inconsistent policy regime. They add the important conclusion that the path for consumption is suboptimal during the interval for which the regime survives, and this distortion continues after the inconsistent regime has ended.

Stabilization with Price and Wage Flexibility

The relevance of sticky prices for very short-run evaluation of policy effects in industrial countries is widely accepted and built into standard econometric models. The relevance of the results depends of course, on the assumption that monetary policy, in fact, is effective in overcoming the distortions generated by inflexible prices.

Economies that have been subjected to high inflation are often highly indexed. In these economies, it has become conventional to assume that monetary policy has very limited power to stabilize real output, even in the short run. Models developed to understand these economies generally assume that real output is independent of monetary policy and the fiscal deficit. These models focus on the role of capital controls in determining the private sector's response to economic shocks with and without the ability to borrow and lend in international credit markets.

An important extension of the Mundell–Fleming model introduces domestic price and exchange rate flexibility. In this version of the model, with perfect capital mobility and flexible exchange rates, changes in the domestic money stock generate proportional changes in all nominal prices so that the stabilization role for monetary policy disappears, and so, too, do the associated arguments for capital controls. If the private sector's consumption decisions are forward-looking, and a number of other conditions are met, Ricardian equivalence also eliminates the effects of bond-financed fiscal deficits. Government spending has real effects but is not useful in generating welfare-increasing changes in the level of employment.

Because effective or even partially effective capital controls push all or a part of the adjustment to shocks to the system to the current account—that is, to net sales of goods and services to nonresidents—it follows that capital controls alter the response of the economy to policy actions. In general, the neutrality of policy discussed above is overturned.

The discussion now turns to papers that address the question of how capital controls affect the relationship between monetary and fiscal policies and other economic variables in a model with flexible prices. It should be noted that in these models, there is no presumption that the effects of controls are welfare-improving. Instead, the objective is simply to understand the interactions of policy shocks and other shocks to the system in a second-best world.

Reinhart (1991) examines the effects of a tax on foreign assets in a model of flexible exchange rates with asset accumulation. In such an economy, the private sector's accumulation of foreign assets is constrained by the current account balance. The model considers the effect of the tax on government revenues, the evolution of asset stocks, and the dynamics of the real exchange rate. The main conclusion is that the imposition of capital controls in the form of a tax on foreign assets generates a temporary trade deficit and an appreciation of the real exchange rate.

Adams and Greenwood (1985) offer a maximizing model of intertemporal consumption for an open economy and explore the welfare effects of capital controls. The model develops several general points that will be important in all the literature to be reviewed below. First, the model shows that dual exchange regimes are equivalent to a program of taxation of capital movements. Second, some program of quantitative restrictions on capital movements is equivalent to a system of taxes or dual exchange markets. Third, any effective capital control program can be manipulated to attain the government's target for the current account balance. Finally, the welfare losses generated by such regimes are analogous to those associated with restrictions on temporal trade in goods and services.

This last point is an important result. In an intertemporal maximizing model with flexible prices, goods available to households at different points of time are analogous to different goods available at a point in time. Just as distortions of relative prices at a point in time are usually welfare-reducing, distortions of relative prices of the same good at different points of time—where the relative price is an interest rate—are also usually welfare-reducing. Optimal capital control programs in such models are possible only in cases where there is some pre-existing distortion to interest rates or if private expectations are systematically incorrect.

Greenwood and Kimbrough (1985) present a model that allows an evaluation of the effects of capital controls in a world where identical households maximize intertemporal utility with perfect foresight and monetary policy has no effects (the monetary sector is not explicitly modeled). In this model, the role of capital controls in limiting the public's ability to trade intertemporally is highlighted.

An interesting feature of the model is that in the absence of capital controls, fiscal deficits have no effect on the equilibrium because households anticipate future tax liabilities. But with capital controls, sales of government debt to the rest of the world are equivalent to a relaxation of the government's prohibition of private capital flows. Moreover, since the public regards the government's debt as equivalent to their own, the government is a perfect financial intermediary.

The model also clarifies the likely co-movement of real macroeconomic aggregates with and without capital controls. If capital markets are integrated, real interest rates must move together across countries in response to a shock to the system, and, in general, real output across countries will also be positively correlated. Capital controls imply that real interest rates can be negatively correlated, and, in turn, output and other aggregates might be negatively correlated. The model suggests that capital controls provide a measure of insulation from foreign fiscal shocks.

Guidotti and Végh (1992) present a model of a large open economy that adds a monetary sector to the model discussed above. They start from the proposition that with prefect capital mobility, domestic disturbances have no real effects. In part this is due to the result that the world money supply is immediately redistributed through international capital flows following a disturbance. With capital controls, money holdings can be redistributed only as the mirror image of current account imbalances. The real effects of these imbalances are felt at home and in the rest of the world. Moreover, important variables such as real interest rates, relative prices, and consumption are affected. Their model suggests that unanticipated and permanent changes in domestic monetary and fiscal policies affect consumption, real interest rates, and the real exchange rates.

Stabilization of Relative Prices

The effects of capital flows on relative prices or real exchange rates has been at the center of much of the literature concerning the economic effects of capital mobility. A stylized fact associated with liberalization of controls over capital flows among developing countries is that the resulting adjustment includes substantial appreciation of the real exchange rate. This, in turn, may be an undesirable feature of an open capital market if temporary relative price changes and associated allocations of productive resources are welfare-reducing. Krugman (1987), for example, argues that temporary real appreciation of the exchange rate might permanently injure export industries if hysteresis is a feature of the correct dynamic model of the economy.

Several authors have suggested that capital mobility should be limited until policies designed to offset the real exchange rate changes are in place. The obvious choice to combat the effects of a capital inflow, for example, would be a reduction in government spending. In this section, it is argued that the welfare implications of these models are far from clear. Moreover, formal explanations of a relationship between capital market liberalization and real exchange rate instability can be generated by very different models.

In the spirit of the sticky price framework, a way to understand a link between liberalization and real exchange rate appreciation is to appeal to a model in which nominal shocks generate overshooting of nominal exchange rates and therefore changes in real exchange rates. Sussman (1992) uses a version of the Dornbusch overshooting model to help explain an apparently unsuccessful liberalization of the capital account in Israel in 1977. Liberalization of the capital account in this model takes the form of eliminating controls that had supported a tax on domestic asset yields and domestic bank loans. Sussman presents evidence that controls in place generated large differentials between onshore and offshore lending and deposit rates in Israel before and after the brief experiment with liberalization.

The model predicts that the reduction in the tax on loans increases investment and aggregate demand and, according to the model, creates an inflationary shock to the system. In addition, the elimination of the tax on domestic assets generates a decline in the demand for money. Since this is equivalent to an increase in the money supply, the model predicts that the domestic nominal interest rate will at first fall, prices will start to rise, and to satisfy the rational expectations interest parity condition, the nominal exchange rate will depreciate by more than the steady-state amount.

The lesson from this model is that the liberalization itself generates an inflationary shock for the economy and a temporary distortion of the prices of traded and nontraded goods. Clearly, an appropriate fiscal policy response could minimize the damage. But if the fiscal system is unable to respond, perhaps because the elimination of the subsidy for government borrowing makes a contractionary fiscal shock impossible, the liberalization will involve short-run costs.

A very different way to introduce real exchange rates into a model is to assume that prices are flexible but to introduce more than one good. Van Wijnbergen (1990) develops a model in which the imposition of a tax on capital imports lowers domestic real interest rates and raises world real interest rates. In turn, current consumption is shifted from goods consumed by residents toward goods favored by nonresidents today, with a reversal of this shift in the future. The change in the composition of current and future demands in turn generates a depreciation of the home currency now and an expected appreciation later.

A useful framework developed by Edwards (1989) considers an export good, an import good, and a nontraded good. The relative price of exports and imports is the terms of trade. The relative price of exports and nontraded goods is usually identified as the real exchange rate. In such a model, capital flows related to liberalization of the capital account can generate real exchange rate changes since excess demand for the nontraded good can increase its nominal price while the price of the traded good is determined in world markets.

Edwards and Ostry (1992) present a model in which endogenous changes in relative prices of traded and nontraded goods interact with capital controls to affect welfare. The basic idea exploited in these models is that distortions in relative prices that are expected to change over time due to temporary policies generate distortions in the consumption rate of interest faced by households. The resulting intertemporal distortion of consumption can be magnified or mitigated by capital controls.

The specific analysis of individual shocks to the system appears to be quite model specific, but the general point is important. Anticipated changes in relative prices alter the "interest rate" relevant for intertemporal consumption and investment decisions. Capital controls also alter intertemporal consumption and sectoral investment decisions. The main message here seems to be that real exchange rate changes associated with shocks to the system (for example, terms-of-trade shocks) might be an important part of a comprehensive evaluation of the effects of capital controls.

This idea is developed further by the introduction of a temporary or variable labor market distortion in the form of a minimum real wage. This distortion generates a variable and suboptimal level of employment. Depending on a number of factors, a subsidy to foreign borrowing (or tax on foreign lending) could tilt demand toward periods during which unemployment is relatively high and, in turn, improve welfare.

This model is interesting because it abstracts entirely from monetary phenomena yet still manages to find a second-best role for capital controls in promoting employment. The lesson, however, is that the level of ingenuity to which the modelers have to resort to create an intertemporal distortion to consumption and employment that can be offset by another intertemporal distortion, capital controls, seems to make the practical importance of the argument remote.

Another potential source of distortions of relative prices is temporary policy reforms, or permanent policy reforms that are expected to be temporary. Calvo (1988) argues that capital movements might magnify the distortion generated by temporary, changing, relative prices generated by changes in commercial policies.

Models of Partial Effectiveness

The idea that capital controls have important economic effects because they move adjustment into the international markets for goods and services has led many authors to consider mixed systems in which controls on capital movements are only partially effective. The intuition is that distorting intertemporal trade and consumption is costly to the private sector, and so it is worthwhile to invest in techniques to avoid controls. It follows that the decision of how to model a capital control regime is an important issue in itself.

At one end of the spectrum are models that assume complete effectiveness. In these models, there is no arbitrage of international interest differentials. In dual exchange rate models, for example, the spread between the commercial exchange rate and the financial exchange rate adjusts to equalize expected yields on domestic and foreign bonds. It is easy to show that the assumption of complete separation of the commercial and financial exchange rate markets is exactly equivalent to an effective prohibition of all net capital market transactions or an interest equalization tax that results in zero net trade.

Such models have been criticized on the grounds that real-world controls are never completely effective. An alternative specification is that controls are effective but can be avoided at a cost. This model is appealing because it seems to explain the empirical finding that the ability of controls to force a wedge between expected yields on securities issued in different countries seems to erode over time.

Bhandari and Decaluwe (1987) and Gros (1987, 1988) have emphasized the endogenous response of speculators to the incentive to avoid exchange controls. Gros (1988) assumes an increasing one-time cost faced by an investor who wishes to acquire foreign assets or liabilities. This model has the property that the long-run interest differential will be zero, but during an adjustment period, relative interest rates can be influenced by policy.

Giavazzi and Giovannini (1989) develop a model in which private-sector traders are permitted to acquire a stock of foreign financial assets or liabilities equal to some fraction of the annual flow of their gross exports or imports of goods. Such positions are often referred to as leads and lags and are typically exempt from capital control programs. The idea here is that controls are effective but allow traders to utilize traditional forms of trade finance as long as the size of such transactions and their term to maturity conform to the usual parameters.

They show that in a maximizing model, such controls distort intertemporal trading patterns and have long-run effects on the economy. The cost of avoiding capital controls in this model is related to the cost of switching domestic production to export markets beyond what would be the competitive equilibrium.

The effectiveness of controls and the possible real distortions to trading patterns generated by avoidance are of considerable practical importance in any decision to impose, modify, or remove a control regime. Indeed, the formal models of the economic effects of capital controls developed above are of little relevance if the private sector easily avoids such restrictions on its financial transactions. This is essentially an empirical question that is taken up below.

Medium-Term Second-Best Arguments

Fiscal Implications of Capital Controls

This section departs from questions of short-run stabilization and focuses on interaction between capital controls and a variety of distortions that might justify such policies. The first example is motivated by the observation that controls over capital outflows are frequently designed to prevent erosion of the tax base for financial repression and inflation. Empirical evidence seems to support the view that governments that employ capital controls have higher rates of inflation, higher revenue from inflation, and lower domestic real interest rates as compared with countries that do not employ controls. If controls are effective in maintaining a tax base, their removal implies a reduction in government revenue and therefore a presumably costly change in another variable that influences the fiscal deficit.

Giovannini and de Melo (1993) argue that the benefits from financial liberalization emphasized by McKinnon (1973) should be compared with the potential costs in terms of tightening government revenue constraints. They provide a direct ex post measure of the differential borrowing costs on domestic and international debt of developing countries. The data support the view that financial repression is a significant source of revenue for many of these countries.

Dornbusch (1988) offers a model in which the government faces two fiscal problems that explain the widespread use of capital controls. First, the government's existing domestic debt service is kept below what would be charged on world capital markets by restricting private capital outflows and thus depressing the domestic real interest rate. Second, in the absence of the implicit subsidy generated by controls over capital outflows, the government would be forced to choose revenue from inflation as the best alternative for meeting higher real debt service costs. Similar results are derived from an overlapping generations model developed by Sussman (1991).

Aizenman and Guidotti (1994) argue that collection costs associated with taxes other than the inflation tax might make capital controls a part of an optimal tax system. The model assumes that the government must service a domestic debt and must use a domestic tax on output that involves increasing costs of collection. The capital control they have in mind is a tax on foreign capital income, and they assume the tax is not avoided. An interesting feature of the model is that the tax base for the foreign income tax is not only the private sector's stock of foreign assets but also the entire domestic debt. The domestic debt is relevant because the tax on foreign income drives a wedge between the foreign interest rate and the domestic interest rate. This, they argue, is equivalent to taxing private holdings of government debt, but unlike other taxes, this one involves no collection costs. They show that countries with large stocks of domestic debt tend to utilize capital controls.

Drazen (1989) shows that the inflation tax is an important source of revenue for several European countries. He also shows that high inflation rates are only part of the story since these countries also have unusually high inflation tax bases in the form of bank reserve ratios. If residents of these countries could freely utilize offshore financial intermediaries, this tax base would erode. It follows that capital controls are an important part of a fiscal system that relies heavily on the inflation tax. Drazen also argues that while such a system might allow the government to avoid even more distorting taxes in the short run, taxing savings and investment will generally lead to slower growth and reduced government revenues in the long run.

Brock (1984) provides an interesting counterargument. He points out that while opening the capital account can generate a decline in the inflation tax base, the government can offset this effect through reserve requirements on capital inflows or through prior import deposit schemes. This is an interesting argument because it suggests that a government with a fiscal problem can open the capital account and minimize the associated loss of revenue from inflation by expanding the inflation tax base.

This is one of the arguments for capital controls that seems quite sensitive to the assumption that the existing shortcomings in the tax system are unrelated to the existence of the controls. In particular, it seems quite likely that a government that imposes controls over capital outflows for some other reason will be tempted to exploit the revenue from financial repression that the controls make possible.

Taxation of Resident Capital Income

Another longer-run feature of some capital control programs is that they are designed to limit secular private capital outflows. It is often argued that countries with relatively low capital–labor ratios (developing countries and countries in transition) should offset a variety of domestic distortions that induce private investors to prefer foreign investments even when the expected private yields on domestic investment exceed the private expected return in world capital markets. There are alleged to be many such distortions.

An obvious potential distortion is taxation or expected taxation of capital income generated within the country while foreign-based capital income cannot be taxed. If capital is mobile, such an optimal tax generates private capital outflows and a deterioration of the tax base, and underinvestment in the domestic capital stock. A limit to capital outflows, or the equivalent interest equalization tax, allows the government to tax capital at the appropriate, second-best, rate.

Razin and Sadka (1991) argue that empirical estimates of capital flight from developing countries suggest that governments cannot tax residents' income from foreign capital at the same rate at which they tax domestic capital income. In their model, it is optimal for the government to restrict capital outflows if it cannot tax foreign assets. Dooley and Kletzer (1994) argue that simultaneous gross capital inflows and outflows are frequently the response of private investors to a variety of government guarantees and subsidies. If it is not possible for the government to credibly refuse to grant subsidies and guarantees, quantitative restrictions on some capital inflows and outflows can be welfare-improving.

Several papers written after the 1982 debt crisis take up the general issue of the optimality of external debt in the face of country risk. Since individual debtors within a country are interdependent in their ability to make debt service payments, and the government can prevent private debtors from making debt service payments, it might be that some collective (government) tax or subsidy to external borrowing is appropriate.

Harberger (1986) presents a model in which country risk generates a risk premium that grows with a country's external debt. This raises the possibility that the marginal cost of additional debt might exceed the average cost and that individual debtors may not internalize the social cost of their borrowing decisions. An important assumption in this model is that default carries costs to the debtor that are not at the same time benefits to the lenders. Under these plausible circumstances, a tax on capital inflows would be optimal.

Aizenman (1990) develops a model in which different attitudes toward default between the debtor country government and the debtor country private sector generate a distortion for domestic capital formation. In this case, it is assumed that the government is known to discount the future at a higher rate as compared with households. This reflects the appealing idea that elected governments may be too interested in the next election. In this environment, domestic investment will be suboptimal since the government will discount the penalties associated with future default too heavily. The result is that private returns will exceed the world rate of interest by a political risk premium. In this environment, the government should subsidize investments in traded goods industries since this increases the vulnerability of the country to penalties for default and therefore increases the credibility of the government's promise not to default.

A somewhat different argument is advanced by Dellas and Galor (1992). In this paper, households located in a number of small open economies make saving and investment decisions that generate a stable but low steady-state level of income and welfare. There is no incentive for capital flows among these economies since the return on capital is the same. A government that can accomplish transfers across generations can engage in external borrowing that can move the economy to another stable growth equilibrium and, through appropriate transfers, increase welfare in all generations. As a part of the external borrowing program, it is also necessary that offsetting private capital outflows be limited through a capital control program. The intuition behind this argument is appealing. Since investment in growth benefits future generations, the present generation might invest at a suboptimal rate. If a government has the tools and wisdom, it might be possible that a superior equilibrium can be attained if the government borrows on international capital markets. During the transition, it is necessary to prevent private capital outflows that the current generation will find optimal.

Uncertain Property Rights

Another argument develops the idea that property rights are often poorly defined in developing countries, and perhaps even more so in formerly planned economies undergoing massive privatization programs. In effect, this allows interest groups of private residents to tax or appropriate the capital income of both resident and nonresident investors. In contrast, investments abroad by residents of these countries are difficult for other residents to detect and appropriate. This leads to overinvestment in the foreign capital stock in order to avoid the political risk associated with investment in a poorly organized country. In such an environment, capital controls might be optimal.

Tornell and Velasco (1992) develop a formal model in which poorly defined property rights imply that investors will prefer external investment even if domestic investments have a higher social but lower private expected return. This model also demonstrates the less obvious point that capital controls may not improve welfare even if capital outflows are reduced. The reason is that the threat of free capital mobility might reduce the amount of appropriation by interest groups.

This is a subtle and important point for all second-best arguments. In a complete model, it is not enough to show that a capital control can offset another distortion. It must also be shown that the existence of controls does not generate even more of the initial distortion. In the Tornell and Velasco model, it is natural to consider the endogenous response to the capital controls because it involves the behavior of private interest groups that must worry about reactions to their behavior. In the more common case in which the government introduces the initial distortion "for a good reason," it is difficult or impossible to evaluate the possibility that the government will be tempted to exacerbate the initial distortion.

Alesina and Tabellini (1989) provide a model in which the initial distortion is the result of behavior of the government. In this model, an alternating sequence of political parties, one representing labor and the other capital, appropriates capital income or labor income in order to make transfers to their constituency, depending on the random outcome of elections. Since neither party can precommit to refrain from appropriation of income, capital controls will be necessary to prevent underinvestment in domestic capital.

This model also explains private capital flight in periods when the government is borrowing on international capital markets. The model assumes that the government borrows a fixed amount per period. In the absence of capital controls, residents, in turn, export capital in an effort to avoid taxation in the event their party is forced from office. This is one of the very few formal models that explain simultaneous private capital outflows and government borrowing.

The interesting feature of such a model is that the change in the private sector's foreign assets is not constrained by the current account imbalance. In fact, the private sector is constrained only by the government's willingness and ability to borrow.

Capital Markets as a Source of Uncertainty

This class of models posits the existence of private investors that are motivated by rumors, noise trading, bandwagons, bubbles, and so forth. In a way, these are the most straightforward arguments in favor of capital controls. In this case, the capital flow is itself the source of the disturbance to the competitive equilibrium. It follows that controlling these kinds of capital flows restores a first-best competitive equilibrium. The difficulty, of course, is to discriminate in the capital control program between stabilizing and destabilizing capital flows.

One of the oldest traditions in international finance is that just such a distinction is possible. The assertion is that short-term capital flows—or more precisely, capital flows with short holding periods—are distortions, while long-term capital flows and direct investment are based on fundamentals. Keynes, for example, made the distinction between enterprise and speculation. If distorting capital flows are associated with short holding periods, it follows that a transactions tax will discourage distorting capital flows.

Tobin (1978) proposed such a tax, and Eichengreen, Tobin, and Wyplosz (1995) update the argument. The basic idea is that adjustment in international goods and labor markets is slow and restricted, and "when some markets adjust imperfectly, welfare can be enhanced by intervening in the adjustment of others" (Eichengreen, Tobin, and Wyplosz 1995, 164). An important aspect of the argument that distinguishes this from the other distortions reviewed above is that a turnover tax is designed to slow the adjustment speed of capital flows and the exchange rate, but not to distort the stock of net flows or the level of the exchange rate over the long run. The authors recognize that a transactions tax on foreign exchange trading would have to be universal but argue that an international organization such as the International Monetary Fund (IMF) could take on such a task. Eichengreen, Tobin, and Wyplosz also advance a quite different argument in favor of temporary taxes on banks' foreign lending, based on a model of self-fulfilling speculative attacks. This argument is taken up below.

In commenting on this paper, Garber and Taylor (1995) review familiar arguments concerning the difficulty in administering such a tax and add the idea that taxing transfers of bank deposits would be ineffective since swaps of securities and other "synthetic" transactions are now very well-developed components of international transactions.

Dornbusch (1986) emphasizes the important point that controls designed to slow down capital flow—in this paper, dual exchange markets—can only be used as a "strictly transitory policy" to offset shocks to capital markets. The model developed by Dornbusch restates the familiar theme that in the long run, a control program that attempts to mask an inconsistent policy regime will generate increasing distortions and ultimately fail to preserve the regime. In cases where deviations between controlled and financial exchange rates have become large, the "resource allocation costs outweigh any macroeconomic benefits" (Dornbusch 1986, 22). This is partly due to the realistic assumption that large differentials generate leakages of some commercial transactions to the free market. The political economy question is whether controls put in place to shield the real economy from financial shocks are likely to eventually generate misalignment in levels of exchange rates and interest rates that are politically difficult to correct.

Van Wijnbergen (1985) provides a more explicit link between variability of government policies and less than optimal domestic investment. The unnecessary variance causes underinvestment because investors will value the option of waiting until the uncertainty is resolved. Tornell (1990) develops a model in which the increased variance resulting from private capital transactions results in less than optimal real investment because investors value the option to wait till more settled times before making irreversible real investments in a country. Finally, Aizenman and Marion (1993) provide some evidence that uncertainty has a measurable negative effect on capital formation in developing countries.

Domestic Capital Market Distortions

In the absence of a formal model involving capital controls, an often discussed distortion in both domestic and international financial markets arises from government insurance of the liabilities of domestic financial intermediaries. The most obvious example of this is deposit insurance for banks, but even in the absence of formal insurance, governments frequently intervene to protect creditors of institutions that are believed to be "too large to fail." The usual reason for such intervention is to prevent contagion of doubts about the solvency of large institutions from generating runs on solvent institutions and associated general declines in asset values.

The well-known problem with this policy is that it encourages financial institutions to reach for risk. The argument is simply that profits from favorable outcomes are paid out to owners of the institution, while losses are shared with the government. The usual prudential regulations designed to limit the government's exposure to losses include requirements that the institution maintain adequate capital—that is, that current accounting profits are not immediately paid to equity holders—and various restrictions on the nature and concentration of assets held.

There is nothing unique about international capital flows in this context except that new types of assets, and therefore new types of risks, are opened to insured intermediaries when they are given access to international capital transactions. Mathieson and Rojas-Suárez (1993, 31) argue that opening markets can generate important efficiency gains but that "potential official credit risks stemming from institutional failures that can be created by the mispricing of risk [or] widespread fraud" provide a strong case for improving the domestic system of prudential supervision. Dooley (1995) argues that commercial banks in the United States acquired claims on individual developing countries in the 1970s that exceeded the concentration ratios that were enforced for domestic lending. The problem was that regulators did not enforce country lending limits, a decision that was justified by the erroneous view that loans to many entities within a country provided a diversified portfolio. Kane (1995) argues that the unwillingness of the authorities to force a write-down of debt following the 1982 debt crisis validated the assumption that the government would provide "free" equity to insured institutions in the event of a bad outcome for their investments.

Akerlof and Romer (1993) argue that exchange risk provides a vehicle for banks to exploit government insurance in developing countries. Using Chile during the 1979–1981 period as a possible example, they argue that the expectation the peso might be devalued led domestic firms and domestic banks to enter into dollar-denominated loans at interest rates that did not fully reflect the risk that the firms would be unable to repay the dollar liability in the event of a devaluation of the currency.

Sequencing of Liberalization of Capital Markets and Trade in Goods and Services

Governments considering liberalization of their capital markets are frequently also considering liberalization of trade in goods and services. This raises the possibility that it might be optimal to sequence the liberalization rather than liberalize all markets simultaneously. This is a difficult area for formal modeling because it requires an explicit dynamic framework. The literature surveyed above focused on several possible sources of expected relative price changes associated with structural reform that might influence intertemporal choices of residents of a country undergoing a reform program. Opening the capital account might either mitigate or magnify the distortion inherent in such anticipated relative price changes.

The distortions that have attracted attention in the context of structural reform include real exchange rate changes associated with liberalization of trade restrictions, slow adjustment of labor markets to changes in relative prices of traded and nontraded goods, and, finally, expected relative price changes generated by reforms that are expected to be temporary.

As argued above, distortions in relative prices due to trade restrictions can generate a role for capital controls under some circumstances. But the sequencing issue is much more complicated. First, there is no very clear reason for the government to have to choose to liberalize one market at a time or to liberalize markets slowly. It is possible that it will take some time to dismantle trade restrictions, perhaps because of administrative problems or because the government wishes to spread out the impact on protected sectors over time. Similar reasoning might also apply to capital markets. If such constraints are taken as given, it is then possible to evaluate the sequencing problem. It should be recalled, however, that the formal models do not provide a rationale for gradual decontrol.

An early argument along these lines is found in McKinnon (1973). Relaxation of trade restrictions would, other things being equal, generate a depreciation of the real exchange rate while relaxation of the capital account is assumed to call for an appreciation of the real exchange rate, given that capital controls had effectively limited desired inflows of capital. This "competition of instruments" problem is resolved by delaying liberalization of the capital account until trade and other distortions are eliminated.

Edwards and van Wijnbergen (1986) develop two ideas that are useful in this area. First, they show in a static model that capital account liberalization in the face of trade distortions can be welfare-reducing. The intuition is that tariffs can distort investment decisions, and capital controls can, in principle, offset this distortion. They also develop a two-period model in which capital inflows are constrained. In this case, gradual liberalization of the trade account generates expected changes in relative prices that can distort investment decisions.

Calvo (1988) develops the idea that any government policy that affects relative prices, and is expected to be temporary, is equivalent to a distortion of intertemporal relative prices. For example, temporary tariff reform implies that the relative prices of traded goods will change when the liberalization program is abandoned. In general, it follows that liberalization of the capital account is not a good idea in cases in which the government really has reformed but the private sector does not find the commitment credible.

Edwards (1988) provides an excellent summary of this literature and a model that attempts to pull together a number of distortions in order to provide some guidance for policy. Not surprisingly, when working with multiple initial distortions, it is difficult to evaluate the welfare implications of alternative sequences of reform. Indeed, an important implication of the model is that the first-best solution is to liberalize all markets immediately.

Quirk (1994) argues that experience with developing countries indicates that simultaneous liberalization is both feasible and manageable given the right combination of other policies. The lesson, perhaps, is that the practical usefulness of the second-best argument is limited to those cases in which one preexisting distortion is clearly dominant and for some good reason can be removed only over time. For example, countries with a record of failed structural reforms might focus on the distortion caused by lack of credibility of their efforts and the time it will take to convince market participants that the reform is permanent.

Multiple Equilibria and First-Best Arguments

Self-fulfilling Speculative Attacks

Turmoil in the ERM that emerged in 1992, and that continues today, has generated a resurgence of interest in models of self-fulfilling speculative attacks. It has long been recognized that changes in the policy regime that are expected to prevail following a successful attack can generate a successful speculative attack even if the government follows fully consistent policies preceding the attack.

A more stringent condition for a self-fulfilling attack is that the change in the exchange rate regime itself generates a fundamental change in the optimal path for monetary policy. If the private sector expects a more expansionary monetary policy following a successful attack, it is possible that such expectations can generate a collapse of a system that is otherwise fully viable. Finally, a much more stringent condition is that a plausible model of the government's behavior implies that a change in policy following a successful attack is optimal given the change in the economic environment generated by the attack.

The lesson from these models is that the exchange rate regime is secondary to the monetary policy the government is expected to pursue, not just in the short run but over the indefinite future. If the speculative attack is interpreted by the private sector as a signal that the government will also abandon monetary restraint in the future, then, by the usual arguments, speculation in financial markets will result in capital movements today in anticipation of this perhaps distant event. It seems to follow that capital controls might significantly slow the onset of the attack. Moreover, an optimistic assessment of the potential role of capital controls might be that the conditions that generate the multiple equilibria will change. For example, the government might find a way to recommit to not altering its behavior following an attack.

It is ironic that the first clear statement of these issues was heavily conditioned by the warning that an announced commitment to a regime, in this model a commodity standard rather than an exchange rate standard, was unlikely to alter the private sector's expectations about monetary policy over the long run. Flood and Garber (1984, 105) are worth repeating at length:

> Behind the sequential transitions from one monetary regime to another . . . must lie a political economy that we have ignored. Such political economic forces determine the complete dynamic panorama of the monetary process. . . . A commodity system can be interpreted as a discipline imposing rule only if the commodity standard's permanence is somehow guaranteed. As there is no means to ensure such performance, the notion of a commodity standard as a stabilizing rule is a chimera.

Flood and Garber (1984) and Obstfeld (1986b) show that if governments are assumed to follow more expansionary monetary policies following a successful speculative attack on the fixed-exchange-rate regime, policy regimes that are otherwise viable can be forced to collapse by self-fulfilling private expectations. Obstfeld (1994b) refines the argument by specifying the political economy that might account for the government's behavior before and after an attack. The analysis sets out a rational government that seeks to maximize a plausible objective function. Since the government's objectives are the same in any exchange rate regime, it follows that policy setting under different regimes must reflect changes in the economic environment rather than arbitrary assumptions concerning the government's behavior.

Both models suggest that the source of self-fulfilling speculative attacks is multiple equilibria consistent with a given set of fundamentals. The first model develops the idea that private expectations concerning devaluation generate high domestic interest rates for long-maturity government bonds in the first period of a two-period model. High domestic interest rates generate a larger fiscal deficit carried into the second period. The government in the second period minimizes a loss function that balances a higher tax rate on income against a higher tax rate on money balances—that is, a higher rate of money creation and inflation. Given the large fiscal deficit, the government chooses to inflate, thereby validating the private sector's expectations. If the government could commit to a low rate of inflation, the nominal interest rate would fall in the first period, the fiscal deficit would fall, and the optimal inflation rate in the second period would be low, again validating private expectations. An interesting feature of this model is that the government could avoid the commitment problem by denominating all its debt in foreign currency.

A second model assumes that government values price stability and the ability to offset negative shocks to output. A sudden shift in expectations concerning the government's preferences for full employment can trigger an attack on a regime that is viable under different expectations. These models are interesting because the government's decision to abandon the peg is fully consistent with an objective function that is the same under both regimes. The only thing that changes over time is private expectations concerning the viability of the regime.

Eichengreen and Wyplosz (1993) and Portes (1993) argue that self-fulfilling models offer a reasonable interpretation of recent ERM crises. Their general point is that the ERM members that were forced to abandon their exchange rate commitments played by the rules of the game for a viable system as long as entry into a European monetary union was a feasible objective.

Eichengreen and Wyplosz argue that the benefits of membership in a European economic union made it rational for governments to pursue conservative monetary policies. An important condition for membership was the maintenance of a stable exchange rate for two years preceding membership. Thus, a successful attack made membership in the first round impossible and perhaps implied that future membership would be more costly to attain. Once this opportunity was removed by a successful speculative attack on the currency, it was then rational for the authorities to relax monetary policy. Thus, the speculative attack generated the subsequent government behavior that validated the attack.

To buttress this interpretation, Eichengreen, Rose, and Wyplosz (1994) offer empirical evidence that the fundamentals behaved differently in the months leading up to the ERM crisis as compared with a sample of crises in other fixed-exchange-rate regimes. In particular, they argue that the ERM crisis was not preceded by excessive money growth, growth in domestic assets, fiscal deficits, or a number of other variables usually associated with inconsistent policies.

A weakness in their interpretation of the evidence, as the authors acknowledge, is that a variety of factors might rationally lead to an expected change in the government's behavior but leave no evidence leading up to the attack. In particular, they consider, but are not persuaded by, the possibility that rising unemployment associated with tight monetary policy in Germany might have generated expectations that monetary policy in other countries would be eased in the future as the political cost of unemployment accumulated.

The role of capital controls in preventing self-fulfilling speculative attacks seems obvious. It is plausible that effective controls would delay the end of a regime that suffered a spontaneous change in private expectations. If the regime remained vulnerable through current account transactions, the extended life for the good equilibrium made possible by capital controls would presumably be desirable. This assumption is reinforced if it is assumed that the ultimate destination for the regime is a credible common currency.

Nevertheless, the contrary argument is equally plausible. If the private sector knows that the system is protected by controls, it would be less impressed by observed stability. Lane and Rojas-Suárez (1992), for example, argue that the use of controls has ambiguous implications for the credibility of a monetary policy regime.

The role of capital controls is also problematic because self-fulfilling attacks can go the opposite direction. For example, a spontaneous decline in private inflationary expectations could set in motion a sequence of falling interest rates and fiscal deficits that generate a good equilibrium. It is perhaps informative that there seem to be few examples of changes in private expectations generating self-fulfilling virtuous responses by governments. Countries that start from a bad equilibrium should shun capital controls since they would delay adjustment to the new, more optimistic private expectations.

A number of papers have exploited the idea that controls themselves might be powerful signals concerning the government's future policies. Dellas and Stockman (1993) show that a speculative attack might be generated by the expectation that capital controls will be introduced. If the government can commit not to introduce controls, the fixed-rate regime is sustainable. In this model, a regime that is otherwise viable becomes vulnerable to expectations that controls will be imposed in response to the attack. This increases interest rates before the attack and generates the conditions for a self-fulfilling devaluation.

Laban and Larrain (1993) argue that removing controls on capital outflows generates capital inflows because controls on outflows make investment irreversible. Thus, by altering expectations concerning the terms on which investments can be reversed, the decontrol of capital flows helps generate welfare-increasing capital inflows.

Bartolini and Drazen (1994) develop the idea that controls themselves are a signal that affects private-sector expectations concerning the government's future treatment of investors. In their model, the removal of controls signals to investors that the government is less likely to tax foreign capital income or reimpose controls once the capital inflow is in place.

Finally, Obstfeld (1986a) shows that capital controls can generate multiple equilibria where none exist with capital mobility. In this model, multiple equilibria are a feature of a maximizing model with effective capital controls. Residents of the controlled economy maximize the utility of real money holdings and consumption over time, subject to their balance sheet constraint. Owing to effective capital controls, residents can accumulate real money balances only through current account surpluses, which have as a mirror image increases in the central bank's net foreign assets. Because the net foreign asset position of the central bank earns the world interest rate, a current account surplus generates an increase in the expected permanent income of residents. An unstable equilibrium occurs if the increase in real money balances, and the associated increase in expected income, is not more than matched with an increase in current consumption. If not, the current account surplus increases and money balances and income continue to rise until a stable equilibrium is reached. This is not an argument for or against capital controls. It only demonstrates that when the domestic interest rate is distorted through a capital control program, the usual assumptions that generate convergence to a unique steady-state equilibrium are not sufficient.

This literature presents a genuine problem for the policy implications of capital controls. On the one hand, an effective capital control program might buy enough time for the government to move the fundamentals to a region where self-fulfilling speculative attacks are less likely. The implication seems to be that controls might be a temporary measure to buy time for a virtuous government to establish its reputation. On the other hand, it is easy to show that the fact that controls might be introduced in the future can generate attacks where none would be observed otherwise. Finally, the removal of controls on capital outflows might be interpreted by the market as a commitment not to pernalize foreign investors and therefore generate capital inflows.

A practical implication of this type of model is that the government probably must be prepared to maintain its fundamental policy stance, even if it is temporarily forced to abandon the exchange rate peg. This may involve significant short-run costs in terms of employment or distorting taxes necessary to finance debt service payments on domestic debt. Unfortunately, the role of capital controls in reducing the costs of maintaining the fundamentals is much less clear. On the surface, it appears that controls might delay or even prevent a speculative attack and the associated costs. But the typical policy of imposing controls as the attack occurs, probably because the authorities believe that the controls are not effective for long, can also be a powerful force to trigger speculative attacks. Finally, a careful treatment of expectations can suggest that policies designed to limit net capital inflows might have just the opposite effect.

Evidence on Effectiveness and Objectives of Controls

Empirical work on the effectiveness of capital controls has suffered from the lack of a widely accepted definition of what constitutes an effective control program. At one end of the spectrum, evidence of effectiveness has been defined as the ability to detect over extended periods different average behavior of selected economic variables for countries with and without capital control programs. At the other extreme, effectiveness has been defined as the ability to maintain an inconsistent macroeconomic policy regime forever.

For this reason, observers have examined the same or similar data sets and reached very different qualitative conclusions concerning the effectiveness of controls. Those who see controls as a short-term device to allow the government time to react and adjust other policy tools generally argue that controls can be effective. Those who study the collapse of regimes and observe that these events are often preceded by the imposition of controls argue that controls are not effective.

The reading here of the extensive empirical literature for the industrial and developing countries is that it generally supports the conclusion that governments can drive a small wedge between domestic and international yields on similar short-term financial instruments for extended periods. This is similar to the conclusions of recent surveys by Epstein and Schor (1992) and Obstfeld (1995a). Thus, capital control programs have had measurable effects on economic variables. Control programs have also generated large yield differentials for a few weeks or months, but these seem to diminish over time as the private sector invests in techniques to avoid the controls.

The more important issue is whether these yield differentials are large enough and last long enough to enhance the effectiveness of a policy regime in attaining the government's economic objectives. Unfortunately, effectiveness in this sense cannot be evaluated without a structural model of what the government is trying to accomplish and the economic constraints it faces.

Perhaps the most direct evidence for the effects of a control program in the very limited sense described above is the spread between the commercial and financial spot exchange rates in dual exchange rate systems. Gros (1988) reports the spread for the Belgian franc over the 1979–1987 period and the Mexican peso over 1982–1986. His interpretation of both these data sets is that the authorities were able to sustain a sizable differential for about one year before the private sector found ways to avoid the controls.

Cairncross (1973) provides data for the United Kingdom investment currency market during 1961–1972. These data indicate that the control system was effective in the narrow sense in that the investment currency premium remained in excess of 20 percent for several years and at times reached nearly 50 percent. Nevertheless, Cairncross finds little evidence that the intended restriction on private capital outflows was effective. Cairncross and others also looked for evidence that controls instituted by the United States to control private direct investment and portfolio capital outflows resulted in lower private capital flows but were unable to find such evidence. For these episodes, the fact that alternative forms of capital flows were not controlled seemed to render the controls ineffective.

For currencies with extensive offshore markets for bank deposits, another simple and informative test of the effects of controls is a comparison of returns on domestic bank deposits and similar deposits offered by offshore branches of the same or very similar banks. An early attempt to measure the effectiveness of controls using these data is reported in Dooley and Isard (1980). This paper presents a model in which onshore and offshore interest rates on bank deposits denominated in the same currency are related to the extensive capital controls program introduced by the German government over the 1970–1974 period and to the risk that such controls might be intensified. A problem for tests of the effectiveness of control programs is that they are complicated legal programs that are difficult to quantify. In this paper, the controls are quantified according to a qualitative evaluation of the size of penalties or taxes on individual types of transactions, as well as the extensiveness of the controls in terms of the types of transactions subject to control. The data suggest that the authorities managed to generate a 4-percentage-point differential for a brief time, during which virtually all private capital inflows were prohibited.

In this respect, the controls had clearly measurable effects. Nevertheless, a speculative attack on the currency generated a very large—by 1970s standards—increase in Germany's international reserves and the fixed exchange rate was abandoned. As the models reviewed above suggest, the control program does appear to have slowed down the demise of the system but could not preserve the par value system.

Gros (1987) reports spreads between Euro and domestic deposits for Italy and France during 1979–1986. He interprets these differentials, which were for short periods as high as 20–24 percentage points, as consistent with his model that predicts that controls are temporarily effective in restraining large changes in investors' positions. That is, during times of turbulence in the ERM, private speculators were not able to adjust their open positions costlessly. Nevertheless, over longer horizons, the interest differentials rapidly returned to very low levels.

Similar evidence for five industrial countries during 1982–1992 is reported in Obstfeld (1995a). He concludes that for industrial countries, the links between onshore and offshore markets are very close but "the data also show that actual or prospective government interventions remain a significant factor in times of turbulence" (Obstfeld 1995a, 17). The data decisively reject the view that capital controls are always ineffective. But the data also suggest that either the governments involved quickly removed the incentives for speculation, through policy changes, or that speculators simply retreated to await another attack.

Chinn and Frankel (1994) report covered differentials for a group of developing countries in Asia. They find that these markets are not as integrated as those of the industrial countries but that during the 1980s, covered differentials seem to have narrowed even though capital controls were generally utilized by the countries studied.

Melvin and Schlagenhauf (1985) extend this approach by explicitly modeling the threat of controls or government-enforced default in addition to controls already in place. They find that for Mexico in the early 1980s, controls had a significant effect on capital flows. In considering the same episode, Spiegel (1990) also finds that political risk was important but estimates it to have the opposite sign of that reported in Melvin and Schlagenhauf. Both papers indicate that the controls in place were effective.

Browne and McNelis (1990) provide a careful study of the imposition of controls over capital flows in Ireland during 1979–1986. Forward exchange rates are available for this data set, and the study is unusual in that it considers a number of domestic and international interest rates. The relative importance of domestic monetary conditions and the yield on similar U.K. instruments are compared before and after the imposition of controls in December 1978.

Their results suggest that there was a jump in the importance of domestic monetary factors in determining some interest rates in Ireland immediately after controls were imposed. However, as with the other studies, the effects of monetary conditions were short-lived, on average only about six months. The usual story emerges that the central bank gained some independence for a short time.

The evidence also suggests that interest rates in domestic financial markets that are poorly integrated with other domestic markets are much more sensitive to domestic money shocks than are bank deposit markets. For example, Browne and McNelis find that changes in domestic monetary conditions had no impact on yields on bank deposits. Yet they find significant influence for domestic conditions on rates of return in relatively noncompetitive domestic loan and mortgage markets.

Fieleke (1994) compares short-term Euro interest rates with similar domestic interest rates for Spain, Ireland, and Portugal during the 1992 ERM crisis. In each case, the authorities enforced controls on capital outflows as part of a defense of the exchange rate arrangement. Although the controls did result in measurable deviations between onshore and offshore interest rates, in the end controls did not prevent a change in the exchange rate.

Fieleke also points out that ERM members that did not utilize controls, Norway and Sweden, experienced much larger fluctuations in domestic interest rates in trying to maintain their exchange rate targets. He concludes, "It may be that Spain and Portugal did acquire some temporary insulation" (Fieleke 1994, 34).

Fieleke offers an interesting alternative test of the expected efficacy of controls by comparing the prices of equities for traded and nontraded goods industries leading up to the exchange rate crisis. If controls are expected to fail in the sense that there is no change in the probability of devaluation, the market value of nontraded goods industries should not rise following an unexpected imposition of controls. Data for Portugal during 1992 and 1993 offer conflicting evidence. The value of nontraded goods equities did rise relative to export-oriented industries but declined relative to import-competing industries. The short sample period and difficulty in identifying the orientation of firms cloud the results.

Eichengreen, Rose, and Wyplosz (1994) challenge this interpretation of the ERM experience. They make the point that focusing on actual devaluations biases the sample toward episodes in which capital control programs have failed. To overcome this, they examine the behavior of a number of economic variables during crisis and noncrisis periods to see if there are systematic differences in the experience of countries with controls as compared with countries without controls. This, they argue, is a more useful measure of the effectiveness of controls. During crisis periods, countries with controls experienced higher inflation, higher rates of money growth, and higher growth of domestic assets. Controls did not seem to affect the loss of reserves, interest rate differentials, or fiscal imbalances. During noncrisis periods, controls appear to affect all the macroeconomic variables tested except reserves.

Their conclusion is quite consistent with the literature surveyed above:

> Controls do not allow countries which pursue policies inconsistent with a peg to keep their exchange rate unchanged forever. They do not prevent attacks, nor do they permit countries to avoid reserve losses or interest rate increases when attacks occur. Controls merely render expansionary monetary policies viable for a longer period by attenuating the link between crises and exchange rate regime collapse (Eichengreen, Rose, and Wyplosz 1994, 8).

An important limitation of this methodology is that well-developed forward exchange markets or offshore deposit markets are needed to control for expected exchange rate changes. For many markets where liberalization is now a policy option, historical controls have inhibited the development of such markets. Thus, empirical research must rely on an alternative estimate of expected exchange rate changes.

Phylaktis (1988) reports results for Argentina based on the model discussed above but uses realized spot rates as a proxy for expected changes in exchange rates. Some types of controls were found to influence the uncovered interest differential. The interesting aspect of these results is that the existence of controls might have contributed to effective taxation of foreign assets, to a political risk premium, and perhaps to the exchange risk premium. The difficulty in sorting out these effects in the absence of forward exchange markets has led researchers to explore alternative models.

Edwards and Khan (1985) propose a direct test for the relative importance of a domestic interest rate and an uncovered foreign rate in determining the demand for money. They found that for relatively open economies (Singapore), only the uncovered foreign expected yield was important in determining money demand. For countries with controls (Colombia), both the foreign rate and domestic market-clearing rates were important.

Haque and Montiel (1990) develop an empirical test for developing countries for which market-clearing domestic interest rate data are not available. This research utilizes an instrumental variable approach to control for the endogeneity of the observed monetary base. The authors conclude that the degree of capital mobility among developing countries is quite high and argue that this indicates the pervasive controls over capital flows in place in most of the countries studied provided little scope for an independent monetary policy.

Dooley and Mathieson (1994) extend this model to test for changes in the degree of capital mobility over time. They also find that capital is quite mobile for countries that have extensive control programs and that in most cases, this degree of mobility has increased over time. In general, this line of research suggests that control programs in developing countries have been of limited effectiveness.

Other authors using similar techniques have reported mixed results. Reisen and Yeches (1991) utilize curb market rates as a measure of effective domestic interest rates and find that capital mobility remained roughly constant for a group of Asian countries, while Faruqee (1991) finds that integration between developing countries in Asia and Japan seems to have increased in recent years. Kwack (1994) develops such a model that identifies the exogenous part of the change in the base using a policy reaction function and reports plausible estimates of the effectiveness of Korean capital controls.

Each of the papers discussed above attempts to measure a counterfactual monetary base that the authorities are assumed to set for an extended period.

However, the observed change in the domestic part of the monetary base is some combination of the exogenous policy change and the response during the period studied to offsetting private capital flows. Since the response to a policy-induced change in the monetary base can be literally instantaneous, it is difficult to identify the policy-induced part of observed changes short of developing a complete model of government behavior. It appears that different techniques for dealing with the endogenous nature of the regressors have important consequences for the results of these studies.

Edwards (1989) provides a qualitative evaluation of capital control programs leading up to 34 devaluations in developing countries. He concludes that governments typically intensified their control programs in the year before devaluations. He also reports data on premia in financial exchange markets as devaluations approached. While there are exceptions, in most cases the financial rate premia increased sharply in the one to three months before the exchange crisis led to devaluation. Nevertheless, data for these same episodes show that current accounts weakened and reserve assets declined in spite of the controls. Edwards concludes, "At most one can argue that these heightened impediments to trade managed to slow down the unavoidable balance of payments crisis unleashed by the inconsistent macroeconomic policies" (1989, 189–90). This evidence seems consistent for the more thoroughly researched data for industrial countries.

Direct Measures of Capital Flows

Johnston and Ryan (1994) examine the effects of capital control programs for recorded capital flows (including errors and omissions) for a cross-section of 52 developing and industrial countries for the period 1985–1992. An important difficulty with this approach is that controlling for factors other than capital controls that shape the structure of capital flows is quite difficult. As the authors point out, models of the capital account typically relate economic fundamentals, such as yield differentials and changes in wealth, to total net capital flows that are the mirror image of the current account balance. Within this constraint, the composition of the capital account between net official flows and net private flows then depends on the behavior of the government. If that behavior is not consistent over time, the behavior of net private capital flows will not be related to economic fundamentals. Moreover, to the extent that control programs respond to capital flows, it would not be surprising to observe that new controls over capital inflows are associated with increased inflows.

Nevertheless, some interesting empirical regularities emerge from the data. The removal of controls on capital outflows by industrial countries did seem to influence the overall volume and structure of net private flows. Direct investment and recorded long-term portfolio investment seem to have been quite sensitive to changes in control programs. In contrast, control programs in developing countries do not seem to have affected either overall private capital flows or their composition. The authors reach the plausible conclusion that the administration of control programs in developing countries has been less effective as compared with that in industrial countries.

A related empirical literature has attempted to measure private capital outflows from developing countries that are not captured by balance of payments reporting systems. Such outflows, generally identified as capital flight, are presumed to be unrecorded because the residents of these countries wish to avoid legal restrictions on outflows and/or taxes on earnings from legal outflows. Dooley (1988) tests the idea that such flows reflect efforts of residents to avoid financial repression.

Mathieson and Rojas-Suárez (1993) test the relationship between capital flight capital control programs and other fundamental determinants of capital flight. They find that during episodes where capital flight responds to increased risk from inflation and default risk, countries with capital controls did not prevent capital flight. The private sector's reaction to a deterioration of the fundamentals was delayed.

Kamin (1988) develops a related idea that capital movements are concealed by misinvoicing of trade transactions. In a case study of the Argentine dual exchange rate mechanism during the period 1981–1990, Kamin (1991) suggests that controls were made ineffective through export underinvoicing and a variety of other leakages.

Tests of the Political Economy of Capital Controls

Recent empirical work has attempted to relate countries' use of capital market restrictions to a variety of structural characteristics of the economy. This literature views policy regimes as endogenous responses to institutional and political features of the economy. Alesina, Grilli, and Milesi-Ferretti (1994) test the relevance of a number of rationalizations for the use of capital controls outlined above by looking for common characteristics of Organization for Economic Cooperation and Development (OECD) countries that seem to be related to the utilization of controls. Their reading of the theoretical literature suggests that the use of controls should be related to the exchange rate regime, to the desire to tax capital income, and to the desire to tax money balances. They find that highly managed exchange rate regimes seem to be associated with the use of controls.

Preferences for taxing capital income and money balances are, in turn, related to a variety of attributes of the political system. For example, inflation might result from weak governments that cannot enforce other types of taxes or strong governments that decide to tax capital income. Governments with independent central banks might resist both inflation and controls designed to preserve the inflationary tax base. Their findings suggest that countries with strong governments and dependent central banks are likely to utilize controls, presumably to generate revenue from inflation and to reduce real debt service.

The authors also test the impact of controls on other macroeconomic variables. Controlling for political stability, they find that controls have a negative effect on the stock of government debt. This is consistent with models discussed above that suggest that revenue from inflation is enhanced by controls and that domestic real interest rates kept below the world rate might limit debt service costs. The structure of the economy also seems to be an important determinant of the use of controls. The data also suggest that, controlling for initial income levels and political stability, controls do not seem to influence growth rates.

Grilli and Milesi-Ferretti (1995) find similar results for a sample of 61 developing and developed countries. In particular, over an extended period, countries with controls seem to experience high rates of inflation, relatively high shares of government revenue from seigniorage, and relatively low real interest rates. These recent results suggest that fiscal considerations are the most important determinants of the use of capital controls and that the controls, or some factor highly correlated with the use of controls, have measurable effects on government revenues.

Integration and Net Capital Flows

The consensus from empirical work reviewed above is that capital markets of industrial countries and many developing countries are highly integrated and that integration has increased substantially over the past 30 years. Capital controls or dual exchange rate systems have been effective in generating yield differentials, covered for exchange risk, for short periods of time but have had little power to stop speculative attacks on regimes that were seen by the market as being inconsistent.

It is surprising, in light of this evidence, that so little supporting evidence is found in the nonfinancial data. What has become known as the Feldstein–Horioka puzzle is the lack of real savings–investment imbalances among countries with apparently integrated financial markets. As argued in Dooley, Frankel, and Mathieson (1987), tests of savings–investment correlations are joint tests of several hypotheses, most of which have little to do with capital mobility or capital controls. The test of market integration might fail because purchasing power parity does not hold, exchange rate risk is a powerful barrier to international investment, domestic financial markets are poorly integrated, the economies studied are near a steady state in which imbalances are very small, or, finally, government policies other than capital controls generate small current account imbalances.

In a recent survey of this literature, Obstfeld (1994a) suggests that the puzzle is real in the sense that current account imbalances appear to be too small relative to historical periods when capital accounts were apparently open or to net capital movements within national boundaries. Several observers have concluded that the most plausible reason for this departure from the expected pattern of international investments is that governments have targets for the current account and manipulate macroeconomic policies to attain these targets. There appears to be no evidence that would suggest that capital controls are an important part of the apparent barriers to real capital mobility.

While not directly relevant to this paper's exploration of capital account restrictions, this observation is interesting and important. Recall that an effective control program is closely related to a government target for the current account balance. It seems clear that if governments are pursuing current account targets using other distortionary policy tools, the welfare effects of imposing controls are much less clear. In this case, the alternative to capital controls is not free trade in financial assets but distortion of another policy tool to eliminate private incentives for intertemporal trade.

A few studies of the real side evidence have looked directly at the effects of capital controls on real capital mobility. Razin and Rose (1994) created a measure of capital controls from the IMF's *Annual Report on Exchange Arrangements and Exchange Restrictions* and tested the impact of these controls for a cross-section of industrial and developing countries. They tested the hypothesis that changes in consumption should be correlated among countries with open capital markets, and investment should be more variable over time. None of these predictions is supported by the data. Like all these studies, these are tests of complicated joint hypotheses. But the data seem to support the view that while real capital markets may not be highly integrated, capital control programs do not seem to be the main reason for this fact.

Gross Capital Flows and Capital Controls: Theory and Evidence

The implicit assumption in the literature reviewed in the previous section is that net capital flows, and the associated redistribution of savings and investment across countries, determine the welfare consequences of capital mobility. Gross private capital flows and the structure of international financial intermediation are, by implication, less important for evaluating the economic consequences of international capital flows and controls on these flows. This section suggests that such models ignore important considerations in the balance of costs and benefits of capital control programs.

Some of the literature already reviewed is relevant for gross capital flows, but in general, this subject is not well developed in the literature. Nevertheless, the evidence cited above suggests that the welfare gains from liberalization of international credit markets are likely to come from better utilization of available domestic savings rather than from net flows of foreign savings. The important point is that direct investment and other international capital transactions might be welfare-improving even if no net capital flow is associated with free trade in financial services.

Obstfeld (1995b) develops the idea that closed national credit markets might be very unlikely to finance high-risk investments because of risk aversion among domestic savers and the inability to diversify within the domestic markets. If high-risk investment projects also have relatively high payoffs in terms of endogenous economic growth, the closed capital market implies that the growth rate of the country is limited. Opening the capital account in this model allows nonresident investors with lower levels of risk aversion to hold high-return investments in the country, while residents hold relatively safe foreign assets. Thus, with no net capital flow, domestic savings are channeled into investments that generate a higher growth rate. As demonstrated in a simulation exercise, the welfare benefits of a higher growth path can be very large.

Partial equilibrium models of the potential benefits for investors of greater access to equity markets in developing countries also suggest that significant welfare gains are available (Lessard 1973, Harvey 1994). These models employ an international capital asset pricing model to evaluate the possibility that opening equity markets would improve the risk-return trade-off faced by an investor currently limited to industrial country equities. Recent work has also tested the effects of restrictions on foreign investment as measured by an investability index compiled by the International Finance Corp. (Bekaert 1993; Claessens, Dasgupta, and Glen 1995). This analysis suggests that existing controls have had significant effect on yields of equities and that removal of such restrictions would benefit investors.

The apparent benefits from international diversification have also led to research that compares optimal portfolios with observed portfolios. While there are many problems with the data on gross international capital flows and even more problems with calculation of stocks of cross-border private financial claims and liabilities, this research suggests a very clear home bias in portfolios of residents of industrial countries. Tesar and Warner (1992) report that residents of industrial countries hold almost all their wealth in the form of claims on residents of their home country. Golub (1990) argues that evidence from gross capital flows suggests that a very minor part of the capital stock of OECD countries reflects gross foreign ownership and concludes that this measure of capital mobility is even more puzzling than the data on current account imbalances discussed in the previous section.

Notes

1. For a recent review of the literature that followed, see Garber and Svensson (1994).
2. See Obstfeld and Rogoff (1994) for a recent review.

References

Adams, Charles, and Jeremy Greenwood (1985), "Dual Exchange Rate Systems and Capital Controls: An Investigation," *Journal of International Economics* 18: 43–64.

Aizenman, Joshua (1990), "External Debt, Planning Horizon, and Distorted Credit Markets," *Journal of International Money and Finance* 9: 138–158.

Aizenman, Joshua (1986), "On the Complementarity of Commercial Policy, Capital Controls, and Inflation Tax," *Canadian Journal of Economics* 19 (February): 114–133.

Aizenman, Joshua, and Pablo E. Guidotti (1994), "Capital Controls, Collection Costs, and Domestic Public Debt," *Journal of International Money and Finance* 13 (February): 41–54.

Aizenman, Joshua, and Nancy P. Marion (1993), "Macroeconomic Uncertainty and Private Investment," *Economic Letters* 41: 207–210.

Akerlof, George A., and Paul M. Romer (1993), "Looting: The Economic Underworld of Bankruptcy for Profit," *Brookings Papers on Economic Activity*, no. 2: 1–60, 70–74.

Alesina, Alberto, Vittorio Grilli, and Gian Maria Milesi-Ferretti (1994), "The Political Economy of Capital Controls," in *Capital Mobility: The Impact on Consumption, Investment, and Growth*, ed. Leonardo Leiderman and Assaf Razin (Cambridge and New York: Cambridge University Press).

Alesina, Alberto, and Guido Tabellini (1989), "External Debt, Capital Flight, and Political Risk," *Journal of International Economics* 27 (November): 199–221.

Argy, Victor, and Michael Porter (1972), "Forward Exchange Market and External Disturbances under Alternative Exchange Rate Systems," *IMF Staff Papers*, 503–528.

Auernheimer, Leonardo (1987), "On the Outcome of Inconsistent Programs under Exchange Rate and Monetary Rules," *Journal of Monetary Economics* 19: 279–305.

Baccheta, Philippe (1990), "Temporary Capital Controls in a Balance-of-Payments Crisis," *Journal of International Money and Finance* 9 (September): 246–257.

Bartolini, Leonardo, and Allan Drazen (1994), "Capital Account Liberalization as a Signal," IMF Working Paper (Washington, D.C.: International Monetary Fund, November).

Bekaert, Geert (1993), "Market Integration and Investment Barriers in Emerging Equity Markets," Working Paper, Stanford Graduate School of Business.

Bhandari, Jagdeep S., and Bernard Decaluwe (1987), "A Stochastic Model of Incomplete Separation Between Commercial and Financial Exchange Markets," *Journal of International Economics* 22: 25–55.

Blackburn, Keith, and Martin Sola (1993), "Speculative Currency Attacks and Balance of Payments Crises," *Journal of Economic Surveys* 7(2): 119–44.

Branson, William (1993), "Comment," in *Financial Opening: Policy Issues and Experiences in Developing Countries*, ed. H. Reisen and B. Fisher (Paris: Organization for Economic Cooperation and Development).

Brock, Philip L. (1984), "Inflationary Finance in an Open Economy," *Journal of Monetary Economics* 14: 37–53.

Browne, Francis X., and Paul D. McNelis (1990), "Exchange Controls and Interest Rate Determination with Traded and Non-Traded Assets: The Irish–United Kingdom Experience," *Journal of International Money and Finance* 9: 41–59.

Cairncross, Alec (1973), *Control of Long-Term International Capital Movements* (Washington, D.C.: The Brookings Institution).

Calvo, Guillermo A. (1988), "Costly Trade Liberalization: Durable Goods and Capital Mobility," *IMF Staff Papers* 35 (September): 461–473.

Calvo, Guillermo (1987), "Balance of Payments Crises in a Cash-in-Advance Economy," *Journal of Money, Credit, and Banking* 19 (February): 19–32.

Chinn, Menzie D., and Jeffrey A. Frankel (1994), "Financial Links Around the Pacific Rim: 1982–1992," in *Exchange Rate Policy and Interdependence: Perspectives from the Pacific Basin*, ed. R. Glick and M. Hutchison (New York: Cambridge University Press), 17–47.

Claassen, Emil-Maria, and Charles Wyplosz (1985), "Capital Controls: Some Principles and the French Experience," in *The French Economy: Theory and Policy*, ed. J. Melitz and C. Wyplosz (Boulder, Colo.: Westview Press), 237–267.

Claessens, Stijn (1988), "Balance-of-Payments Crises in a Perfect Foresight Optimizing Model," *Journal of International Money and Finance* 7: 363–372.

Claessens, Stijn, S. Dasgupta, and J. Glen (1995), "Return Behavior in Emerging Stock Markets," *World Bank Economic Review* 9 (January): 131–51.

Delbecque, Bernard (1993), "Dual Exchange Rates Under Pegged Interest Rate and Balance-of-Payment Crisis," *Journal of International Money and Finance* 12: 170–181.

Dellas, Harris, and Oded Galor (1992), "Growth Via External Public Debt and Capital Controls," *International Economic Review* 33 (May): 269–281.

Dellas, Harris, and Allan Stockman (1993), "Self-Fulfilling Expectations, Speculative Attack, and Capital Controls," *Journal of Money, Credit, and Banking* 25 (November): 721–730.

Dooley, Michael P. (1995), "A Retrospective on the Debt Crisis," in *Understanding Interdependence: The Macroeconomics of the Open Economy*, ed. P. Kenen (Princeton, N.J.: Princeton University Press).

Dooley, Michael P. (1988), "Capital Flight: A Response to Differences in Financial Risks," *IMF Staff Papers* 35 (September).

Dooley, Michael P., Jeffrey Frankel, and Donald J. Mathieson (1987), "International Capital Mobility: What Do Saving-Investment Correlations Tell Us?" *IMF Staff Papers* 34 (September).

Dooley, Michael P., and Peter Isard (1980), "Capital Controls, Political Risk, and Deviations from Interest-Rate Parity," *Journal of Political Economy* 88 (April): 370–384.

Dooley, Michael P., and Kenneth M. Kletzer (1994), "Capital Flight, External Debt, and Domestic Policies," *Economic Review* 3: 29–37.

Dooley, Michael P., and Donald J. Mathieson (1994), "Exchange Rate Policy, International Capital Mobility, and Monetary Policy Instruments," in *Exchange Rate Policy and Interdependence: Perspectives from the Pacific Basin*, ed. R. Glick and M. Hutchison (New York: Cambridge University Press), 68–95.

Dornbusch, Rudiger (1988), "The EMS, the Dollar and the Yen," in *The European Monetary System*, ed. F. Giavazzi, S. Micossi, and M. Miller (Cambridge, England: Cambridge University Press).

Dornbosch, Rudiger (1986), "Special Exchange Rates for Capital Account Transactions," *World Bank Economic Review* 1(1): 3–33.

Drazen, Allan (1989), "Monetary Policy, Capital Controls and Seigniorage in an Open Economy," in *A European Central Bank?: Perspectives on Monetary Unification After Ten Years of the EMS*, ed. M. de Cecco and A. Giovannini (New York: Cambridge University Press), 13–32.

Edwards, Sebastian (1989), "On the Sequencing of Structural Reforms," NBER Working Paper Series, no. 3138 (Cambridge, Mass.: National Bureau of Economic Research, October).

Edwards, Sebastian (1989), *Real Exchange Rates Devaluation and Adjustment* (Cambridge, Mass.: MIT Press).

Edwards, Sebastian (1989), "Tariffs, Capital Controls, and Equilibrium Real Exchange Rates," *Canadian Journal of Economics* 22 (February): 79–93.

Edwards, Sebastian, and Mohsin S. Khan (1985), "Interest Rate Determination in Developing Countries: A Conceptual Framework," *IMF Staff Papers* (September).

Edwards, Sebastian, and Jonathan Ostry (1992), "Terms of Trade Disturbances, Real Exchange Rates, and Welfare: The Role of Capital Controls and Labor Market Distortions," *Oxford Economic Papers* 44 (January): 20–34.

Edwards, Sebastian, and Sweder van Wijnbergen (1986), "The Welfare Effects of Trade and Capital Market Liberalization," *International Economic Review* 27 (February): 141–148.

Eichengreen, Barry, Andrew K. Rose, and Charles Wyplosz (1994), "Speculative Attacks on Pegged Exchange Rates: An Empirical Exploration with Special Reference to the European Monetary System," NBER Working Paper Series, no. 4898 (Cambridge, Mass.: National Bureau of Economic Research, October).

Eichengreen, Barry, James Tobin, and Charles Wyplosz (1995), "Two Cases for Sand in the Wheels of International Finance," *Economic Journal* 105 (January): 162–172.

Eichengreen, Barry, and Charles Wyplosz (1993), "The Unstable EMS," *Brookings Papers on Economic Activity*, no. 1.

Epstein, Gerald A., and Juliet B. Schor (1992), "Structural Determinants and Economic Effects of Capital Controls in OECD Countries," in *Financial Openness and National*

Autonomy: Opportunities and Constraints, ed. T. Banuri and J. Schor (Oxford, England: Clarendon Press), 136–161.

Faruqee, Hamid (1991), "Dynamic Capital Mobility in Pacific Basin Developing Countries: Estimation and Policy Implications," IMF Working Paper 91/115 (November).

Fieleke, Norman S. (1994), "International Capital Transactions: Should They Be Restricted?" *New England Economic Review* (March/April): 27–39.

Fischer, Bernhard, and Helmut Reisen (1993), *Liberalising Capital Flows in Developing Countries: Pitfalls, Prerequisites and Perspectives* (Paris: Organization for Economic Cooperation and Development).

Fleming, J. Marcus (1974), "Dual Exchange Markets and Other Remedies for Disruptive Capital Flows," *IMF Staff Papers*, 1–27.

Flood, Robert P., and Peter M. Garber (1984), "Gold Monetization and Gold Discipline," *Journal of Political Economy* 92, 90–107.

Flood, Robert P., and Nancy P. Marion (1982), "The Transmission of Disturbances Under Alternative Exchange-Rate Regimes with Optimal Indexing," *Quarterly Journal of Economics* (February): 43–66.

Frankel, Jeffrey A. (1992), "Measuring International Capital Mobility: A Review," *American Economic Review* 82 (May): 197–201.

Garber, Peter M., and Lars E.O. Svensson (1994), "The Operation and Collapse of Fixed Exchange Rate Regimes," NBER Working Paper Series, no. 4971 (Cambridge, Mass.: National Bureau of Economic Research, December).

Garber, Peter M., and Mark P. Taylor (1995), "Sand in the Wheels of Foreign Exchange Markets: A Skeptical Market," *Economic Journal: The Journal of the Royal Economic Society* 105 (January): 173–180.

Giavazzi, Francesco, and Alberto Giovannini (1989), *Limiting Exchange Rate Flexibility: The European Monetary System* (Cambridge, Mass.: MIT Press).

Giovannini, Alberto, and Martha de Melo (1993), "Government Revenue from Financial Repression," *American Economic Review* 83 (September): 953–963.

Giovannini, Alberto, and Jae Won Park (1992), "Capital Controls and International Trade Finance," *Journal of International Economics* 33 (November): 285–304.

Golub, Stephen S. (1990), "International Capital Mobility: Net Versus Gross Stocks and Flows," *Journal of International Money and Finance* 9: 424–439.

Greenwood, Jeremy, and Kent P. Kimbrough (1985), "Capital Controls and Fiscal Policy in the World Economy," *Canadian Journal of Economics* 18 (November): 743–765.

Grilli, Vittorio, and Gian Maria Milesi-Ferretti (1995), "Economic Effects and Structural Determinants of Capital Controls," IMF Working Paper 95/31 (Washington, D.C.: International Monetary Fund, March).

Grilli, Vittorio, and Nouriel Roubini (1993), "Liquidity, Capital Controls, and Exchange Rates," *Journal of International Money and Finance* 12 (April): 139–153.

Gros, Daniel (1992), "Capital Controls and Foreign Exchange Market Crises in the EMS," *European Economic Review* 36 (December): 1533–1544.

Gros, Daniel (1988), "Dual Exchange Rates in the Presence of Incomplete Market Separation: Long-Run Effectiveness and Policy Implications," *IMF Staff Papers* 35 (September): 437–460.

Gros, Daniel (1987), "The Effectiveness of Capital Controls: Implications for Monetary Autonomy in the Presence of Incomplete Market Separation," *IMF Staff Papers* 34 (December): 621–642.

Guidotti, Pablo E., and Carlos A. Végh (1992), "Macroeconomic Interdependence Under Capital Controls: A Two-Country Model of Dual Exchange Rates," *Journal of International Economics* 32 (May): 353–367.

Guitián, Manuel (1993), "Currency Convertibility: Concepts and Degrees" (Seminar on currency convertibility sponsored by the IMF Institute and the Arab Monetary Fund, December).

Haque, Nadeem Ul, and Peter Montiel (1990), "Capital Mobility in Developing Countries—Some Empirical Tests," IMF Working Paper 90/117 (Washington, D.C.: International Monetary Fund, December).

Harberger, Arnold C. (1986), "Welfare Consequences of Capital Inflows," in *Economic Liberalization in Developing Countries*, ed. Armeane M. Choksi and Demetris Papageorgiou (Oxford, England: Basil Blackwell), 157–183.

Harvey, Campbell, R. (1994), "Predictable Risk and Relative Returns in Emerging Markets," NBER Working Paper Series, no. 4621 (Cambridge, Mass.: National Bureau of Economic Research, October).

Helpman, Elhanan (1981), "An Exploration in the Theory of Exchange Rate Regimes," *Journal of Political Economy* 89(5): 865–890.

Johnston, R. Barry, and Chris Ryan (1994), "The Impact of Controls on Capital Movements on the Private Capital Accounts of Countries' Balance of Payments: Empirical Estimates and Policy Implications," IMF Working Paper 94/78 (Washington, D.C.: International Monetary Fund, July).

Kamin, Steven B. (1991), "Argentina's Experience with Parallel Exchange Markets: 1981–1990," International Finance Discussion Papers, no. 407 (Washington, D.C.: Board of Governors of the Federal Reserve System, August).

Kamin, Steven B. (1988), "Devaluation, Exchange Controls, and Black Markets for Foreign Exchange in Developing Countries," International Finance Discussion Papers, no. 334 (Washington, D.C.: Board of Governors of the Federal Reserve System, October).

Kane, Edward J. (1995), *The Gathering Crisis in Federal Deposit Insurance* (Cambridge, Mass.: MIT Press), 119–28.

Krugman, Paul (1987), "The Narrow Moving Band, the Dutch Disease, and the Competitive Consequences of Mrs. Thatcher: Notes on Trade in the Presence of Scale Economies," *Journal of Development Politics* 27: 41–55.

Krugman, Paul (1979), "A Model of Balance-of-Payments Crises," *Journal of Money, Credit, and Banking* 11 (August): 312–325.

Kwack, Sung Y. (1994), "Sterilization of the Monetary Effects of Current Account Surpluses and Its Consequences: Korea, 1986–1990," in *Exchange Rate Policy and Interdependence: Perspectives from the Pacific Basin*, ed. R. Glick and M. Hutchison (New York: Cambridge University Press), 287–313.

Laban, R., and F. Larrain (1993), "Can a Liberalization of Capital Outflows Increase Net Capital Inflows?" Pontificia Universidad Catolica de Chile, Instituto de Economia, Working Paper no. 155.

Lane, Timothy, and Liliana Rojas-Suárez (1992), "Credibility, Capital Controls, and the EMS," *Journal of International Economics* 32 (May): 321–357.

Lanyi, Anthony 1975, "Separate Exchange Markets for Capital and Current Transactions," International Monetary Fund Staff Papers 22 (November): 714–49.

Lessard, Donald (1973), "International Portfolio Diversification: A Multivariate Analysis for a Group of Latin Countries," *Journal of Finance* 28: 619–633.

Marston, Richard C. (1993), "Interest Differentials under Bretton Woods and the Post-Bretton Woods Float: The Effects of Capital Controls and Exchange Risk," in *A Retrospective on the Bretton Woods System*, ed. Michael D. Bordo and Barry Eichengreen (Chicago: University of Chicago Press).

Mathieson, Donald J., and Liliana Rojas-Suárez (1993), "Liberalization of the Capital Account: Experiences and Issues," IMF Occasional Paper no. 103 (Washington, D.C.: International Monetary Fund, March).

McKinnon, Ronald, I. (1973), *Money and Capital in Economic Development* (Washington D.C.: The Brookings Institution).

Melvin, Michael, and Don Schlagenhauf (1985), "A Country Risk Index: Econometric Formulation and an Application to Mexico," *Economic Inquiry* 23 (October): 601.

Obstfeld, Maurice (1995a), "International Capital Mobility in the 1990s," in *Understanding Interdependence: The Macroeconomics of the Open Economy*, ed. P. Kenen (Princeton, N.J.: Princeton University Press).

Obstfeld, Maurice (1995b), "Risk Taking, Global Diversification, and Growth," *American Economic Review* 84 (December): 1310–1329.

Obstfeld, Maurice (1994a), "Are Industrial-Country Consumption Risks Globally Diversified?" in *Capital Mobility: The Impact on Consumption, Investment, and Growth*, ed. Leonardo Leiderman and Assaf Razin (Cambridge and New York: Cambridge University Press).

Obstfeld, Maurice (1994b), "The Logic of Currency Crises," NBER Working Paper Series, no. 4640 (Cambridge, Mass.: National Bureau of Economic Research).

Obstfeld, Maurice (1986a), "Capital Controls, the Dual Exchange Rate, and Devaluation," *Journal of International Economics* 20: 1–20.

Obstfeld, Maurice (1986b), "Rational and Self-Fulfilling Balance-of-Paymetns Crises," *American Economic Review* 76 (March): 72–81.

Obstfeld, Maurice, and Kenneth Rogoff (1994), "The Intertemporal Approach to the Current Account," NBER Working Paper Series, no. 4893 (Cambridge, Mass.: National Bureau of Economic Research, October).

Park, Daekeun (1994), "Foreign Exchange Liberalization and the Viability of a Fixed Exchange Regime," *Journal of International Economics* 36: 99–116.

Phylaktis, Kate (1988), "Capital Controls: The Case of Argentina," *Journal of International Money and Finance* 7: 303–320.

Portes, Richard (1993), "EMS and EMU After the Fall," *The World Economy* 16(1): 1–16.

Quirk, Peter J. (1994), "Capital Account Convertibility: A New Model for Developing Countries," in *Frameworks for Monetary Stability*, ed. T. Baliño and C. Cottarelli (Washington, D.C.: International Monetary Fund).

Razin, Assaf, and Andrew Rose (1994), "Business Cycle Volatility and Openness: An Exploratory Cross-section Analysis," in *Capital Mobility: The Impact on Consumption,*

Investment, and Growth, ed. Leonardo Leiderman and Assaf Razin (Cambridge and New York: Cambridge University Press).

Razin, Assaf, and Efraim Sadka (1991), "Efficient Investment Incentives in the Presence of Capital Flight," *Journal of International Economics* 31: 171–181.

Reinhart, Carmen M., and R. Todd Smith (1995), "Capital Controls: Concepts and Experiences," mimeo, March, 1–32.

Reinhart, Vincent (1991), "The 'Tobin Tax,' Asset Accumulation, and the Real Exchange Rate," *Journal of International Money and Finance* 10: 420–431.

Reisen, Helmut (1994), "Pension Funds, Capital Controls and Macroeconomic Stability," OECD Working Paper 2(47) (Paris: Organization for Economic Cooperation and Development).

Reisen, Helmut, and Helene Yeches (1991), "Time-Varying Estimates on the Openness of the Capital Account in Korea and Taiwan," *Journal of Development Economics* 41 (August): 285–305.

Spiegel, Mark M. (1990), "Capital Controls and Deviations from Proposed Interest Rate Parity: Mexico 1982," *Economic Inquiry* 28 (April): 239–248.

Stockman, Alan C., and Alejandro D. Hernandez (1988), "Exchange Controls, Capital Controls, and International Financial Markets," *American Economic Review* 78 (June): 362–375.

Sussman, Oren (1992), "Financial Liberalization: The Israeli Experience," *Oxford Economic Papers* 44: 387–402.

Sussman, Oren (1991), "Macroeconomic Effects of a Tax on Bond Interest Rates," *Journal of Money, Credit, and Banking* 23 (August, Part 1): 352–366.

Tesar, Linda, and Ingrid Warner (1992), "Home Bias and the Globalization of Securities Markets," NBER Working Paper Series, no. 4218 (Cambridge, Mass.: National Bureau of Economic Research, October).

Tobin, J. (1978), "A Proposal for International Monetary Reform," *Eastern Economic Journal* 4.

Tornell, Aaron (1990), "Real vs. Financial Investment: Can Tobin Taxes Eliminate the Irreversibility Distortion?" *Journal of Development Economics* 32: 419–444.

Tornell, Aaron, and A. Velasco (1992), "The Tragedy of the Commons and Economic Growth: Why Does Capital Flow from Poor to Rich Countries?" *Journal of Political Economy* 100(6): 1208–1231.

van Wijnbergen, Sweder (1990), "Capital Controls and the Real Exchange Rate," *Economica* 57 (February): 15–28.

van Wijnbergen, Sweder (1985), "Trade Reform, Aggregate Investment, and Capital Flight," *Economic Letters* 19: 369–372.

Williamson, John (1993), "A Cost-Benefit Analysis of Capital Account Liberalization," in *Financial Opening: Policy Issues and Experiences in Developing Countries*, ed. H. Reisen and B. Fisher (Paris: Organization for Economic Cooperation and Development).

Wyplosz, Charles (1986), "Capital Controls and Balance of Payments Crises," *Journal of International Money and Finance* 5: 167–179.

Appendix B to Part VI

Are Recent Capital Inflows to Developing Countries a Vote For or Against Economic Policy Reforms?

Michael P. Dooley
University of California, Santa Cruz
Working Paper No. 295
May 1994

Abstract

Recent private capital inflows to emerging markets are usually seen as a vote of confidence for economic prospects and policies of recipient countries. However, this good news is tempered by still-fresh memories of the economic pain many emerging countries suffered after the debt crisis in 1982, when a similar round of capital inflows suddenly dried up.

We argue here that there is good cause for concern. Conventional analyses assume that investment opportunities in emerging economies are the force that has driven the boom in emerging markets. These analyses are useful to a point but miss the essential nature of recent capital inflows.

We offer an alternative interpretation in which international investors have little interest in what the emerging economies do with the resources made available by private capital inflows. Investors are instead interested in the ability and willingness of the recipient government to honor a chain of guarantees that temporarily promise investors yields in emerging markets that exceed yields available in international markets.

A useful analogy is that recent capital inflows are like inflows to U.S. savings and loans after deregulation of these institutions in the early 1980s. In retrospect, it is clear that such capital inflows were not a ringing endorsement of the management of the savings and loans but a correct guess that relatively high yields were available at little risk to the depositor. Such an arbitrage capital inflow is a vote of confidence that the government will honor foolish commitments, not a vote of confidence for good economic policies.

Two ingredients are necessary for massive arbitrage capital flows. First, international investors must have access to emerging markets. Second, the emerging government must have sufficient net worth to make guarantees credible. Deregulation of emerging markets and fiscal reforms in many of these countries have created the conditions under which arbitrage opportunities can be exploited by international investors.

Our conclusion is that developing countries will have to choose from an unappetizing menu of reforms to avoid another crisis in international lending markets. Private capital inflows have recently become a widespread and surprising problem for macroeconomic policy in a variety of developing countries. Although sustained private capital inflows are something that most governments would be happy to live with, there is the concern that what flows in for reasons we don't fully understand could flow out for those same reasons. While capital inflows can be inconvenient, unexpected reversals of access to foreign capital can, as we learned after 1982, have disastrous and lasting effects.

In most cases, developing countries have attempted to offset the domestic effects of capital inflows through some combination of sterilized exchange market intervention, exchange rate appreciation, and, in some cases, restrictions on nonresidents' access to domestic investments. In early 1994, for example, Malaysia imposed restrictions on capital inflows reminiscent of the control program launched in Germany and other European countries with "strong" currencies in the waning days of the Bretton Woods system of fixed exchange rates. In other cases, capital market liberalization has been put on hold or slowed substantially.[1]

In this essay, we develop the argument that there are very good reasons for governments to be concerned about what we will call arbitrage capital flows. Such capital inflows share the unfortunate properties of capital inflows to U.S. savings and loans in the 1980s and are likely to have the same consequences for taxpayers in developing countries.

The basic motivation behind these capital flows is the opportunity to exploit a government subsidy or guarantee. They do not reflect confidence in the investment climate in the country but in the government's ability to give away money. The only lasting way to deal with this type of capital inflow is to remove the subsidy or guarantee. As discussed below, this involves difficult choices for countries that have graduated to the ranks of nations that participate fully in the international financial system.

What Lies Behind Private Capital Inflows?

Conventional pessimists argue that capital inflows since 1989 are mainly the result of depressed yields available in industrial countries.[2] Really dedicated pessimists allege that low yields in the industrial countries have pushed poorly informed investors to reach for higher returns available in emerging markets without understanding the risks involved. Once under way, resulting booms in emerging equity and other financial markets have generated speculative inflows that seem to be unrelated to the fundamental value of the securities traded. Such inflows are a misguided vote of confidence for economic policies in recipient countries.[3] The conventional optimistic interpretation is that private capital inflows reflect fundamentally improved risk-adjusted expected returns on investments in recipient countries. In this case, net capital inflows, and the associated current account deficits, help reallocate real capital formation to countries where risk-adjusted returns have improved. Such inflows are naturally limited by the supply of superior investment opportunities. Inflows of this type are clearly a vote of confidence for economic policies in recipient countries.

In this essay, we argue that neither of these arguments helps much in understanding the scale of private capital inflows in the past few years. Both sides of the debate have focused on the incentives for net investment in emerging markets. Thus, it is natural that the focus is on real or imagined opportunities to add to the productive capital stock of countries receiving capital inflows.

The view developed is that large capital inflows reflect private investors' efforts to exploit financial arbitrage opportunities generated by governments of developing countries. Two ingredients are necessary for these types of capital flows. First, the government must be wealthy enough to credibly offer a subsidy or support a guarantee. Second, emerging markets must be accessible to international investors. If these two conditions are met, the size of the position taken by private investors for arbitrage incentives that may have been around for a long time will grow explosively.

Such inflows do not reflect investors' confidence in the economic performance of the recipient economies but in the ability of their governments to guarantee abnormal rates of return (at the governments' expense) for a limited but predictable period of time. In many ways, recent inflows into emerging markets are analogous to the spectacular inflows to U.S. savings and loans before 1989 or the convergence play inflows to high-inflation European Monetary System (EMS) currencies before the exchange market crisis of 1992.

Recent Private Capital Inflows into Developing Countries

Only three or four years ago, a prevalent view was that developing countries that had trouble servicing external debt in the 1980s would not reenter international capital markets for a generation. The useful life of this prediction was even shorter than the average for economic predictions, as very large inflows to developing countries in Asia, Latin America, and the Middle East were widespread after 1989.

Tables VIB–1 and VIB–2 show private capital flows into developing countries in Asia and the Western Hemisphere expressed as a percentage of the recipient country's gross domestic product (GDP). In some respects, the experience of the two regions has been remarkably similar. For the Western Hemisphere, private capital inflows were reduced dramatically following the 1982 debt crisis as eight of ten countries experienced private capital outflows during 1984–1989. In contrast, during 1992–1993, nine of ten of the Latin countries shown experienced private capital inflows. For Asian developing countries, private inflows were less affected by the debt crisis, but here, too, inflows increased sharply after 1989, with six of the eight countries listed experiencing sizable inflows during 1989–1993.

The counterparts of these private inflows can be divided into official capital outflows, conventionally measured by increases in international reserves, and current account deficits. This is an interesting division because reserve gains probably have minor implications for the real economy, while current account deficits measure the contribution of foreign savings to real domestic consumption and capital formation.

For the Western Hemisphere, small private inflows before 1989 financed current account deficits. During 1990–1993, much larger private inflows were matched by current account deficits of about $100 billion and reserve accumulations of about $60 billion.

For Asia, almost all the private inflow before 1989 was matched by reserve accumulations. The much larger private inflows since then have increasingly

Table VIB–1. Private capital inflows as a percentage of GDP, Asia.

	Indonesia	*Korea*	*Malaysia*	*Philippines*	*Singapore*	*Sri Lanka*	*Taiwan*	*Thailand*
1970	2.70	5.58	−1.87	−.36	74.37	1.72	.54	2.66
1971	2.30	6.40	1.97	−.52	87.07	1.18	.32	3.42
1972	6.49	3.81	4.60	.80	48.60	1.62	.67	4.03
1973	5.17	4.51	−1.25	2.06	28.77	1.31	−6.06	2.16
1974	−.86	9.38	6.43	4.75	41.48	2.77	8.38	4.91
1975	−3.22	8.74	4.28	4.43	24.52	1.70	2.72	5.23
1976	3.23	4.53	−.64	5.00	15.11	1.55	−.39	3.12
1977	1.95	3.52	−3.37	2.75	9.27	2.12	−6.08	6.00
1978	4.05	−.39	−1.73	7.54	15.58	1.98	−6.39	3.75
1979	.86	5.55	−2.15	5.50	15.96	9.60	−1.20	7.49
1980	−.75	5.51	.29	4.30	24.48	8.99	3.60	5.23
1981	−.63	4.13	5.80	1.02	18.66	9.36	8.61	7.84
1982	−1.19	2.02	10.94	3.40	17.28	12.55	−2.74	.70
1983	9.16	−.42	10.38	.96	5.04	9.61	−2.72	7.93
1984	3.74	.27	3.81	−1.38	11.91	6.12	−5.76	6.59
1985	2.20	.42	5.70	−4.48	11.21	4.58	−3.90	3.78
1986	−2.25	−4.08	4.58	−5.05	4.97	5.92	9.25	2.53
1987	1.58	−6.41	−3.75	−5.45	10.05	3.31	9.67	3.10
1988	−.76	−3.10	−8.22	−2.19	2.23	5.08	−9.55	7.00
1989	1.17	−.57	3.88	.58	−3.50	4.56	−8.31	10.29
1990	8.71	−.40	8.47	1.93	.23	4.72	−9.35	14.87
1991	8.11	2.94	12.10	2.12	−7.84	5.20	−1.32	12.56
1992	6.64	2.70	15.04	−1.27	−6.40	2.66	−3.15	8.76
1993	3.42	1.22	4.89	2.70	−11.05	4.26	−.06	7.87
Averages								
1984–88	.9	−2.6	.4	−3.7	8.1	5.0	−.1	4.6
1989–93	6.7	1.6	10.1	1.4	−6.3	4.2	−3.5	11.0

Source: IMF, IFS

Table VIB–2. Private capital inflows as a percentage of GDP, Western Hemisphere.

	Argentina	*Bolivia*	*Brazil*	*Chile*	*Colombia*	*Ecuador*	*Mexico*	*Peru*	*Uruguay*	*Venezuela*
1970	.98	–3.46	2.48	1.16	3.94	6.89	3.40	–2.56	–.79	1.19
1971	–.09	–4.83	3.26	–.90	6.66	3.21	2.39	–.01	–.96	1.84
1972	.46	–4.97	6.11	–.13	5.17	7.90	2.72	–.70	–5.85	3.71
1973	.28	–6.06	5.20	–.69	2.73	4.37	1.90	2.86	–3.43	–3.00
1974	–.02	–4.00	5.58	–3.49	1.92	1.86	3.13	7.84	–.93	–8.13
1975	.52	1.32	4.32	–.51	1.51	8.13	3.17	4.62	.88	3.05
1976	.09	–.91	5.76	1.90	4.16	5.37	–.48	–.09	3.90	–1.07
1977	–.15	–.47	2.94	5.96	1.90	11.06	2.91	2.97	8.62	6.74
1978	–4.27	–1.36	5.32	11.15	1.77	10.55	3.19	–.23	5.95	12.49
1979	2.30	5.78	3.50	10.56	5.87	7.02	4.59	–.94	5.88	5.97
1980	–2.22	–26.27	3.82	11.95	5.35	8.36	5.50	.35	9.16	.03
1981	–3.27	–6.31	4.59	15.23	5.55	.65	3.94	5.55	4.39	–3.12
1982	–7.50	–11.04	3.18	3.48	7.91	5.79	–4.73	5.32	–4.01	–9.13
1983	–1.17	–19.63	–1.26	–2.32	3.73	–16.90	–3.24	–5.99	–5.87	–8.18
1984	.43	.68	1.36	6.79	1.45	–7.21	–2.71	–8.80	–.50	–8.57
1985	–.84	–1.94	–4.36	–.62	4.70	–9.55	–2.53	–8.65	–2.95	–4.27
1986	–1.61	5.45	–3.16	–8.58	1.79	–13.06	.10	–5.45	–2.06	–5.19
1987	–3.86	–.67	–2.95	–6.02	–.39	–6.84	2.46	–5.86	–2.84	1.60
1988	–.12	7.46	–3.37	–7.22	1.64	–1.30	–1.71	–5.98	–4.87	2.17
1989	–7.11	2.35	–1.38	–2.08	1.01	–5.45	1.74	–4.02	–4.29	–3.00
1990	–.93	4.52	–1.00	4.74	.01	–4.28	2.73	–2.09	–1.37	–10.21
1991	–1.38	3.48	–.81	4.49	–.73	–2.68	7.27	3.50	–3.61	3.15
1992	5.05	7.04	1.34	8.63	1.04	–7.91	7.64	1.26	3.67	3.39
1993	7.33	5.36	–1.16	5.71	2.53	.15	6.75	.19	–1.51	2.92
Averages										
1984–88	–2.2	2.2	–2.3	–3.0	1.7	–7.2	–.4	–6.5	–2.9	–2.9
1989–93	2.5	5.1	–.4	5.9	.7	–3.7	6.1	.7	–.7	–.2

Source: IMF, IFS

supported larger current account deficits, although for the past three years the reserve buildup has still accounted for two-thirds of the private inflow.

In summary, a widespread response to capital inflows has been official intervention in foreign exchange markets and increases in international reserve assets. This response suggests that differences in formal exchange rate arrangements might be less important than governments' attitudes toward the effects of inflows on exchange rates and the monetary base. Second, renewed access to international capital markets has allowed many countries to increase investment and/or consumption relative to GDP. Finally, a sudden reversal of private capital inflows would constitute a significant shock to a majority of the countries in these two regions.

Arbitrage Capital Flows

It would be a mistake, however, to conclude that investors care what the developing countries are doing with the capital inflows. The key to understanding such inflows is a careful evaluation of the contingent liabilities taken on by governments. These implicit liabilities can create powerful incentives for private financial transactions.

In a tightly controlled financial system, government guarantees are difficult to exploit. But as capital markets become more integrated and direct controls on financial transactions break down, investors will find new and better ways to take advantage of explicit or implicit government guarantees. The volume of such capital flows may have little to do with the economic fundamental we usually associate with private capital flows. Instead, the scale of transactions is determined by the resources available to support the government guarantee.

The important difference between this and a speculative bubble is that, when a bubble bursts, some private speculators lose to others. When an implicit guarantee is called, the government loses. One can find dramatic examples of this process in both developed and developing countries. The combination of deposit insurance and a relaxation of controls over deposit rates and portfolio selection in the United States led to explosive growth in inflows into savings and loans and to their eventual collapse. The problem, clear in retrospect, was that the contingent liability of the U.S. government provided the private investor with a virtual guarantee that high yields offered by savings and loan deposits would not be matched by depositors' losses. Depositors did not question the ability of some savings and loans to offer deposit rates 200–400 basis points over the market. As long as deposits were "probably" guaranteed, there was little downside risk.

The important lesson is that the size of the capital inflow to the savings and loans did not depend on the fundamental quality of the assets they were acquiring. To extend the analogy with a developing country, depositors did not care if the savings and loan bought a junk bond (international reserves), a shopping center (domestic investment), or a new car for the bank president (imports of consumer durables). Depositors were protected by the very considerable ability of the U.S. government to bail them out.

Moreover, the interest rate offered by savings and loans did not accurately reflect anyone's expected rate of return on the assets, although the savings and loan executives probably thought their boats, cars, and vacation homes were extremely good investments. For these reasons, it was a mistake to interpret the capital inflow to savings and loans as reflecting either a rational or irrational evaluation of their solvency.

In developing countries, a similar process helped generate the debt crisis of 1982. In this case, the governments of debtor countries offered guarantees of the dollar value of residents' liabilities. The rapid buildup of private external debt in the 1970s was matched by a buildup of contingent liabilities of the governments. This contingent liability became an important, but at the time little noticed, part of the developing country governments' overall positions. To some extent, the offer of the guarantee caused the private capital inflow. Perhaps more important, the usual market checks to private inflows were short-circuited by the government guarantee.

About half of the private capital inflow before 1982 was recycled to international markets through unrecorded private capital outflows, what ex post has been labeled capital flight. The other half was matched by current account deficits, a pattern quite similar to the balance of payments of developing countries today.

The most recent example of arbitrage capital flows was the so-called convergence play inflows to high-inflation EMS countries during 1987–1991. Over this period, an estimated $300 billion flowed into high-yield EMS member countries as investors calculated that the governments' commitment to maintain the exchange rate arrangement was credible for long enough that they could reverse their positions before the exchange rate peg was abandoned.

At the same time, the central banks of the countries receiving inflows resisted the fall in nominal interest rates that would have occurred if inflows were permitted to augment the money supply. As argued below, this is exactly the problem facing monetary authorities in emerging markets. With the benefit of hindsight, it is easy to see that the huge losses suffered by EMS governments as the exchange rate arrangement was abandoned in 1992 justified private investors' faith in the guarantee, rather than in the economic policies of the governments involved.

Recent Capital Flows

Is it possible that such a process is again at work in international capital markets? It is interesting to note that the overlending hypothesis for the buildup of external debt of developing countries is often associated with the view that a bubble can occur once in every generation of investors. Thus, as the story goes, memory of the widespread defaults by developing countries in the 1930s died off with the bankers of the 1930s and set the stage for irrational, follow-the-leader lending to the same countries in the 1970s. A repeat of the same argument to explain recent widespread inflows to developing countries implies a dramatic reduction in the half-life of investors, or at least their memories. In this business, one learns not to rule out an explanation simply because it assumes a high level of incompetence, but in the current circumstances, I believe there is a much better and more important lesson to be learned.

The alternative explanation is that a combination of fundamentals and arbitrage transactions is again at work. First, the fundamentals clearly favor a repatriation of funds to many debtor countries. Fiscal reform has been impressive in many countries; debt restructuring has been put in place; privatization, in fact as well as intention, has been remarkably successful. At the same time, interest rates available in industrial countries are at their lowest levels in many years. All these factors make a net private capital inflow to developing countries unsurprising. But are these factors sufficient to explain the large private capital inflows in recent years? I have serious doubts.

It seems likely that once again, private capital inflows are being sustained not only by the more favorable investment climate but also by arbitrage opportunities generated by the governments of developing countries. The form of the incentive is a little different as compared with the external debt-capital flight pattern that led up to the 1982 debt crisis. But in one important respect, the recent private capital inflows are similar, in that they are sustained by a contingent claim on the government.

The distinguishing feature this time is that recent private capital inflows to developing countries have taken the form of domestic-currency-denominated instruments, including equities, corporate bonds, bank deposits, and government securities.[4] This is certainly different from the dollar-denominated, government-guaranteed, syndicated credits that comprised the buildup in debt before 1982.

In the current pattern of capital flows, it is not obvious that the government of the borrowing country has provided a guarantee. However, an implicit guarantee is provided by the increasingly popular use of the exchange rate as an anchor for inflationary expectations. In basing its credibility on the maintenance of a fixed or managed exchange rate, the government, in effect, provides an exchange rate guarantee for the investor in domestic-currency-denominated instruments similar to that offered by high-inflation European exchange rate mechanism (ERM) countries.

This, of course, seems to leave the investor with a credit risk. But in most emerging markets, the government is very likely to provide a credit guarantee as well as the exchange rate guarantee. In cases where international investors buy government securities, the guarantee is explicit. Commercial bank deposits are also guaranteed, especially where the deposit is denominated in domestic currency.

Finally, even the liabilities of domestic nonfinancial corporations carry a strong government backup. This is because such firms are heavily indebted to the domestic banking system. If nonresident creditors want out, these firms can be expected to ask for and receive credit from the domestic banks. To refuse to do so would depress the market value of the banks' existing claims on the domestic firms and call into question the solvency of the domestic banking system.

What limits this process? As long as the developing country central bank maintains domestic nominal interest rates at levels above those available on similar foreign assets, there is, in principle, no limit to the private capital inflows generated. Of course, in reality, the government's resources are limited. At some point, the market will begin to doubt the government's ability to maintain the exchange rate peg and the negative carry resulting from the low return earned on reserves relative to that paid on the domestic liabilities issued in sterilized exchange market intervention. But the scale of private capital inflows necessary to exhaust the central bank's expected net worth can be very large indeed.

Solutions

The only solution is to break the chain of guarantees now being offered to international investors. The chain has several links. The first is the commitment to allow free access of international investors to domestic financial markets. The second is the commitment to a nominal exchange rate target. The third is the commitment to sterilize the monetary effects of capital inflows in order to resist declines in domestic interest rates and overheating the domestic economy. The fourth is the implicit guarantee of deposits and solvency of the domestic banking system. If any one of this chain of guarantees is broken, the losing position now being taken by governments will evaporate. But none of the links can be broken without cost.

A threat to withdraw the guarantee of bank deposits or the solvency of the banking system is unlikely to be credible. The historical involvement of the governments of developing countries with their banking systems makes the threat to allow bank failures a hollow one. Authorities in developing countries recognize the dangers of external borrowing by their commercial banks. For example, the government of Mexico has had some success in limiting Mexican banks' borrowing in international markets, and this has forced investors to acquire direct claims on nonfinancial firms. But as argued above, investors expect the firms to call on their banks during a crisis, and the banks are expected to provide funds that will allow a profitable exit for the foreign investor.

Another option that is probably not feasible is to turn back the clock on capital market integration. Experience in the industrial countries suggests that once private investors have "found" a market and incurred the fixed costs of operating in that market, governments are not able to materially restrict access to profitable investments. For developing countries that retain effective controls, as appears to be the case in some Asian developing countries, a slowing or reversal of liberalization might be a short-term option.

By default, this leaves the exchange rate monetary policy regime as the only option. Unfortunately, there are no easy answers here either. A flexible exchange rate regime would allow an independent monetary policy but seems to be associated with excessive volatility in real exchange rates. Recent research on the behavior of flexible rates for industrial countries is not encouraging, in that there seems to be no correspondence between the variance of the fundamentals and the variance of the real exchange rate. The prospect of an "unnecessary" real exchange rate appreciation is not attractive to countries that have prospered with export-led growth.

A few emerging-market countries will find it feasible to fix the exchange rate and allow capital flows to influence domestic monetary conditions. But this is a particularly difficult policy choice for most developing countries. For economies that are attempting to reduce entrenched inflation and inflationary expectations, a capital inflow that is not sterilized means an increase in the monetary base and a fall in domestic interest rates. This is not the normal recipe for a successful stabilization program. While a few very open economies will find it optimal to fix the exchange rate and import monetary policy, most will find the complete loss of control over monetary policy unacceptable.

Our view is that relinquishing the exchange rate target is the best of a nasty list of choices for most developing countries. Although the exchange rate is a powerful way for the government to signal its intention to fight inflation, a nominal exchange rate target does not contribute to credibility of those intentions in an environment where private expectations for the real equilibrium exchange rates change rapidly. Surely, developing countries engaged in important stabilization and reform programs are those for which we have relatively little ex ante information on the equilibrium real exchange rate. Greater exchange rate flexibility will greatly affect the net private capital inflow that is fully justified by the economic reform packages that have been put in place in many developing countries. It will stop arbitrage capital flows that have dominated the economic environment for the past few years. The collapse of the EMS in 1992 should be a reminder that as much as we might yearn for stability in everything, the reality seems to be that difficult choices are necessary.

Notes

1. D. Mathieson and L. Rojas-Suárez, "Liberalization of the Capital Account: Experiences and Issues," IMF Working Paper WP/92/46, 1992.
2. G. Calvo, L. Leiderman, and C. Reinhart, "Capital Inflows and Real Exchange Rate Appreciation in Latin America: The Role of External Factors," *IMF Staff Papers* 40, 1993.
3. The recent sharp declines in prices in emerging equity markets and markets for sovereign debt are apparently related to the rebound in interest rates in industrial countries that began late in 1993. See M. Dooley, K. Kletzer, and E. Fernandez-Arias, "Is the Debt Crisis History?" World Bank Working Paper, 1994.
4. S. Gooptu, "Portfolio Investment Flows to Emerging Markets," World Bank Working Paper, March 1993.

Part VII CENTRAL BANK COORDINATION IN THE MIDST OF EXCHANGE RATE INSTABILITY

Should the world return to a more coordinated monetary and exchange rate environment? What are the dangers or benefits of a return to a Bretton Woods type of system?

Moderator:
Harvey Rosenblum
Senior Vice President and Director of Research
Federal Reserve Bank of Dallas

Panelists:
John W. Crow
Adviser
American International Group of Companies

Ricardo Hausmann
Chief Economist
Inter-American Development Bank

Allan Meltzer
Professor of Political Economy and Public Policy
Carnegie Mellon University

Miguel Urrutia
Governor
Central Bank of Colombia

Rosenblum:
When we started thinking about holding this conference, the one thing I knew I wanted was a wrap-up session with people who have been on the firing line, veterans in dealing with currency fluctuations that are responding to real shocks and financial shocks. So what we have assembled here on this final panel are four people who have had to deal with these kinds of shocks in one form or another. We have a former central banker, John Crow, formerly governor of the Bank of Canada. We have a current central banker, Miguel Urrutia, from the Central Bank of Colombia. We have Ricardo Hausmann, chief economist of the Inter-American Development Bank and former planning minister of Venezuela, who has had to deal with some of the enormous shocks that country has been exposed to in recent years. And we have Allan Meltzer, who is the first person I always want to turn to for advice on how to deal with economic problems. He's not just an advisor, indirectly, to the Federal Reserve System by virtue of being chairman of the Shadow Open Market Committee, but he's advisor to numerous central banks and ministries of finance around the world.

This session will deal with what this entire conference has been leading up to, which is, Where do we go from here? Do we want to take a step backward, toward the Bretton Woods system that we have left behind? If not, where do the world's financial and currency markets evolve from here?

Crow:
This conference's theme is certainly very relevant and timely. Indeed, this continent has a wide variety of just about everything that I think anybody would want to consider in the way of an exchange rate regime. There's something for everyone. We even had in Mexico, for a while, a kind of precursive target band. Until recently, there is one thing we didn't have. This is not exactly a continent of strong currencies, but we have one, at least now, in the U.S. dollar, which is a bit stronger than it was a few weeks ago. Perhaps economists shouldn't really care whether currency is strong or weak, but central bankers certainly do. It makes for a slightly easier life. More important, you need these respites of strength to balance out periods of weakness and thereby keep market expectations reasonably balanced as well.

My underlying theme in these initial remarks is that, yes, of course, exchange rates matter, and they matter a lot, of course, to central banks. They are the ratios of national moneys, and central banks are deeply concerned with the behavior of money, obviously. At the same time, domestic policies come first, as they should. So the real question is how a country can adopt an exchange rate regime that enables it to pursue good domestic policies. That's the underlying issue.

My own country, Canada, is certainly a floater. We're almost the dean of floaters, having done it for 25 years now, rain and shine. We exited from Bretton Woods, in fact, in 1970, a bit before the general collapse. And there was an earlier period of 10 years in the 1950s when Canada also was floating, violating the Bretton Woods Agreement in the process.

In fact, Canada has been floating longer than the Bretton Woods system was in effect. I think that's worth bearing in mind when we talk about pegged exchange rates, because there's been a bout of nostalgia recently, apparently occasioned by the fiftieth anniversary of Bretton Woods. But the Bretton Woods system didn't last that long. It really didn't start until the late 1950s, when current account convertibility became more general in Europe. In Japan, current account convertibility didn't start until 1964, and by 1971, the Bretton Woods system was effectively out the window. So it is not quite the long-term shining example of a silver age, as it tends to be portrayed with the benefit of nostalgia.

In Canada, we are pretty comfortable with floating. I'm not sure we understood why we did it when we started to float, but with 25 years' practice, I think we've become better at it. And it works for us. Of course, it works better with sound domestic policies, but so does any exchange rate regime. What is important to emphasize is that floating does not get in the way of good domestic policies. In fact, I would say floating is useful in the sense that it makes you focus on the quality of domestic policies.

The one thing about floating that I had to persuade many Canadians of involved their belief that the reason we have a floating exchange rate is so we can depreciate. I had to insist that it was appropriate, even if unwelcome to some, for the exchange rate to appreciate on occasion. That was somewhat difficult to get across. Indeed, many Canadians seemed to think that the central bank really didn't care about the exchange rate because of the very fact that the bank was allowing it to appreciate. We cared about it, but the bottom line was that we cared about some other things more than the exchange rate.

The title of this panel discussion—"Central Bank Coordination in the Midst of Exchange Rate Instability"—looks rather daunting. I think the phrase "putting a finger in the dike and seeing the holes appear somewhere else" was used this morning. Well, this title certainly smacks of the dike analogy. Central bankers are running around in all this instability, putting fingers in dikes. And, lo and behold, they are not very successful. Look at all the exchange rate instability!

But it isn't really that difficult. I wouldn't say it's easy, but it's not that difficult, especially if central banks bear in mind their fundamental domestic responsibilities.

With that background, let me turn to the questions, and let me take the second one first, which I think I've almost answered: What are the dangers or benefits of a return to a Bretton Woods type of system? Not a good idea. Peg rates are not on the menu, for the kinds of reasons discussed at this conference. They didn't work very well before, when governments had some control over the rate because they had all kinds of capital controls. They work even less well now, as the Europeans discovered in the early 1990s. The Europeans had to liberalize their domestic financial systems for the sake of efficiency and competition. That meant liberalizing the external side of financial systems. It also meant facing up to the implications of international capital markets, and, bingo, the exchange rates came under pressure. Canada learned this much earlier. We had an open financial system way back, and that's essentially, I think, why we have been floating since way back.

As for a more coordinated monetary and exchange rate environment, clearly an exchange rate is a ratio; there's interdependency built in. I wouldn't want to argue against coordination; it sounds like a good idea. But while trying to do a little good, you may end up doing substantial harm. The harm comes from confusion about responsibilities and the objectives of domestic monetary policies because of excessive focus on the exchange rate—in other words, putting the cart before the horse.

Let me go into a bit more detail about coordination. The classic definition of coordination is Henry Wallich's: "a significant modification of national policies in recognition of international interdependence." The key word here is *modification*; it's not *cooperation.* You don't just tell people what you are doing in hopes that information will lead to better policies in general. With coordination you change your policies; you modify them. But I would argue that coordination is not a task for central banks. What they should do, above all, is keep an eye on their domestic objectives, although they are, of course, very internationally minded, maybe the most internationally minded of all government agencies. But they do have, or should have, domestic objectives, and they each have, after all, just one monetary instrument, their balance sheet. Let me be unambiguous about this: they should use that instrument to promote domestic monetary stability. That's what they are there for.

Let me dwell for a moment on thè piece of coordination I really know something about, which involved the Group of Five and the Group of Seven (G5/G7), and how it relates to this issue of central banks. The other thing I'll talk about is how exchange rates get taken into account in pursuing domestic objectives. By the way, I think Agustín Carstens was on the right track this morning in this latter regard when he commented on the Mexican experience.

Bear in mind that while there were trucks on the road in the G5/G7 period, central bankers were not the drivers. In a sense, central bankers were the passengers. One example of coordination is the Plaza Accord. In fall 1985, the U.S. dollar had overshot on the upside, and there was concerted intervention to bring it down. I think it was all basically sterilized intervention. Perhaps the markets thought there would be some follow-up in terms of policies, but there wasn't very much, if any. The follow-up that would have been important, given the underlying causes of the U.S. appreciation, would have been a prompt shift in U.S. fiscal policy. That didn't happen. The follow-up that would have been absolutely terrible, and also didn't happen, fortunately, was an easing of monetary policy in the United States. That would have been quite direct in bringing down the U.S. dollar, but it would have been a big mistake for domestic reasons because U.S. demand was buoyant at that point.

The only time that I recall, in fact, monetary policy—or even fiscal policy, for that matter—changing after invention was the shift in Japan to an easier monetary policy after the Louvre Accord, when the object of the game changed from pushing the U.S. dollar down to trying to hold it up or even push it back up a bit. That situation left a bad taste in the mouth of the Bank of Japan, and maybe other Japanese, in terms of being the cause of the asset bubble. From their point of view, the very easy monetary policy in Japan, designed to keep the yen down and the U.S. dollar up, was one factor in the asset bubble that caused so much trouble. The moral here is keep your eye on the domestic ball and don't get seduced by the coordination mirage.

The verdict on intervention is, I think, that it sometimes may do some good, especially if concerted, and it is unlikely to do a lot of harm as long as it doesn't confuse a country about what it is really trying to do. It won't do any harm, I guess, if it's sterilized.

Let me dwell for a moment on the recent episode of intervention, involving the United States, Japan, and Germany. I think in the case of the United States, the intervention was sterilized. In the case of Japan, it probably was not. Japan has moved to a more expansionary policy. While the Japanese can't get interest rates down very much, if they can print enough yen, they can certainly move the exchange rate. So if you really want an expansionary monetary policy, the intervention comes rather easily, as long as you don't worry too much about the kinds of monetary base numbers being generated. Let me also emphasize that the Japanese have very good domestic reasons for pursuing a more expansionary monetary policy, and they have the tools to reflate even if they can't get interest rates down. In other words, they can always operate on the exchange rate through, let's say, aggressive intervention. They have the yen to buy the dollars; they print them.

The last thing I will talk about relates to the technology of central banking. Here you are, you have a floating exchange rate. You affect your exchange rate by monetary policy, as you do interest rates. The effects of central bank actions spill out onto the markets for both domestic and foreign money. The way we try to assess what is happening in Canada in terms of the thrust of monetary policy actions is by using a broad definition of monetary conditions. In our case, it includes both changes in short-term interest rates and in the exchange rate. Both have effects upon demand. You shouldn't exclude exchange rates from the equation. That is, you should look at the transmission of monetary policy through the exchange rate as well as through interest rates. I think that's helpful in organizing your thinking about where you are in monetary policy terms.

Of course, monetary conditions are linked across countries. If one country's exchange rate changes, another country's is going to, and so you change their monetary conditions and then you get into interdependence again and, potentially, coordination. Clearly, you could have somewhat of an iterative process, but all policy is iterative and progressive or gradual to a degree. You don't get there overnight. And there's a fairly wide range of tolerance on these things. For one thing, every country has a somewhat different effective exchange rate because each has a different pattern of trade and capital. My view is that this can all be worked out without any great strain, provided people keep an eye on their domestic responsibilities.

Finally, what I've just discussed is clearly not itself a cure for exchange rate instability. We have different national monetary policies around the world, and, of course, there are different fiscal policies. But if all monetary policies were anchored in domestic monetary stability, that would represent a very powerful force indeed for underlying exchange rate stability.

Hausmann:
Let me start by saying that Latin America is a pretty volatile place. Gross domestic product (GDP) volatility in Latin America was about 4.5 percent per year, on average, for the period 1970–92, about two and a half times the average GDP volatility of OECD countries. Latin America's terms of trade volatility is about double that of the OECD countries. Real exchange rate volatility in Latin America is about three times that of OECD countries, and it has about two and a half times the consumption volatility. Consumption volatility in the OECD is about 2 percent annually, compared with 5.6 percent in Latin America. Obviously, Latin America is a pretty volatile place. And as Vittorio Corbo said yesterday, volatility is bad. It's bad for growth and for income distribution. It's bad for a number of things we care about. So we need to be concerned about volatility.

What's behind this volatility? Is it all imported? Is it homegrown? Is it the result of bad policies? Is it essentially incompetent policy-making? Or is there more to it? I am going to take a somewhat nonpartisan view. Is volatility in Latin America external? Yes, in part. We have more in terms of trade volatility and more capital flow volatility, although some could argue that capital flows, if they are volatile, may be reacting to domestic factors. But there is some international context. Latin America's economies are much less diversified than those of the OECD countries, so each economy is much more sensitive to specific shocks.

But Latin America also has pretty volatile policies. Fiscal policy is about three times as volatile as it is in OECD countries. The standard fiscal surprise in an OECD country is about 1.3 percent of GDP. The standard fiscal surprise in a Latin American country is about 3.6 percent of GDP. Why is fiscal policy in these countries more volatile? Part of the reason is that fiscal policy is somewhat dependent on terms of trade, because national income is affected by terms of trade, exports contribute to taxes, and imports contribute to taxes. So shocks to the terms of trade are likely to generate fiscal consequences. It's also interesting that when you do econometric cross-country regressions, you find that measures of political instability also seem to be related to fiscal instability. So fiscal volatility also reflects political problems.

Latin America's financial volatility has been, historically, disproportionately larger than it has been in OECD countries. In the past 20 years, the region's inflation rate has averaged some 200 percent, orders of magnitude above the average of OECD countries. Why is it that Latin America has become so financially unstable? We all think there's a fiscal reason for this financial instability and that the fundamental problem is fiscal policy. Fiscal policy is pretty volatile, as I just mentioned. But it is three times more volatile; it is not 200 times more volatile. So why does this fiscal instability generate so much financial instability, exchange rate instability, and, perhaps, GDP instability?

Studies we've conducted at the Inter-American Development Bank reveal that Latin American fiscal policy is unstable, but not in an anticyclical manner (see Inter-American Development Bank 1995; Hausmann and Gavin 1996; Hausmann, Gavin, Perotti, and Talvi 1996). For 22 of the 23 countries we studied in detail, fiscal policy has been, on average, procyclical. So it's not that fiscal policy is trying to compensate for other problems in the economy. Many times, it's accentuating those problems, or at least it was in 1970–92, which is the period we looked at.

We also looked at a very interesting comparison: the size of the standard Latin American financial system is about 20 percent of GDP, compared with about 70 percent of GDP in the OECD. So the standard fiscal surprise in an OECD country represents about 1.8 percent of the financial system's assets. The standard fiscal surprise in Latin America, which is some 3.6 percent of GDP in a much smaller financial system, implies that the standard surprise is about 18 percent of the financial system. So the surprise represents a much larger proportion of financial assets and, consequently, leads to much higher monetary volatility. In other words, monetary volatility is very much impacted by this amplifying role that shallow financial markets have. You might think that real exchange rate volatility is very much related to real shocks to the economy, like terms-of-trade volatility. It just so happens that real exchange rate volatility for the period we studied was essentially a monetary phenomenon. So monetary instability leads to real exchange rate instability and is also an important explanation for GDP volatility.

This very quick interpretation of some of the causal relationships involved points out the crucial role financial systems play in either absorbing or amplifying the amount of volatility in an economy. If an economy suffers surprises, the financial system may be an element that helps absorb these shocks, or it may be a source of trouble, amplifying their consequence. We find deep financial systems help an economy stabilize itself, but financial systems are themselves affected by volatility. So countries in the region may be in a kind of volatility trap: if they are volatile, they have shallow financial markets because people are afraid something might happen and so financial markets don't develop very much. But if the financial markets don't develop very much, then you will have high volatility. In other words, high volatility leads to shallow financial markets, and shallow financial markets lead to high volatility.

What is needed to get out of this trap? First, I will explore some extreme, absurd ideas, and then I'll return to the real world.

The first argument I'm going to make is that part of the problem is that the world's banks are essentially national banks. The reason we have national banks is not because economic forces, per se, make banks national institutions. It's because governments charter banks nationally; governments make banking a national industry. So the solution I'm going to imagine is that we have global banks. National banks in a volatile economy are likely to be weak because in a volatile economy, money demand shocks are likely to be very large. Banks better be very liquid because if they are not, when they get a bad demand shock on their deposits, they will run into trouble. So banks are well advised not to intermediate too much and to keep a lot of their assets liquid. Also, a small volatile economy is likely to have real shocks that change the value of the real assets that underlie the loans that have been made.

So if you will allow me this solution for a moment, there would be an international organization, involving several countries, that charters global banks, and member countries would allow these banks to operate in their national economies, simply taking deposits and making loans, in each country's own currency, if that is what that government wants. There would not have to be monetary union in a single currency; these banks could operate in several currencies. The point is that if there is a shock to the demand for money in a country, it would be just one more little shock for one of these global banks. If you have a real shock to the economy that hits the balance sheets of banks, it would be just one little part of a balance sheet that is in just one more country where this bank is operating. So the transmission of shocks to the real side of the economy through the financial system would be greatly reduced.

The point I'm trying to make is that one major problem in small open economies like those in Latin America is the fact that we have national banks that make these financial systems operate more as amplifiers of shocks than as absorbers of shocks. If we had a global bank system, the transmission mechanism would be removed.

Since we cannot wait for an international accord establishing global banks to be reached, what can national economies do in the meantime? Is there a case to be made for the stabilizing role of foreign bank branches in the domestic financial market? There is some evidence that may be the case. For example, a significant portion of Uruguay's banking system is foreign owned. When Argentina was in serious trouble this year, Uruguay seemed to be unscathed.

There is evidence that pegging the exchange rate can imply very difficult pressures on the financial system. And as somebody said earlier, before you peg, you had better ensure your financial system is strong enough, and you have to know whether pegging is going to be viable. We have evidence that if it is not viable, when you abandon these pegs, the economy is hurt a great deal.

But what do you do if you are, for example, the Bahamas, Bermuda, or Belize? They have to peg because they are obviously not optimal currency areas. I'm wondering whether some international agreement can be considered, especially for the very small economies that represent no significant costs for the rest of the world but that have to peg and do not have the preconditions for it.

Meltzer:

What John Crow said earlier was very much along the same lines of what I'm going to say. But I believe I'll say some things that he didn't because he's more diplomatic than I, and because, as a teacher, I know that reinforcement is always useful.

We were asked to talk about three topics. The first was whether there should be more coordination of exchange rates; second, whether in some way or another we should return to a type of Bretton Woods agreement of fixed but adjustable rates; and third, whether the role of the International Monetary Fund (IMF) and the World Bank should be different than it has been in the past.

On the subject of coordination, there are two types of coordination, which I'll label *good* and *bad.* Within the two types, there are two others, called *sterilized* and *unsterilized.* An article on coordination in yesterday's *Wall Street Journal* is an excellent example of the confusion between sterilized and unsterilized intervention. What the article said, very briefly, is that Secretary Rubin is a clever trader; he spent a lot of years at Goldman, Sachs, where he learned how to trade in markets, particularly in exchange markets; so he figured out how to surprise the market. That's one of the reasons, the article says, exchange rate intervention has been successful, particularly recently, and why the dollar has been appreciating against the yen.

One thing that's wrong with this thinking, of course, is that there has been very little American exchange rate intervention during this period. But let's put that to one side. The article contrasts Rubin with David Mulford, who engaged in exchange rate intervention much more frequently. It misses what I think is the more important difference: Japan is now engaging in unsterilized intervention. No one ever believed that unsterilized intervention, which is an increase in the monetary base by buying foreign exchange reserves, would have a different effect than an increase in the monetary base achieved by buying domestic securities. The Japanese are choosing to buy foreign exchange for what I think are good reasons, under the circumstances. What has happened is that they have gone from a policy which in my judgment was deflationary (that is, prices actually would have fallen in equilibrium at a rate of 3 to 4 percent a year) to a modest inflation of perhaps zero to 1 percent. It had been anticipated that the Japanese would continue a policy of deflation, but now there's new information that, lo and behold, that's not going to be true. Some problems in the banking system also are coming to light, which I expect causes some outflow from Japan. But apart from that, this change in policy, the unsterilized intervention, is clearly an important factor about current intervention.

Let me go, now, to *good* and *bad*. Good intervention is my kind of intervention. That is, policymakers don't meet and decide to tighten fiscal policy. I can just see the day that Fed Chairman Alan Greenspan or his successor goes to Congress and says, "We have to raise taxes or tighten money because the Japanese are having a problem." I think that's a nonstarter. Central bankers will cooperate, even in that sense, when they see it is in their national interest. Many central bankers will tell you that when they engage in coordination, it's because it fits, in one way or another, with their domestic objective.

In any case, that's not what I mean by good intervention. Good intervention is when central banks adopt a common policy objective; they all choose, in their own ways, a low or zero rate of expected inflation. If they do that, then exchange rates will be less volatile because there will be less—not none, but less—currency shifting, and exchange rate volatility will primarily reflect changes in real exchange rates and real opportunities. This is a very good way of responding to real changes. The world's economies will be not completely stable, but they will be more stable than they would otherwise be.

I have often proposed a rule for monetary policy that does exactly that: the United States, Germany, and Japan, the three principal moneys in the world, would aim for zero inflation. And my rule tells them how they might do it. That doesn't mean they would all do the same thing, but they would all follow the same rule, and that would produce a public good. If they all achieved low or zero rates of inflation consistently and kept their exchange rates more stable, that would be good coordination. Coordination through policy rules would provide an opportunity for third countries to voluntarily peg to one of the major currencies and thereby obtain something that they could never obtain by themselves—both fixed exchange rates and price stability. Large countries would provide a public good for the smaller or less economically important countries, and everyone would be better off. The large countries would get the benefits of their fixed exchange rates; smaller countries would get the benefits of our low inflation. Our currencies would continue to float to buffer the real shocks that occur in the world when there are changes in the terms of trade, changes in taste, changes in productivity, and the like. Good coordination solves the public good problem.

Bad coordination is when countries intervene and mistake the objectives for the object. This is what I call the King Canute Syndrome. Remember King Canute? He didn't build a seawall to keep the waves from coming in; he sat on the beach and ordered them not to come. That's the kind of coordination I consider bad coordination; we all get together and try to prevent the inevitable from happening. That isn't going to work. Good coordination can work.

Now, economics is not physics, so it's true that at times, coordinated intervention can affect the exchange rate briefly. For example, speculators can be forced to cover, so there is some small but rapid response to intervention. The market can be uncertain whether the intervention is sterilized or unsterilized. Market participants may say, "Hey, if these guys are going to throw a couple of billion dollars into the market, we'll wait until tomorrow when they stop throwing it in and then we'll resume what we're doing." For those reasons and many more, we can briefly get some initial effects from unsterilized or even sterilized intervention.

But what are the long-term effects? What does intervention have to do with the ability of countries to export and import? Very little. If we look, for example, at the Deutsche mark-dollar rate for the years 1980 to 1994, what do we find? We find that the differences in the rates of inflation are about half a percent a year (Germany's being lower) and that the difference in productivity growth is about 0.2 a percent a year (Germany's being higher). If we add those two numbers together, we get 0.7 percent per year. How much has the Deutsche mark-dollar exchange rate changed over that period? Approximately 0.65 percent per year, so we are really very close to being able to say that that exchange rate reflects long-term fundamentals. Whatever one may think about short-term effects of intervention, they don't make very much difference. What matters is the long-term effects.

Now, if we do the same calculation for Japan, we don't come out with quite as good an answer. At least a part of the reason is something Alan Blinder mentioned last night. What he said was that there has been a doubling of the yen share of currency holdings. More people were holding more yen over the period from 1980 to the mid-1990s than earlier. The yen share of total reserves has gone from 4.3 percent in 1980 to 8.5 percent in 1994. For the yen, differences in productivity growth and inflation explain about 75 to 80 percent of the average annual depreciation of the dollar against the yen since 1980. And I expect, but I've not actually measured, that the shift in the demand to hold dollars and yen explains most, if not all, of the rest.

Now, let me turn to the question of what is currently happening to inflation. Countries are formally and informally adopting low- or zero-inflation targets. We have five countries now formally committed, in one way or another, to a zero-inflation policy or a very low inflation policy: New Zealand, Great Britain, Sweden, Finland, and Canada. Those countries have committed to a zero- or low-inflation policy and have taken steps to implement it. They may not be entirely adequate steps; it may be much more difficult to achieve zero inflation, on average, than people currently imagine. Nevertheless, this is certainly a change in the way these central banks operate.

Informally, Germany, Switzerland, Japan until 1986, and I believe once again, and now, finally, the United States, have adopted low- or zero-inflation targets. Then there are countries like Argentina, which has come from 6,000 percent inflation down to a very low level of inflation. So we have a movement of countries towards zero inflation, which is going to reduce exchange rate volatility. There's going to be less volatility because two things are different. One, we're not going to get quite so much churning from the monetary side if all these countries follow a low- or zero-inflation policy. And second, markets will have much less of a problem trying to distinguish between real and nominal changes, between those changes that ought to occur in exchange rates and those changes that are the result of bad monetary policies that may eventually be reversed.

I'd like to say a word about Argentina, which I think is a very interesting case. Argentina not only has a currency board, it has a very effective mechanism for enforcing that currency board. There is an extensive economic literature on trigger strategies. I have never thought much of that literature because it seemed to assume away the most important problem, How does the public coordinate its efforts to punish the central bank or the government for inflating? Well, Argentina has found an effective answer. It involves allowing dollar deposits and allowing them to be used for ordinary transactions, not only as the medium of exchange but also as the standard unit of account for many different types of transactions, although not all.

This means people can quickly and easily shift from peso deposits to dollar deposits and punish the central bank very quickly if it deviates from its strategy. That's a very effective policy. Moreover, there are interest rates on pesos and interest rates on dollar deposits, so the central bank has a very good measure of what the market thinks about the risks involved in the two types of deposits. That is a very effective mechanism. It just involves opening your market to allow another currency to operate in your country. In most of Latin America, the dollar already is operating, so all that needs to be changed is for the practice to be legalized.

Now I want to say two words about a move back to the Bretton Woods Agreement: "No chance." Bretton Woods broke down because it was a flawed system. It lasted—here I depart a bit from John Crow—from 1959, the start of convertibility, to March 1968, when President Johnson effectively embargoed gold, refusing to sell it except to central banks and then rapping the knuckles of most of the central banks that asked to buy it. Johnson imposed a type of capital control on the world's principal currency. Effectively, the system came to an end in March 1968. The next three years were simply the death throes. It was a crisis-prone system, so there's no real reason to resurrect it.

Some people did resurrect it as a small Bretton Woods system in Europe called the European Monetary System. That system broke down also. Let's look at how well and effectively it worked. France removed exchange controls, if I remember correctly, in 1984, and seven years later, it was in a plus or minus 15 percent band. Italy and the U.K. remained in the system for a short time. Why? Because there are three mechanisms of adjustment: wage flexibility, which is made difficult in Europe by the existence of the welfare state; labor mobility, which is made difficult by differences of language and custom and historical animosities in Europe; and exchange rates. Now, if the other two mechanisms don't work, it seems to be a rather foolish idea to throw out the one that might. So a zero-inflation policy with relative prices adjusted to real exchange rate movements seems to me to be a good idea for Europe.

Let me just say two last things. One is about the IMF and the World Bank: huge bureaucracies with a great deal of wealth. Parkinson's Law has clearly operated. They no longer have their original functions, but they have many, many more people employed. Numerous IMF studies have produced no evidence, as far as I know, that conditional lending works. That doesn't mean that it never works; it just means that on average it is very difficult to show that it works.

Recently, the IMF has been doing what I regard as counterproductive things, like wanting to issue SDRs (special drawing rights) to Russia, serving as a lender of last resort to Mexico, asking to increase the general agreements to borrow by $28 billion. Most of these I regard as wasteful, bad policies that create moral hazard. There is no problem is North Asia, there is no problem in

Southeast Asia, and there would be fewer problems in Latin American countries if there were fewer people to rush to their defense with financial aid.

Let me conclude with three proposals for reform. First, for the principal currencies (the U.S. dollar, the Deutsche mark, and the yen), adopt or maintain a low-inflation rule—that is, adopt it as a rule. That would increase the stability of exchange rates and produce a public good for third countries. Second, either most countries should close the monetary side of their central banks or, at least, allow foreign currencies to be used as legal tender. There are far too many central banks. What possible good can the central bank of Argentina, or Bolivia, or Mexico, or of many other countries do to offset the damage they've done over the years? Any country that destroys its currency as many times as Argentina, Bolivia, Chile, and Brazil have would be better off without a central bank. Third, close the IMF and end most of its redistribution and bailouts. This practice produces moral hazard and delays adjustment, as it did in the 1980s when the IMF continued to lend money to Latin American countries so they could pay their interest by increasing the amount of their debts. It would have been much better for these countries to have defaulted on the debts early, wiped them out, and never have accumulated the additional debts, which they acquired through the efforts of the IMF.

Finally, the IMF makes government-to-government loans, and what we need are many, many more private-to-private loans.

I'm aware that these three recommendations, or at least some of them, are politically difficult. That doesn't make them wrong or make the present arrangements less costly. I'm also aware, and I hope you are, that when some of us began arguing that zero inflation should be the aim of central banks, many people thought that was politically naive and very difficult to do. But we are getting there now, and I hope that we will move forward on these other recommendations.

Urrutia:
I will deal with a rather small part of this whole issue: the problem of central bank coordination in Latin American free-trade agreements.

Despite the existence of common markets and free-trade agreements in Latin America, the foreign exchange crisis of the 1980s decreased trade among Latin American countries much more than it decreased trade between Latin American countries and the rest of the world. This, of course, created a crisis for the free-trade agreements or common markets that had been set up. One explanation for the crisis was the difficulty of maintaining free trade between countries that were following very divergent macroeconomic policies and that reacted to external shocks with extensive controls, both in trade and in the capital account. As a result, most of these free-trade agreements essentially fell apart.

In the 1990s, there was a resurgence of interest in economic integration. This second attempt at integration had some rather surprising and positive results.

One case involved Colombia, Venezuela, and Ecuador, the core of the Andean Group. For Colombia, trade with Ecuador and Venezuela went from 4.6 percent of total trade in 1989 to 12 percent in 1995, a threefold increase. It was, as far as one can tell, quite a welfare-enhancing increase because contrary to what everybody had said for the previous 30 years, it turned out that the economies were much more complementary than competitive, and there was a clear increase in efficiency that contributed to these countries' rapid rates of growth in the 1990s.

In 1995, despite the crisis in Venezuela, Colombian exports have grown 41 percent in dollar terms to that market and 59 percent to Ecuador. These are very large figures, so something very interesting is going on. In addition, much of that trade is of nontraditional exports, which generates future exports to other areas through the process of learning by doing.

However, divergent macroeconomic policies and exchange rate regimes are creating serious tensions in this system. Can integration attempts survive these major divergencies in macro policies? Or are we bound to revisit the problems that occurred at the time of the debt crisis? What happens when one partner has a fixed exchange rate against the dollar and the other floats? Maybe nothing happens. But much more important than that, what happens if there is a very substantial divergence in macro policies, for example, as may be the case with Venezuela and Colombia and to some extent Argentina and Brazil?

In the case of Venezuela and Colombia, the result of these very substantial differences in macro policies has been large changes in bilateral real exchange rates. In the period from January 1994 to July 1995, the Venezuelan real exchange rate was devalued by 25 percent with respect to the Colombian peso. And then in the second half of that period, it was revalued by 25 percent against the Colombian peso. What advantage is there in having a 25 percent real devaluation followed by a 25 percent real revaluation, or vice versa, in such a short period? The impact of all this on trade and on the free trade agreement is substantial.

What happened in this particular case, of course, was that Venezuela did a maxi-devaluation and then fixed the exchange rate, but this was followed by very high inflation. So the nominal devaluation was very rapidly eroded. This did not have a particularly negative effect because Colombia could afford to absorb massive imports from Venezuela due to its very solid balance-of-payments situation. So in this particular case, the free-trade agreement, I think, was quite helpful to the country that was in trouble. But at the present time, we are in the opposite situation. The Venezuelan exchange rate continues to be fixed, inflation continues to be very high, and so very likely the opposite will happen. Venezuela will have to start absorbing a lot of Colombian exports, and it's not clear it can do so easily. This is most likely going to cause a major problem in the free-trade agreement.

In comparison, very little has happened to the free-trade agreement between Colombia and Ecuador. Why? Because their macro policies have been much more similar. This has culminated in the fact that Ecuador decided to adopt a crawling exchange band very similar to Colombia's in the last few months, so not only are the exchange rate regimes now fairly similar, afloat within a crawling band, but macro policies are quite similar. The result has been an almost constant real bilateral exchange rate between Colombia and Ecuador in the past year and a half. And despite the constancy of this exchange rate, both countries' exports to each other have grown at the rates I suggested. So the similarity in macro policies has made viable what is probably a welfare-enhancing reform—these two countries' free-trade agreement. If you look at the newspapers, at least the Colombian ones, you never see news of trade conflicts between Ecuador and Colombia. The private sector sometimes complains about some problem of certificates of origin of some good, but there have been no major trade conflicts.

In the case of Venezuela and Colombia though, because of tremendous changes in the real exchange rates generated by different macro policies, conflicts are surfacing, are becoming rather serious, and may endanger what I think is a very positive thing—the opening up of these economies, which should, in the natural course of things, do a lot more trade with each other than they did in the past.

The question is, then, Can these trade schemes survive when basic macro policies differ? They did not survive in the 1980s. At present, central bank coordination may not be very viable. I agree that central banks have to look at the effects of their policies on their internal markets. But maybe if, let's say, central bank dialogue were introduced into the policy-making process of both countries, it could help broad macro policies become more similar or, at a minimum, make explicit the costs of very different macro policies. And one of the costs of maintaining these very different macro policies might be to destroy those agreements and the welfare they have produced. In some cases, making that cost explicit might be helpful. If the threat to the integration process were made more explicit, policymakers might develop somewhat better macro policies.

Questions and Comments from the Floor

Question:
I very much like Mr. Urrutia's last point about the relationship between monetary policy and the integration processes. All integration processes apparently have been affected since the Mexican collapse. Policymakers say everything is proceeding, but there is a delay, particularly because the viability of Argentina and Brazil is being questioned.

After the Mexican collapse, a couple of ideas were proposed. One was the creation of a last-resort facility to take the position that the U.S. government took in that case. The other proposal was for the creation of regional central banks or strong coordination in macroeconomic policy and emergency policies to deal with speculative attacks on the currencies of countries with stabilization problems. I would like the panel to elaborate on these proposals.

Urrutia:
The Andean Group does have a small central bank, the Fondo Andino de Reserva, whose record is rather good. The Fondo Andino has not lent a great deal of money, but it has lent and done so very rapidly. So in the middle of a crisis, it can be quite useful. When Peru and Ecuador had their problem, Ecuador had a run on its currency that lasted a very short time. It asked for support from the Fondo Andino, and in about a week, the Fondo Andino gave Ecuador $200 million. Interestingly enough, Peru voted for the support. So some of these schemes, even if they are small, are very flexible and can be helpful in the integration process.

Meltzer:
I'd like to make two comments. One is on this proposal for a lender of last resort. The lender of last resort has to lend a currency that is common. Presumably, it has to be able to create that currency. The current proposals involve using the IMF as a lender of last resort. But what are they going to create, SDRs? Those are not a medium of exchange. The IMF could force them on central banks, but central banks can create their own currency. So I don't see what problem that solves. A lender of last resort has to be able to create base money. There is no base money for the world, and so a lender of last resort for the world seems to me to be a not very interesting idea. Regional central banks have the same problem. They have to be able to create currency.

A much more useful step is to have some standby lending authority that will lend you money to tide you over in a crisis. That is probably a good idea, particularly if you go the direction that I urge of closing down central banks in small countries, replacing them with something like a currency board, and allowing foreign deposits in the banks so that people have a chance to shift their asset mix.

Question:
Governor Crow made a parenthetical comment, if I heard him correctly, that there had been no change in U.S. monetary policy associated with the Plaza Accord. My reading of the data is that there was a very large change in U.S. monetary policy, that growth of reserves got up to a range of around 25

percent in 1986, and the depreciation of the currency was hardly surprising in that setting.

Crow:
I will have another look at the data, but my impression was that demand was pretty strong in the United States and there was no good reason for the United States to ease monetary policy. However, I guess you may be right in one sense. Some would argue that the whole coordination exercise was a way for the U.S. Treasury to get around the Fed and force Fed officials to do things they didn't want to do from a domestic point of view. The Treasury had the Fed take easing action via the international route. If the Treasury succeeded, that was a big mistake. I am not totally convinced that it did succeed, however.

Question:
When I was in graduate school, I was taught that fixed exchange rates were better than flexible exchange rates because fixed exchange rates force countries to run responsible monetary policies. Now, I was taught this by Robert Mundell, so there's a context to this. But it's interesting to me to see how close Allan Meltzer came to this, which is to say that fixed exchange rates are better than flexible exchange rates for all countries of the world except the United States, Germany, and Japan. What I'm wondering is, where do you draw the distinction? Should France have a flexible exchange rate? Should Sweden? Should Bermuda? Is it that a country has to be big enough so that fixed exchange rates can't control its policies? Where do you draw the line?

Meltzer:
You misheard or I misspoke, one or the other. I divided the world into three groups. The three largest countries, I said, should float. I think everyone agrees that they will continue to float. For the many very small countries, my recommendation was to close their central banks because they are a source of problems. For many countries that are in between—and I would include Canada and France in that group—it's up to them to decide what they want to do; that is, they can peg their currencies, or they can float their currencies and import zero inflation from the principal countries. But I didn't say that they should do that; that's for them to decide. If Canada wants to float against the dollar and sees some advantage in it, either political or economic, why should I tell them not to do it?

Hausmann:
First, there is very little evidence on the question of whether fixed exchange rates generate responsible monetary policy. We know that fixed exchange rates

allow you to postpone inflation until the time when you've lost all your reserves. Therefore, it is not clear that fixing necessarily leads to responsible monetary policy. Flexing your exchange rate implies that if you do something stupid today, they'll attack today, and you'll pay the cost today, so it may provide more discipline.

Second, I do believe that there is a very important trade-off in choosing between fixed and flexible exchange rates. We have some evidence from a study we've done on whether GDP volatility is affected by the choice of exchange rate regime. What we find is that fixed-exchange-rate regimes generate larger GDP volatility. So it means that output is going to be more volatile if you have a fixed exchange rate. And if you take that evidence to bear, then there is a trade-off between a fixed exchange rate and a more volatile output or a flexible exchange rate and maybe a more stable output.

Crow:
I want to jump in because, after all, Bob Mundell is Canadian. A few years ago, he recommended that Canada fix. The argument is that Canada's economy is no bigger than California's, maybe a bit smaller, and California uses the U.S. dollar satisfactorily, so why not Canada? But he also said that we should fix at a lower initial point. He was trying to have it both ways. We had an appreciated currency, which I mentioned before is not a popular thing in Canada. We don't have a floating rate, apparently, to appreciate. Before the last election, the opposition, at one point at least, was arguing that they—and this is, in a sense, contrary to what you were suggesting—didn't see why Canada should have a lower rate of inflation than the United States. We have a floating exchange rate, but we have a lower rate of inflation. The logical argument, I think, but I don't think it is one they would buy, is that Canada should fix to the U.S. dollar and have the same inflation rate as the United States, a higher inflation rate than it has now.

Coming directly to your point, let me single out three countries with floating exchange rates—Australia, Canada, and New Zealand. New Zealand is a pretty small country, and it's done rather well with its monetary policy and that whole series of institutional reforms. All three have engineered major reductions in inflation over the last several years. That's pretty responsible in terms of monetary policy. Maybe if I see Bob Mundell, I'll make a point of telling him that.

References

Hausmann, Ricardo, and Michael Gavin (1996), *Securing Stability and Growth in a Shock-Prone Region: The Policy Challenge for Latin America* (Washington, D.C.: Inter-American Development Bank).

Hausmann, Ricardo, Michael Gavin, Roberto Perotti, and Ernesto Talvi (1996), "Managing Fiscal Policy in Latin America and the Caribbean," prepared for the seminar Fiscal Institutions to Overcome Volatility in Latin America, 37th Annual Meeting of the Board of Governors, Buenos Aires, March 24.

Inter-American Development Bank (1995), "Overcoming Volatility in Latin America," *Report on Economic and Social Progress in Latin America: 1995* (Washington, D.C.).

MIX
Papier aus verantwortungsvollen Quellen
Paper from responsible sources
FSC® C105338

If you have any concerns about our products,
you can contact us on
ProductSafety@springernature.com

In case Publisher is established outside the EU,
the EU authorized representative is:
Springer Nature Customer Service Center GmbH
Europaplatz 3, 69115 Heidelberg, Germany

Printed by Libri Plureos GmbH
in Hamburg, Germany